More Praise for HONOR THY CHILDREN

"A vital message.... Traces [the Nakatani's] ordeal with graceful compassion and delicacy, demonstrates that wholeness and healing can be achieved under what seem like impossible circumstances, and that love, trust and acceptance are necessary in every family."
  —*San Francisco Chronicle*

"From great tragedies emerge stories of people showing exceptional strength. Molly Fumia brings to life one of those stories with her writing about a family robbed of its children through aids and violence. In the face of such misery, this family's response strengthens us all. It is a story worth reading and strength worth witnessing."
  —Donald P. Francis, M.D., President of Vax Gen, Inc.,
    and former head of the Center for Disease Control AIDS
    Laboratory Activities

"Here is a story ripe for tragedy. Then comes the awareness that we are, all of us, human—and hard behind that comes love. This is a story proving, again, that the most remarkable victories belong not to those who are hardened, but to those who are vulnerable."
  —Mary Fisher, author and founder of the Family AIDS
    Network

HONOR THY CHILDREN

One Family's Journey to Wholeness

Molly Fumia

CONARI PRESS
Berkeley, CA

Conari Press books are distributed by Publishers Group West
Cover design: based on the movie poster for *Honor Thy Children* (a feature
   documentary) courtesy of León Entertainment. Poster design and layout
   by Francisco J. León and Judi S. Kaminishi
Cover illustration: Daniel Jacobo
Cover photos courtesy of Al and Jane Nakatani
Cover photo of Al and Jane Nakatani: Eugene Tanner
Interior design: Jennifer Brontsema

Library of Congress Cataloging-in-Publication Data
Fumia, Molly.
   Honor thy children: one family's journey to wholeness / Molly Fumia.
        p.   cm.
   ISBN 1-57324-077-X (hc)
   ISBN 1-57324-198-9 (pbk)
        1. Family—United States—Case studies.   2. Japanese American families—
   United States—Case studies.   3. Sons—United States—Death—Case studies.
   4. AIDS (Disease)—Patients—United States—Biography.   5. Parents of AIDS
   patients—United States—Biography.   6. Violent deaths—United States—Case
   studies.   7. Bereavement—United States—Case studies.   I. Title
   HQ536.F96   1997
   306.85'089956073—dc20   96–43773

Printed in the United States of America on recycled paper
00 01 02 03 RRD(C) 10 9 8 7 6 5 4 3

DEDICATION

For Melissa, Mark, Nicholas, Gino, Kristen, and Joel
I believe in you

ACKNOWLEDGMENTS

When a mother of six writes a book, it is a community activity. For the support—both practical and spiritual, unceasingly or just when I needed it—given me by the following people over the past three years, I extend endless gratitude: Debbie and Joe Biondolillo, Tim Blue, Dean Brackley S.J., Bob Brown, Judie and Tony Buldo, Bobbie Carcione, Mary and Bill Carry, Kate Chimenti, Peggie and Pete Crisham, Sue Eschelbach, Evelyn and Tom Freeman, Rena and John Fumia, Debbie and John Fumia Jr., Kathy Gibson, Will Glennon, Tom Gumbleton, Helen Menden, Bill Muller S.J., Nancy Ottoboni, Addie Pearson, Jennifer Pearson, Jeanette Phelps, Sue Sattler I.H.M., Janet Schultz, Nikki Segall, Marita Trobough, Gerry Wade S.J., Sharon Wulf, Mary Yates, and Kathy Zapala.

To Steve Wozniak, Janice Enright, Pam Dunnett, and Jean Izumi: The spirit of your generosity accompanies my words.

To the memory of Paul Monette and Randy Shilts: You informed my writing. Thank you.

Special, heartfelt thanks to Anne Takeuchi and James Martin. You are, indeed, brave.

My deepest appreciation to Joyce Kumamoto and Allison Tom, as well as Harriet and Takeo Kawakami, Stacy Izumi, Dawn Waszkiewicz, Teresa Velcamp, and Brittany Hennig, for the remarkable gift of your memories; to Eugene Tanner, for your brilliant images; and to Kent Granath, for your passionate interpretation of one brief life.

And finally, to Chuck: I only hope you can begin to know the love and gratitude I feel for you. And to Mary Jane Ryan: You were my friend before time. Thank you, including whatever that was we experienced on Maui.

CONTENTS

A FAST BALL 1

THE TOUR 9

THE CIRCLE 25

JAPANESE BORN IN HAWAII 33

THE AMERICAN WAY 45

THE THINGS WE DEMAND OF A MAN 59

WEDDINGS AND GRANDCHILDREN 76

FULL-BLOWN 87

MEASURE OF SUCCESS 101

NO COMPARISON 113

ELDEST SON 125

THE OYSTER CLUB 136

GOING PUBLIC 150

SAVING LIVES 162

JUST BE YOURSELF 172

GAYDAR 181

THE CHANGING SEASON 196

SECRETS 214

REVELATION 224

IN FIRST PERSON 240

DYING WELL 257

THIS IS MY SON 265

OUTSMARTING THE ANGEL 276

CALL ME TOSH 292

HONOR THY CHILDREN 307

This is a true story. Conversations and reflections were based on hundreds of hours of interviews. In the interest of privacy, some names and details have been changed, and in one case a composite character created.

A FAST BALL

I have a friend who says the best things in life ruin you, because they throw you off your well-worn track and challenge you to grapple with the unexpected.

"Surprise is life," he says.

I remember the telephone call, on May 5, 1993, that at least temporarily ruined me.

"Hi," Guy began, friendly, immediately intimate, luring me into conversation by not identifying himself—as if I was supposed to recognize his "famous" voice.

"Hello," I replied, wondering why Guy Nakatani was acting like we dallied daily on the phone.

I had met him once, at his presentation on HIV and AIDS at my son's high school. We had talked together, his family and I, about Guy's work and about my books on grieving. They had three sons—two dead, one dying. During those few moments with them, no amount of personal experience could have kept me from feeling like a freshman who had wandered into a graduate seminar; their grief and the reasons for it defied interpretation. But still, there had been some sense of connection.

I propped the phone under my chin, about to say something, although I don't know what. *How are you?* Somehow, that didn't seem appropriate. But then he proposed we meet for breakfast, informed me of the time and place, and hung up. I made a note in my calendar.

On the way to our date, I replayed the scene at the school where Guy had spoken. He was introduced as a "victim of HIV"; hardly a victim I felt; "conquering hero" was much more to the point. I watched while he worked his magic, coaxing four hundred teenagers and their parents to listen to him, the kind of listening that spreads beyond the ears to involve the whole body, the wide-eyed, pin-drop, edge-of-the-seat kind of listening that preachers pray for. I saw him invade their minds and dissolve their illusions, with simple words that evoked wild laughter and quiet tears, and finally I felt their fear and their sudden, startled uncertainty. He had done it. He had awakened them.

Swept up in the emotion of it all, I moved forward to speak with him. I introduced myself. "Can I do anything?" I stammered, the timeless question offered to the afflicted and the grieving.

Guy did not reply but turned to his parents, who were standing next to him. "This is Molly," he said, nodding my way.

"I'm Alexander Nakatani." His father extended his hand. He was a handsome man, lean and compact, only a little taller than me. The lines on his face were not harsh, and although it appeared that he spent time in the sun, his skin was still smooth. Heavy waves of silver ran through his dark hair. Behind his glasses, warm brown eyes met mine.

"And this is Jane, my wife."

"Thank you for having us here tonight," said the woman beside him. When I found out much later that Jane is only five feet one, three inches shorter than me, I was surprised. From the very beginning, I held fast to the ways we were the same. Once I found a T-shirt that had on its front a drawing of two women walking on a beach, their arms around each other, one dark-haired and possibly Asian, one light-haired and probably Caucasian, their heads bent in conversation. "We're sisters," Jane laughed when I gave it to her. And when she cut her hair short, in a style that resembled mine, she remarked that now no one would be able to tell us apart.

We were both mothers; that much united us, gave us our common language, entangled our feelings. But while I could forget my troubles once in a while, her burdens would never let her go. I understood her captivity in that moment, when we met for the first time. I looked into her beautiful face and saw, still lingering there, a capacity for joy that would never be fulfilled.

Pressing, I came up with an idea of my own. "Maybe I could write something for you. I mean, if there's anything you need written. . ." I could feel my voice retreating into my throat as I became aware of how silly I must have sounded. Guy was obviously articulate, as was his father. The presumption that they might need better words was insulting. Thankfully, the moment passed.

But now as I approached the cafe, I wondered if they wanted to take me up on my offer. I knew that Guy had just returned from Washington; perhaps he wanted me to write a letter to the president, demanding that he get serious about HIV. Maybe he wanted me to help him write an epitaph.

Guy was waiting for me. I surprised myself by looking him up and down. I couldn't help it, really, because Guy Nakatani was the most remarkable-looking person in the place. He was wearing a long-sleeved denim shirt, crisp and freshly ironed. His jeans were fashionable, his belt and shoes perfectly matched. A thin sweater vest of soft earth tones hung lightly over the shirt, and topping off his outfit, he wore a gray wool baseball cap, backward, tipped a bit sideways, showing off his mop of still luscious black hair. On the table next to him lay a large brown leather personal planner with a brass clasp.

He got up to greet me, and I embraced him. Beneath the vest and the shirt, I could feel an object protruding from his chest, his Hickman catheter, I later learned, the device that had been surgically installed to feed medicine directly into his heart.

"Is it okay to hug you?" I asked.

"Absolutely, just don't squeeze too tight."

Over breakfast, I expressed my admiration and gratitude for his work. Being the mother of six children, four of them teenagers, I knew that his message was not for somebody else.

"You got to me, Guy," I admitted.

His forehead wrinkled. "I hope I got to your children."

I felt a little chill.

"There are so many kids out there searching," he said thoughtfully, "and these are the ones who won't know what's happening to them, you know?" He peered at me intently from underneath his hat. "They're vulnerable. Whatever, whoever comes along, they'll just go with it. Like, you know, what's that animal that just follows?"

"Sheep."

"No. Lemmings."

"Lemmings?"

"Those dumb little creatures that follow the crowd over the cliff and into the sea, where they drown or get eaten by sharks."

I returned his gaze. He was quite serious about this analogy. We finished breakfast and ordered coffee. For a while, silence settled over our table.

"Why am I here?" I finally ventured. I was sure we weren't two old friends just catching up.

He asked me if I had read the recent article about him and his family in the newspaper. I had. It was a long, well-written account of the Nakatani family tragedies and Guy's commitment to informing young people about HIV and AIDS. On the front page was a color photograph of Guy sitting beneath his own portrait, as well as those of his dead brothers. Later I would see them lined up on the living room wall, windows into the past—Glen at the seashore, Greg with the dog, and Guy looking like a model from *Gentlemen's Quarterly*. The long article struggled to explain the mystery once again: Why would talented young men be so quickly put to death?

"That reporter got me thinking. I want a book about us."

I suspected what was coming and experienced that quickening sensation of going out to meet an interesting idea. He leaned toward me. Never in my life had I been confronted with such an earnest, engaging presence.

"I don't want our legacy to be about a family who lost three sons.

4

There's nothing wrong with our family name." Guy reached across the table and pulled my coffee cup toward him, as if I would eagerly follow. I did, until we were literally nose to nose.

"Our family is an example of honor, dignity, and pride. We've never lost ourselves as a family."

Taken back by the vehemence of his declaration, I started to comment, but he waved me off.

"I've read your books. You understand that it's possible to survive tragedy, and let me tell you, Molly, that is what my family is about. Do you see?"

I was unable to formulate any kind of sensible response to this statement in the allotted time. This family's tragedy was tremendous, unspeakable. I had no idea what he meant by survival. One brother murdered, another already claimed by a devastating disease; none would reach the age of thirty. Despite all I had written about the transforming power of the grief process, I wasn't sure Alexander and Jane Nakatani would survive the complete destruction of their family.

But he had just flattered me with the possibility that I understood it all, so I said, stupidly, "Yes, Guy, I see."

He sat back and smiled, this time a Cheshire cat grin that failed to hide his satisfaction with our discussion. "I want my story told, and you can tell it. You should do this."

At this point I was reeling, wondering how my life had been so easily snatched from my control. Of course, I was interested; but I needed time to think about it.

Guy just kept smiling.

I look back now on that moment with great affection. But make no mistake about it: I'd been had.

• • • •

Later, he was triumphant, or was it smug? "I knew you would do it," he teased.

"You did not, Guy," I insisted, not wanting to give anything away. "I didn't know I would do it."

5

I had gone home and had several thousand discussions about Guy's proposal with various friends and loved ones. The sides of the argument lined up in front of me: I had already begun another book, which, I decided, could be temporarily abandoned. I would have to spend a great deal of time with Guy, away from my own family, and yet my husband, Chuck, and our older children were unconditionally supportive, even excited about the project. And finally, the Nakatani story was drenched in sadness; would I eventually become too weighted down with their burdens to enjoy my own life?

I called the friend who thinks so highly of surprise.

"Molly," he said solemnly, "what do you do with a fast ball over the middle?"

Even if I hadn't been a baseball fanatic since childhood, I'd been to enough Little League games since then to know how things work at the plate.

"You gotta swing."

And so it was decided. Whatever plans I had carefully prioritized for the immediate future were tossed aside like yesterday's newspaper. I would opt for the unexpected.

However, I did not jump fearlessly into the Nakatani family abyss. And I'm sure that many others, once acquainted with their story, moved away quickly, unable or unwilling to stay. Some of that I understood. For the compassionate, there is more than enough human misery to go around. And some tragedies are so staggering, so foreboding, one is compelled to stare straight ahead and walk by. A father and a mother lose all their children—to even begin to feel their pain is a threat to my own well-being.

However, I perceived the presence of other, more subtle dangers. This father, viewed through the scratched glass of the American way of life, had done everything right. He had worked hard to provide shelter and security for his sons and every opportunity for them to succeed. He had played by the rules and then passed them on, assuming his children would be like him, behaving honorably, staying away from trouble. "I value my life," Alexander once told me, "and I figured my kids

6

would, too. Doesn't everyone value their life? Who the hell would risk that?"

What parent among us could answer: my child? Is it my child who might be at risk, at his own hand or that of another? And the scariest thought of all: Could it be that my child is not like me?

For Alexander and Jane Nakatani, that possibility never crossed their minds. Now, sitting amid the smoldering ruins of their family, they confront all those who still have the opportunity to parent with yet another question: How can we make the world safe for gay children?

Say that Alexander and I dare them to consider our story, sex and all. Say that there isn't anything about our lives that was recognizable from the start. The deaths of all our children, of course. But their lives, too, were a surprise to us. This is our greatest regret, not to have known what terrified them. But to other parents, to anyone who has a child in their life to care about, tell them: It was one tragedy that could have been avoided.

I must admit that once immersed in their lives, there arose within me one other pesky, irrational fear. Could their misfortune spread, as surely as the plague? Jane would speak of it periodically, when my car broke down, or when my mother had a heart attack: I had gotten too close and somehow been infected. And dread, sharp and insistent, would hover over me for a moment, until we waved away the Nakatani bad luck with their secret weapon: clear, decisive laughter.

Undoubtedly, anyone who avoided all this unpleasantness also missed the fun. Laughter, a surprisingly common event amid tragedy—some special human quirk, I suppose. Often, when I was with them, we would find ourselves laughing, not just nervous giggles, but belly laughs, gleeful tears streaming down our cheeks. And inevitably, someone would remark, "If anyone saw us now, they wouldn't believe it." It was a nightmare, yes; but it was also something of a fairy tale.

There was the day the man walking his dog on the road to the middle of the island asked, "How are you this morning?" And Jane replied darkly, "You don't want to know," and we found secret merriment in his short glance, the stricken look that crossed his face. Soon, all of Jane's children will be dead. Of course he didn't want to know. Later, we laughed out loud, not in mockery, by any means, but in triumph. A remnant of control had been seized; a small, irreverent pleasure claimed; death ignored once more.

It's just that even with this story's sad opening lines, things weren't as they seemed. Death was only a single player in a colorful cast of many more interesting characters. I came to expect so much more than sadness, and in the end I ran to them. I held dear my own small part. Their victory washed over me and cleansed me of my secret fears—of death, and of life. Their unexpected laughter gave me hope. Ultimately, nothing could have kept me away. Nothing.

THE TOUR

Two days later, I found myself driving to the Nakatani home for the first of many interviews with Guy and his circle of family and friends. As I parked my car in front of the house, I was desperate to calm down. This was not as I had expected. Instead of being overwhelmed by the sadness of it all, I was excited, seduced by a sense of the remarkable.

Their house on Copeland Place was at the end of the street. The split-level resembled others on the block; they had been built during the sixties, when the city of San Jose had burst and spilled its residents into the morass of suburbs which now covered the perfect soil of the Santa Clara valley. I looked up at the house from the end of the driveway. Under the roofline, two long windows with half-drawn shades canopied the garage door, creating a curious effect. It was as though the house was smiling.

Along the pathway that led to the house, the grass still flourished, green and freshly cut. I walked up the steps that led to a comfortable porch and confronted the front door. As I reached for the bell, my eyes came to rest on a wooden plaque of a man swinging a golf club. It read, "Welcome to our Clubhouse: The Nakatanis." Beneath the golfer a black metal mailbox with gold trim screamed of normalcy. Two letters, stamped and addressed with a perfect hand, awaited the day's pickup. On the mailbox, a strip of plastic identified the inhabitants of this house in neat letters: "The Nakatani Family: Al, Jane, Glen, Greg, and Guy." I pondered these words—how could it be that they had not simply, mercifully, faded away?

Just in time, I remembered that Guy had told me to come in without ringing. Two steps inside the door, a voice greeted me from somewhere down a stairway to the left.

"Hel-lo-o," the voice sang, as Guy's style of greeting was established.

"Hi, Guy," I responded, aware of the rhyme.

"Did you take your shoes off?" he called. I looked down and saw a neat line of shoes, slippers, and sandals next to the door. The voice below explained. "We take our shoes off in the house, just in case you weren't aware of the Japanese tradition. We don't want to bring bad luck in on the bottom of our shoes."

As quickly as the irony grabbed me, the voice below continued, laughing. "Of course for us it didn't work!" And I laughed too, not because of the satire on life played out in a single comment, but because it was funny. I added my shoes to the end of the row.

There was no sign of Alexander or Jane. Later, I wondered if Guy had ordered them out, so that the arrangement between the two of us would be understood as Guy's thing. His father and mother had important supporting roles, but there could be only one leading man: Guy's story, Guy's legacy, produced and directed by Guy, with a little help from me.

Shoeless, I took a few steps. To the right of the large entryway was the living room, and across the room on the far wall, the three portraits. Artwork that reflected their Japanese-Hawaiian heritage clung to other walls: a Wyland painting of a family of whales, an Otsuka serigraph of a Japanese bride in her flowering headdress. To the left were shelves containing a music system, a few books, and some framed photographs. Everything was in order; no dust, none of the debris of life that cluttered my own living room.

"Down here," Guy called. I walked forward, peering into the kitchen on my right, past a table and sliding glass doors into their backyard. I could see a long deck, freshly painted white, and at the end a lattice-work gazebo shading a patio table and several chairs. Below the deck was a concrete area and some grass; later I would learn there had once been a swimming pool, but it had been filled in.

"Molly?" I turned to the left and descended the stairs quickly into a cozy den. He was on the couch, his arm propped under his head, a long tube protruding from under his T-shirt—new, blue, with the word "Polo" emblazoned across the front. Guy was hooked up to some kind of machine, which was gurgling a little tune.

Across from him on a comfortable-looking chair sat a handsome young man dressed in a gray suit.

"I want you to meet my friend James." Without waiting for me to respond, he continued, "James, get up and let Molly sit down."

James stood up and politely extended his hand. He didn't appear thrilled. Watching him being tossed out of that plush chair, I wasn't surprised.

"James, please stay where you are," I protested, grabbing several cushions from a stack near the fireplace and beginning to build myself a comfortable spot on the rug. Guy, meanwhile, would not be derailed.

"No, Molly, sit there. He's just leaving." James started up the stairs. "Bye, James. Make lots of money." Guy leaned over to follow James' stocking feet as they disappeared out of view.

"Wait," he commanded. "Are you wearing my new socks?"

After a moment, during which time I realized that James must be putting on his shoes, his voice floated down the stairway.

"No, silly, these are mine. Don't you remember when I bought them?"

"James, I'm not dead yet."

"Bye." The front door slammed.

"They sure look like mine," he commented, eyeing me as if he expected me to agree.

Instead, he grinned broadly. "How should we start?"

"Let's start with you," I returned his smile. "How are you feeling?"

We had a conversation about his machine and his medicines, about the disease that held him captive on the couch for four hours every day. Gancyclovir, a drug battling CMV retinitis, that part of the cytomegalovirus that destroys the retina, was dripping from an intravenous machine into his body through the Hickman catheter. The drug made worse his regular bouts with nausea and diarrhea, but kept him from going blind in his right eye. His left eye had been sightless for a year.

We talked about his work in the schools and his dreams for an AIDS program that would live longer than he would, finding others to tell their stories the way Guy had. I asked questions, and he responded simply and sincerely, and yet, an odd feeling wrapped itself around our conversation, like we were making small talk about the end of the world.

Guy's machine made a series of beeps, and he sat up to attend to it. He punched a few buttons on the control panel and after untangling the tube between his catheter and the machine, he unhooked himself and stood up.

"After my bathroom break, do you want a tour of my house?" he asked cheerfully.

I didn't, particularly. I was marveling at Guy's composure—his certainty. He spoke easily, in the same breath, of death and life, of diarrhea and new socks.

He returned from the bathroom with words of encouragement. "Don't you want to get the ambience of Guy's environment?" Standing by my pile of pillows, he gestured dramatically.

"This is my hospital room." The sweep of his arm came to rest in the direction of the fireplace. The brick hearth was laden with medical supplies, bandages and syringes, tubing, scissors and tape, sterile washcloths, bottles of water, lotions and oils, and a pile of towels. He moved to the couch and patted its pillows. "And this is my couch. I'll spend a lot of time here as long as I'm living at home, hooking up."

"Are you moving?" I asked. I was so far adrift.

"I'll probably have to go to the hospital, eventually." My sudden discomfort must have played across my face, because Guy added kindly, "Maybe not.

"This is my machine. See the bag up there? It's usually full. This tubing feeds through the machine and monitors how much of the medicine is dripping into my body. If air gets into the tube, the machine stops and goes 'beep, beep,' and it's really annoying. This is the sharps container, and this is the garbage can for all my other stuff."

Guy looked at me expectantly, but I was still contemplating the "sharps container." How rarely, in all of this, did I think about the deadliness of the virus that was as close as Guy's body, or the used needles that piled up in the bottom of a special wastebasket that had as its sole purpose to protect the rest of us. One tends to move past all of that quickly. And this was a house that had long since learned to live with the intruder; the lingering threat was not to those within these walls.

He stood behind the bar and opened up a small refrigerator, revealing dozens of plastic bags full of intravenous medicine. "I keep them all right here. No big deal. It's just that they have to be refrigerated." Guy leaned over and moved a few of the containers. "Want a soda?" he asked, fetching a can from the back.

"No, thank you," I replied.

"Am I boring you?"

"Not at all."

"Well, maybe we ought to skip to the heart of the matter." He leaned over the bar and lowered his voice to the level of conspiracy.

"Wanna see my closet?"

I told my parents I was gay after my senior year in high school. I know it was a shock to them, because I had all the prettiest girlfriends during high school. It was the last thing on their minds, that it could happen to me.

It was hard to tell them, because Glen was also gay. He hurt them terribly when he left at the age of fifteen. All his pictures came down off the wall.

13

I was nine when that happened. One night Glen and my mom were arguing, and he pushed her. Not real hard—they were standing at the top of the stairs, but she didn't fall.

From that moment on, I disowned him. Everybody from high school thinks I have only one brother. All I saw was the pictures coming off the wall, and nobody talking about Glen. So, I thought, I'm not going to talk about it either. I'm going to learn to cope. I didn't want to cause any more pain for my parents.

And it happened just the way I feared it would. My mom said, "Now you're going to turn out like Glen." I hated him for that.

On the way to the closet, Guy continued to recite a litany of his possessions. His videotapes, his scrapbooks, boxes overflowing with envelopes and folders.

"This is my collection of all the letters ever sent to me and all the articles ever written about me." He pulled out a scrapbook and opened it up. I turned the pages.

Guy was apologetic. "I know there's a lot here. You can read it later."

To date, he had spoken to almost thirty thousand people. Did Guy expect me to read every letter?

He seemed to be divining my thoughts. "It's just that I want you to feel what I feel when I get them," he said.

I surprised myself by reaching for him, aware that I was excusing his self-absorption, separating him from the rest of us who might have more time to make our mark. I'm not dead yet. His legacy in folders and boxes, his most recent memories, recounted over and over again, perhaps to imagine the effect they would have on those he was leaving behind—these were Guy's preoccupations, pure and sweet, stripped of judgment by the living.

Buried beneath a scrapbook, I noticed a copy of *Tales of the City* by Armstead Maupin. "Are you reading this?"

"Oh, yes, this is my current book." Guy picked it up and opened it. "To tell you how smart I am, I've been reading for two weeks, and this is how far I've gotten." He revealed his bookmark to be resting on page thirty-nine. "At this rate I'll have to finish up in my next life." Tossing the book on the couch, he started up the stairs.

"This kills me, especially lately." His words appeared to be painfully true as he shuffled up the steps one at a time. We passed by a pair of neatly folded trousers sitting on the top step. "Excuse the mess," he remarked.

He pointed through a doorway. "This is my room. Actually, this is James' and my room. Except that he doesn't keep his stuff in here, because I take up all the space." Guy moved me to the center of the room and planted himself in front of me, leaning forward, eyes sparkling.

"Here it is," he said, turning slowly.

Behind him, an enormous closet stretched over one whole wall of his room. It had no doors. An impressive arrangement of shelves and rods at various heights were filled with geometric precision with a grand array of clothing of every type imaginable.

Suddenly, I felt wildly out of place. Guy was talking to someone who didn't know Polo from K-Mart. In my world, I spent a lot of time rearranging; moving clothes from the floor to the hamper, my best sweater out of my daughter's closet, or that old lamp in the garage into the living room. Furniture that matched and an empty laundry basket were long-term goals.

I shifted from one foot to the other, trying to appreciate the perfection before me, while my tour director launched into his presentation.

"These are my casual shirts," he began, indicating two lines of hangers, perfectly spaced on two rods, one in back of the other, extending across the top half of the closet. "All the short-sleeve shirts are in front, and they're done by color, as are all of my clothes. Actually, this one's out of place." Guy moved one shirt over two places.

I lowered myself slowly onto his bed. Guy smiled but didn't hesitate. He moved to some of the shelves on the side of the closet. "I have a special section for my underwear and socks, and it's divided up by Polo socks and workout socks. These are all my sweatshirts, and the first shelf is devoted to all my Polo sweatshirts."

"Polo is, uh, like a theme," I commented.

He moved to the other half of the closet. "This is my work side, my pants, and it goes from more casual to dress, and these are my work clothes, and each suit must be put into a bag for me." He pushed one of the suits over gently, and a long tie rack swung out. "And, of course, my ties, which are harder to categorize, but I have my own system."

"With my CMV retinitis," Guy rambled on, "there's a good chance I'll lose sight in my other eye before this is over. So when I can't see anymore, I'll still know where everything is."

Oddly, his explanation didn't move me very much. I didn't think feeling sorry for him went along with the closet.

If I go blind, I'll be okay. I won't be able to shop, and that's going to kill a lot of my good times. But I can still give my talks. I know it all well enough.

I'm most afraid of when dementia hits. I think that will be hard on everyone. I don't want them to watch me. The spinal cord will go, the brain will go. I don't want to live that long.

At some point, I might have to say, I've got to go. I think my father would help me. I'm serious about that. I don't want to say I'm dead serious, but I am. We'll see.

I'm willing to deal with being blind. Blind is fine. Lots of people are blind.

It's not because I would give up. I would just move on. The life of Guy is not going to stop. I'll keep going somehow. I don't feel like I would be giving up or quitting. Far from it.

Guy was in high gear. "I get such a charge out of spending money on great clothes that make me look good. I have a full wardrobe, in fact, I'm having a hard time remembering everything I've got. And I've got to know where to locate everything in case James has been around."

His face turned somber. "I can tell you where the clothes are that have the most meaning to me."

I pondered this for a moment. How could a shirt or a pair of pants mean anything, when pressed against the fate of the man who wore them?

"So," I said, clearing my throat, "there is significance in these things for you?"

"Oh yeah. The significance is that I'm completely anal and everything must be a certain way and a certain plan."

I fell back on his bed, laughing. Guy ignored me, moving to the shelves next to his suits.

"These are my sweaters. My shorts are on the bottom. I don't really like them there. It bothers me, but I have no other room for them. They're organized by their frequency of use. I have some shorts that I love much more than others."

I watched him, thoroughly entertained, as he narrated this very personal peek into his life. For the moment, he was clearly in control and enjoying that small victory. He moved to the dresser built into the closet and pulled open the top drawer.

"And here my drawers are set up for my T-shirts. These are all my sleeping shirts, with the exception of the first row." I stood up and went over to inspect the shirts. "T-shirts that I use for dress," he paused, glancing at me sideways. "Go ahead," he said, "pull it open." Obediently, I opened the second drawer. "All Polo in the first three rows. Then it goes to Gap."

What are we doing? I thought; even Guy was giggling now. "These are my Hawaii T-shirts." The third drawer came open. "I had a Stussy section when I was in high school, but I'm no longer into Stussy."

His voice, punctuated with amusement, belonged to a tour guide at a theme park—the one who has been there a long time, who really knows how to give a visitor a good time.

"Then we have long-sleeves and tank tops. You know, long-sleeve knit."

"Hmm."

"And the rest is a mishmash."

"Oh, dear," I laughed, "close that drawer."

"So that kind of tells you exactly where I'm at."

I plopped back down on the plush white comforter that covered Guy's bed.

"You must be special," he said softly.

"Why is that?"

"Because I never let anyone sit on my bed."

I had to command myself not to stand up immediately, struggling to maintain distance between us, to elude the suggestion of mutuality. I am wiser than you, some voice within me shouted.

The tour was winding down. Guy moved to a little gallery of photographs on the wall and on his dresser. "You're going to see basically the same people in all of these pictures."

"That's you."

"Yes."

"Your hair's different."

"It's permed." We moved along the row. "This is Anne. She's my best friend. Every night, she comes home from work and gives me a back rub. I've known her forever."

September 9, 1989

Dear Annco, Nastasia, Diarreahead AKA: Anne,

Today I told our dear friend Catherine. Getting those words out, "Cat, I'm HIV" was kinda tough. All day yesterday I thought about it. So all day today I was a basket case. And then during dinner I felt nauseous. (How do you spell that?) Anyways, near the end of my meal I had to go to the bathroom because I was getting wiggly. Well, while I was in the bathroom Cat paid the bill and got up. That's when I wanted to tell her but the time just got messed up.

So we got into the car and I said, "What do you feel like doing?" And she said, "something exciting!" I thought to myself, Oh great. Now I'll never be able to tell her. So I just started driving and I went into how I wasn't going to school anymore and I was just doing what I want to do. Finally, I told her why. I've never heard Cat stay so quiet (outside of sleeping). It was almost scary.

I had to argue with her that I wasn't kidding. Then, besides the initial shock words, she didn't say much. I wish she'd said more. I'm kinda wondering what she's thinking. Maybe you should call her and see if she's okay.

So anyways, at least there are no more secrets. I feel relieved that she knows. All I hope for now is that this won't change things between all of us.

   Love, Guico

P.S. Nastasia—have you ever humped a bike cop? Just kidding.

"And this is James, of course. In front of the Beverly Hills Hilton. I took him there to surprise him, because he had never done anything like that before."

Guy picked up the photos of Anne and James and regarded them thoughtfully. "You know, when I first met Anne, she had no style at all. I had to start at the beginning, help her build a wardrobe, show her how to walk, teach her everything. Ditto James. He was clueless, dressed like a slob. Now," Guy put them back in their places, "he's classy. Most of the time. I can't really leave him alone very long."

"James is your lover, Guy?"

"Uh-huh," he nodded, adding, "but that's not public."

In the next picture, Guy was holding a laughing girl in his arms at what might have been a New Year's Eve party, given the cardboard hats. "That's Catherine," he explained. "She's the third friend."

"The third friend?"

"Besides James and Anne. If she lived around here, I'm sure she'd be around, you know, in the circle." He tapped the photo thoughtfully. "That's a perfect example of how we are together."

I leaned forward to get a better look.

"Or, how we used to be. I can't be that way anymore. But if you ever wanted to get a picture of the fun, wild Guy, talk to Cat."

He handed me the remaining picture: Guy in his wheelchair, flanked by James, Anne, and Mickey Mouse.

"Disneyland. James was so excited. You'd think he'd never been anywhere."

I handed it back. "What do you mean, you and James aren't public?"

Guy frowned. "We decided that for the talks we wouldn't deal with the issue of my sexuality. I don't want to lose them."

He faced his closet for a moment, legs apart, hands on his hips. Slowly, he turned back, until I was confronted with a different person than had been with me only minutes ago, as if he'd been replaced by a company spokesman, who was going to give my question an official response. "Like when someone asks, 'How'd ya get it?' Some of them want to ask, you know, and then some kid finally brings it up."

Guy began to pace a little and gesture dramatically, but his eyes never left mine. I was being given a lecture or a scolding; I wasn't sure which. Whatever it was, it was masterful.

"So I say to the kid, 'If I tell you I got it from having unprotected sex with a woman, you'll say oh, how terrible. If I tell you I got it from a man, you might stop listening or even feel disgusted and forget about what we're talking about.

"If I tell you I got it from a tainted blood transfusion, you'll feel sorry for me. If I tell you I got it from sharing a needle, you'll think what I'm saying has nothing to do with you."

Guy's voice was rising, and I found myself preparing for a blast.

"My question for you is, which one of these ways will scare the shit out of you? Because let me tell you, there's no good way to get this disease. You don't die any better, one way or the other!

"But this," Guy thundered, searing the air with each word, the cadence mesmerizing, the intonation perfect, "is not about how I got it! This is about how you're *not* going to get it!"

He studied me for a long moment, as if he could rate his effectiveness by the degree of distress registered on my face.

"Yeah," Guy's face relaxed, and his voice softened pleasantly. "Why would I do it any differently?"

Downstairs a clock chimed.

"Oh, did you see the three portraits over the couch in the living room, of me and my brothers? Did you notice the frames? Mine is the only one that's made of koa. I don't know if you know what koa is, but it's a very rare wood from Hawaii and my absolute favorite."

He chattered on, his words tumbling out on top of each other, as if speaking faster might explain it better. "Now I tell you, Polo is all of me. It's everything I buy. So I was really, really surprised at myself, that I would have all these things from Hawaii."

Guy sat down on his bed and patted the spot beside him, giving me permission to join him. He picked up a bright blue pillow and waved it around. "These pillows were made by an aunt in Hawaii. They're hand sewn." Sunlight streamed in from his window, and specks of dust could be seen dancing in the wake of the pillow.

"I just didn't get it before, you know, like don't call me *kamaina*, I'm just visiting from the mainland. So she made my quilt, too, and how this influence has come into my life, during the last couple of years, Hawaii and my appreciation of it, because if it was my choice, and you can see by the cherrywood in here it's really not," Guy ended breathlessly, "what people see of me."

He looked up. "Does that make sense?"

I had no idea what he had just said, but I nodded.

"It's a weird acceptance that I've gone through. I'm more in touch with my feelings. And my really true feelings are back in that direction, you know, toward the people of Hawaii, who really understand the importance of family.

"It all means so much to me. For instance, that koa mailbox." His eyes twinkled. "I told my Mom it would be the perfect urn."

I could only imagine his mother's reaction.

"But it's koa," he emphasized, picking it up. "I think it's big enough to hold all my ashes." Guy cleared his throat. "Yeah. There's a lot of significance in the things that I have and display today."

I could make no reply, rattled as I was by his earnest attempt to paint an accurate self-portrait, to entertain the still-warm possibilities of the present. It was difficult for me to enjoy him and this good-natured seduction, without being hastily sobered by the lurking specter of regret.

Guy, on the other hand, seemed to grasp the present eagerly. The comfort of denial must lure him, I thought, to tangible pleasures. We all enjoy our possessions—the signs and symbols, the stuff of life that announces who we are at the moment. His moment gone, Guy was simply finding things that would announce him forevermore.

He stood up again and poked through a case of compact discs. "This music is for special occasions. Like when I spend special time with James or even when I spend special time with myself. I really appreciate lighting my candle, dimming the lights, and just absorbing the moment. I don't do any evaluating of my life during this time."

How scary it would be to lie still long enough to evaluate his circumstances; I turned away from the thought.

"I used to be the type of person who had to go, go, go. Much worse than you've seen with me today. But," his voice became urgent, "I'm starting to value space by myself."

There were a dozen questions running through my head, but I didn't want to appear insensitive or stupid by asking them.

Again, he read my mind. "Go ahead, ask me anything."

I forged ahead. "When did you know you were gay?"

"Okay," Guy was nodding, "good question. When I was five years old we went to the beach in Hawaii with some old friends of my parents. The first day Uncle Aki, that's what I called him, carried me across the sand down to the water. It felt so good being carried by him. Every day after that I had him carry me. I would pretend like I didn't want to walk on the sand and whine and cry until Uncle Aki picked me up. He had to be the one. Yeah, I knew then."

"When you were five?"

"It's a lifetime thing, Molly."

"Yes, Guy." I didn't want him to think I doubted any of that. "But in our society, the sexual feelings of a gay five year old aren't noticed or smiled at, like when a five-year-old girl gets curious about the body parts of a five-year-old boy."

"That's exactly it!" Guy said triumphantly. "What is normal anyway? When he held me, I felt warm, wonderful feelings that I now know to be the beginnings of sexual attraction, and it all felt perfectly normal. I didn't know I was screwed up."

I looked up at him sharply. "You aren't . . ."

"I know, I know. I didn't mean to say that. It just got so hard, later."

I put my hand on his arm. "I know."

He raised an eyebrow.

"I mean, I want to know, Guy. I want to know everything about what you went through."

From the depths of Guy's deep brown eyes came some far-off feeling . . . fear? I wondered. Yearning? But the moment rushed by.

He turned back to his dresser and picked up two small frames containing young, smiling men. "My brothers," Guy said quietly. "That's Glen on the left. And that," he touched the face gently, "is Greg."

He replaced the photos and led me next door into another bedroom. "This is James' room, just for clothes. We spend all our time together in my room. This is the collection room—for his junk. He's not as picky as me. I guess that's obvious."

James' room was highly normal, clothes strewn about, shoes tumbled on the floor, a pile of mail tossed on the desk. The bathroom was next. Guy ushered me in and sighed heavily.

"This is my bathroom. It's, uh, where I'm at. I love my toilet because its the kind of plastic that doesn't get cold. The other day we were somewhere, I don't know, at least twenty minutes away, and I came all the way home to go. That's how I feel about my toilet."

I thought about the comfort of a warm toilet seat while we crossed the hall to the doorway of the master bedroom.

"My parents," Guy shrugged. "This is the way they always live. A mess."

Ditto Molly, I thought.

"Drives me crazy."

Inwardly, I smiled. Now this was a room I could really get into. Pictures of the three sons were everywhere. One side of the room was obviously Jane's, with a sewing machine and stacks and boxes of items clearly belonging to an elementary school teacher. A beautiful antique dresser caught my eye. This cluttered, lived-in room felt familiar, like any two people enjoying the decorations of the present, naively confident in a future where pretty things would comfort them still.

"Guy, I need to tell you that I love this room. You should avoid my closets. You'd have a breakdown."

We went downstairs and stopped in the hallway by the front door so I could slip into my shoes. Our eyes met, and we contemplated each other for a moment. "Are you ever angry, Guy?"

His hand tensed on the doorknob, as if he might be thinking about flinging the door open quickly to usher both me and my question out. "Sometimes. Not too often. The most frustrating thing for me is knowing in the end what has happened to this family, not only with me, but with everybody else."

I gazed at him, not really understanding.

"Everybody died."

To imagine the unimaginable . . . Inevitably, as I drove home, the thought of losing all one's children invaded my consciousness, staying with me for a long, harsh moment, until I revolted, shaking my head until the idea had been tossed away.

I turned my thoughts to Guy. I felt set upon, like a gullible tourist lured to the home of a nice, twenty-five-year-old man who turned out to be a cat burglar, charming and irresistible, like Cary Grant in *It Takes a Thief*, but who had stolen something from me that I wouldn't discover until later.

And finally, I remembered the closet without doors, framing an alcove of spectacular color and perfect order. A thought came to me, unbidden, that perhaps it was all an illusion. Where once doors had been, clothes now concealed a hiding place.

THE CIRCLE

Later that night, Guy lay on top of his comforter, feeling lonely. His parents had gone to bed. Anne had called at nine to say she was still coming to give him his massage. Guy rolled over to face his clock. 10:07. Anytime this century, Anne.

James wasn't home yet from the second of his two jobs, as a supervisor at a home for mentally impaired adults. Guy had urged him to abandon it. Put all your energy into becoming a manager at Nordstrom, he advised him, like I did; make it your career. But James enjoyed working at the home; everyone told him he was good with the people there, loving and patient.

I don't know how James does it. I mean, the work at Nordstrom can be tedious—really hard work at times, but still, there are those moments when everybody is bustling around, getting ready for a sale, making the store dazzle. Or when we're previewing a new line of clothes and deciding where to put it, how to display it, what to tell the customers to make them buy it. I loved all that. And even though I have my new career now, talking to kids, keeping them alive, I still miss it sometimes.

James leaves Nordstrom and goes to a place full of crazy people. Nice crazy people, he tells me. He really likes them. I admire him for that. And

I can understand, because James can be very gentle and caring. When he's not being a weenie.

He was just drifting off when he heard doors and voices downstairs.

"Annie?" he called out, leaning up on his elbows to peer into the hall. But it was James who bounded up the stairs and filled the doorway.

"She's here. Should I tell her to come up?"

"Not until I get a kiss hello."

"Wow, that's a switch."

"Don't start."

James leaned over the bed and obliged Guy with a playful peck.

Stripping off his tie and shirt as he went into the room next door, James declared, "Let's get her up here and get this back rub going. I want to go to bed."

"You can just go sleep somewhere else," Guy called after him. "I want to take my time. Everything hurts."

Each night for months, Anne had arrived with her bottle of oil and her experienced hands to give Guy one of the few physical pleasures he still looked forward to. No matter how tired she was, Anne was faithful to the routine, and Guy appreciated her devotion, though he expected as much from a best friend. For now, being Guy Nakatani's best friend defined her. Anne had come to accept that role, with far less difficulty than she accepted the fact that soon Guy would be leaving her, taking their friendship with him into eternity, and she would have to find herself all over again.

Clad in cut-off jeans and a Grateful Dead T-shirt, she entered Guy's room just behind James. They lined up next to Guy's bed.

"James, move your big booty," Anne teased, giving him a shove.

"Who's got the big booty?" he inquired sweetly.

She frowned. "I'm running every day."

"No, Anne," came the voice from the bed. "You're not running every day. You didn't run today or yesterday. Did you run yesterday?"

"No, but I'm going to run tomorrow."

"That's not every day. You never stick to anything."

"Don't make me mad, Guy. I'll rub you away." She handed James the oil. "You do his legs; I'll do his back."

Guy was taking his shirt off with some amount of difficulty, having already donned a pair of sweat shorts. The down comforter was rolled back. "No oil on my comforter," Guy always reminded Anne. He stretched out on his stomach and breathed out a happy sigh of anticipation.

James and Anne spread oil on Guy's body and began to massage his light brown, flawless skin. His once robust gymnast's build had slowly shriveled down to acceptably thin.

"Does that hurt, Guy?" James asked. "You don't have any fat anymore. I'm bumping into your bones."

Guy murmured something about not caring, and they worked quietly for a while.

If I had been James and James had been me, I don't think I would have stayed. Oh, by the way, I'm HIV-positive. Honestly, the way I used to function, I probably would have bolted. I hope he never thinks, what a fool I am.

Of course I was searching for intimacy, but James and I managed that for only a little while. Sometimes I still get the feeling, though. When he calls me the day I go to the doctor. How was it? What did he say? Or when he knows I woke up feeling terrible. He waits about two hours and then he phones. Are things better? Just the normal things people that love each other do. I like that. I've never had that before.

Like the time he said, you know we're supposed to be honest about everything, right? So he sits me down and tells me: A man brought me flowers. Of course, I was jealous. But for him to be consciously aware that this is something he needs to tell me, yes, these are the things that make me feel intimate.

A back rub emotionally satisfies me. It's the feeling of someone touching my body, massaging my scalp, touching my back and not my penis.

It's an innocent touch. I can relax.

Maybe it goes back to when I was little and my dad used to give me back rubs. I thought they were just the most wonderful thing. I think having that experience as a child comforts me now as an adult. I remember what life can feel like.

The door to Jane and Alexander's room opened.

"Guy" came a loud whisper across the hall. Jane entered her son's room and eased herself down onto the bed next to his head. "Well, aren't you spoiled," she admonished him with a tender touch to his damp forehead.

"Massage my scalp, Mom?"

Guy turned over. Jane worked her fingers lovingly through her son's hair and onto his face, carving out gentle lines across his cheeks and up to his temple. James and Anne moved over the rest of his body, massaging any spot they may have missed.

A chuckle coming from the doorway caused them all to look up. "This is nice. Where do I get in line?"

"Hi, Dad," Guy purred underneath his mother's hands.

Without a word, James and Anne shifted a little, making room for Alexander. Together, they comforted Guy, until his breathing slowed and he slept, his burdens put temporarily to rest.

· · · ·

James and Anne went downstairs to the kitchen, looking for a snack. Back in their own room, Jane joined her husband in bed.

"Aren't you going to turn off the light?" Alexander asked after a minute. He rolled over to face his wife, who was lying on her back, eyes open, her arms folded tightly over her chest.

"You look relaxed," he commented.

"You'll never believe what happened to me today. I was so mad, I wasn't even going to tell you." Jane paused, and Alexander waited. "I got stopped by the police."

Her husband suppressed a smile. "And what crime did you commit?"

"A traffic ticket," she said, giving him a look of total exasperation. "I got a ticket!"

Alexander simply raised his eyebrows.

"I was in front of Bradley's, you know, that bookstore where I like to go, and there weren't any cars at all, so I made a U-turn in the middle of the street."

"Was there a yellow line?"

"No."

"No yellow line?"

"Well, there was this little tiny thing in the road."

"You went over a divider?"

"It was very low. Not like those big dividers on big streets. I don't know what it was, really—I don't think it was there before. They probably just put it in."

Two words floated through Alexander's head. *Wheel alignment.*

"Oh, brother," Jane sighed, turning to him. She curled up on her side, her head resting on her arm.

Alexander regarded his wife. She looked so pitiful, like a naughty child who'd been scolded and left to think about what she'd done.

"So what did the cop say?" he asked delicately. Are you crazy, lady? That probably would have been my opening line, he thought.

"He said I'd made an illegal turn. I said I was sorry, but that I'd had a lot on my mind lately. He said, like what? So I told him the whole story. First I told him about Greg and then about Glen and then Guy. Can you believe it? He gave me the ticket anyway."

"So did you get out of the car and let him have it?"

"Oh, Al, of course not. Why would I do that?"

"Why not? Remember that tenant, the really filthy guy who ruined our rental house in San Luis? You ran after him with a bat. You were swearing at him, all the way down the street. You called him names."

"That was different. He made me really mad."

"I guess so," Al grinned at her. "You called him a dirty fag."

"Oh God," Jane groaned, scrunching up her pillow. "See how terrible I was? I didn't know what I was saying."

"You're not so terrible."

"You know, I felt silly. I finally figured out the cop didn't believe me. I mean, who would believe all that?"

"How hard were you crying?"

"I wasn't crying at all."

"You mean to tell me that you got through the whole story without shedding a tear, and any other time, when someone even looks at you funny, you're a weepy mess?"

"I was trying to remain calm."

"Jane, this was a time for hysteria."

"You're right. I don't know what happened."

Their eyes met and they laughed together, conscious of their shared understanding, feeling, as they often did, all the things that both united them and set them apart, two against the world.

"You know," said Alexander, "I got out of a ticket once. It was the simple truth that did it. After Greg died, I was on my way down to San Diego to attend the trial, and a cop stopped me and said I was speeding, and I said, 'Yes, I was.' I acknowledged it. Why bother with denial? I didn't care anyway.

"So he's writing up the ticket, and I'm sitting there, and then for some reason, I think I was talking to myself, really, I said, 'It's been a bad day.' The cop stopped writing and asked me what I meant. So I told him about Greg and the trial."

"Were you crying?" Jane interrupted.

He understood that she was teasing him, but he searched his memory anyway. "You know, I may have shed a tear. I don't remember. My feelings were still a little raw, you know, and I had a hard time saying out loud, 'My son is dead.' Those words didn't come easily."

"I remember at the trial, you broke down several times talking to the reporters."

"I know," Alexander nodded thoughtfully. "I would see them coming, holding their microphones or their notebooks, and I would ready myself, plotting out what I was going to say so I could stay in control. It didn't always work."

So much, Jane thought. Such a long list of terrible memories. Sometimes she reviewed them in her mind, not to continue the torture, but out of curiosity. How could anyone live through this, she would muse, confronting each ghost, considering each moment which, when lined up one next to the other, formed the incubus that haunted them.

"So," said Jane, shaking off the vision, "he believed you."

"Yeah. He said, 'Okay, I'll buy it.' He told me to take care of myself and drive slower and he sent me on my way."

Jane considered this for a moment. "I should have cried. That's where I went wrong."

Alexander grinned and leaned across her, extinguishing the light. They were quiet for a moment, and he thought she was asleep.

Jane's like that. She emotes. I brood. She's mad as hell and then she lets it all out and it's over, just like that. I carry my anger around for days, until it finally goes away because I've analyzed it to death.

We're okay, though. We've survived so far because we always seem to end up here, in this bed, in the middle of the night or early in the morning, talking things over. Most people spend time in bed sleeping or making love. We spend time surviving.

Jane wasn't asleep.

"Al, have you ever thought about where we live?"

"Hmm. We live in San Jose."

"No, our street."

"We live on Copeland Place." It took only a moment. Laughter, long and hard, rose up between them.

"Maybe we should put up a sign," said Al.

"Yeah," Jane agreed, "welcome to cope-land."

They began laughing again, the bed shaking, reaching over to hush each other and keep the rest of the household from joining them.

• • • •

In the flickering darkness made by his favorite candle, Guy floated dreamily under the soft down of his comforter. From somewhere, the sound of laughter drifted through his semiconsciousness.

He opened his eyes. In the soft light, he could view the landscape of his room. He closed his eyes again, feeling safe, his possessions surrounding him like sentries on their last watch, protecting the last little prince in the castle tower.

The laughter got louder. Guy listened, more aware now of where it was coming from. He leaned his head toward his parents' room, enjoying the sounds. Then he heard the front door close behind Anne, and James' step on the stairs. He smiled.

The circle. Guy, Jane, Alexander, James, and Anne. Guy had no need for anyone else to come close. It was good to have the affirming applause of his audiences, and thousands of letters from thankful kids, assuring him that he would be remembered. But to spend precious, borrowed time, Guy had no need, no desire for others.

JAPANESE BORN IN HAWAII

Alexander Denichi Soares was born on June 25, 1936, in Hilo, Hawaii. The nurse who prepared his birth certificate noted quietly his Russian, Japanese, and Portuguese names.

His maternal grandfather, Koi Nakatani, migrated from Japan because there was no work for him there. On his way to Seattle, he jumped ship in Hawaii. Since he imagined himself to be a fugitive, he changed his name from Nakatani to Mitani and slipped quietly into island life.

Eventually, Koi married and had two daughters, Harriet and Marian. When his wife died, he felt he could not care for both girls, so Harriet went to live with a Caucasian family. They were wealthy and well connected during the war. Accompanying them, Harriet could enter military bases for social functions despite the fact that she was Japanese and at that time subject to great suspicion. Harriet's benefactors made over their tiny, doll-like guest, barely four and a half feet tall, indulging her much like they did the family poodle, whom they also adored.

The fact that Koi had no sons put both his given and adopted names in peril. According to custom, the oldest daughter, Harriet, would lose the family name to that of her husband, which she did when she married Alexander Soares. Harriet named her first son Alexander Denichi, after her husband and because he was *ichi*, the first.

After five years in Hilo, Harriet and Alexander divorced. Harriet chose a new home in Honolulu, and the real family name, Nakatani, which was how she designated her son when he started school. This was helpful, because in the estimation of his teachers and his mother's friends, he didn't look at all to be half Portuguese. Harriet, too, was relieved to clear up this problem.

That same year, the Japanese military bombed Pearl Harbor. Alexander wouldn't be able to recall the sounds of the bombs or the panic of the island's people. He does remember that the school where he was scheduled to attend first grade was mistaken as a military installation and completely destroyed a mere three weeks before school was to begin.

For Alexander and the children he played with near the small house where he lived, it was an exciting time. They knew that the United States was at war with Germany, Italy, and Japan, and that they, as children born in Hawaii, were Americans. They practiced blackouts and civil defense in their school and in the chicken coops and woodpiles of the neighbors' yards. A great day was one spent in a bomb shelter.

Although Harriet Nakatani was tiny, she was a towering parental figure, who taught her son to turn his back on Japanese ways. He skipped Japanese-language school, and they never spoke Japanese at home. She even tried stubbornly to gossip in English with the neighbors. If her son learned English and got an education and did things right, he would be a success in America, which was all she wanted for him.

Her influence was profound; for all his childhood, Harriet was his sole caretaker. The man whom Harriet married sometime during the fifties, Takeo Kawakami, was never "father" to Alexander, or even "stepfather," but rather "uncle." A teenager by then, Alexander was struck by the fact that although he honored Takeo, he would have no one to call "Father" for the rest of his life.

There were many times when Alexander was aware that he was

alone. He learned to value his cognitive processes, noticing at a very early age that thinking seemed to be his talent. Later, he would wonder about feeling. The day would come when he would view himself harshly and with bias, as a Japanese male, defined by the mind but betrayed by the heart.

Socially, Alexander didn't develop at the rate of his peers. Dating was a frightening frontier for him. But during his sophomore year, he joined the Junior ROTC program, and his identity, which had been blurry and unsure, came into focus as a cadet. He would immerse himself in that special society for the next seven years.

His self-worth rose as rapidly as his rank. Once he passed the level of field-grade officer to company, and then battalion, commander, he was given a sponsor, and with that came a pretty girl who dressed up and escorted him to the military balls, staying at his side throughout those heady evenings. There were eight schools with an ROTC program, and therefore eight military balls. During high school, Alexander had eight dates.

He was very thankful for this arrangement. He could count on one hand the number of girls he was infatuated with in high school, and significantly reduce that number as to girls he actually approached. To ask for a date, and then to be turned down: It was a terrifying yet probable outcome, and the thought rankled, considering his other accomplishments.

Alexander loved being a cadet. It moved him beyond the limitations of his childhood and showered him with recognition for his achievements. It was with great confidence that after two years at the University of Hawaii, he applied to several high-ranking universities on the mainland and was accepted at them all. He chose the University of Michigan, the one farthest away from the islands.

I was the first Japanese American in the history of the University of Michigan to rise to the rank of Army ROTC commander, which made me the highest-ranking cadet on campus, in charge of the Army, Navy, and Air Force on Armed Forces Day. After graduation, I was offered a regular

Army commission rather than a reserve commission, which meant I was in the elite part of the officers' corps. It meant they were offering me a career.

What was important was the discipline, the esprit de corps, the gauntlet of preparing for hostilities. I was responsible for myself and those under me. What I did reflected on the lives of others. It was a social relationship I relished.

My achievement amazes me still. I was a skinny little runt. My regiment towered over me, and yet I commanded them. The fact that I was Japanese did not hold me back and actually was of surprisingly little significance.

Graduating from the University of Michigan, I set forth my life down the narrow path of certainty. I would be a social worker during my two years of active duty, passing up my alternate dream of flying a helicopter which, although enticing, was not a practical plan. I would continue my social work at the prestigious Veterans Administration in Palo Alto, California, where my reputation would precede me. And I would end my career as chief of Social Services and enjoy the fruits of my labor with my family. I would not be expected to fail.

It wasn't real, I suppose. It never occurred to me that just off the path were things I could never have imagined—terrible, unexpected things with which I had absolutely no relationship. The illusion of predictability. Despite what you may have heard, the military fails to prepare its warriors for the surprise attack of life.

I remember the pride I felt each time I prepared my dress uniform. Wearing it meant still another moment of recognition, of honor. I stood before the mirror and admired the starch and shine that I had become. I didn't know I had trapped a creative being beneath the stiff clothes. I didn't know I had polished a two-edged sword.

• • • •

Jane Toshiko Souka was born on February 15, 1938, in the town of Kahului on the island of Maui. The house that held Toshio and Claire Souka and their eight children was in back of the Island Market. Jane

and her sisters and brothers knew that others saw them as an important family. Their father owned the store, featured prominently on
Pulehu Avenue, and their mother, who was known for her generosity,
had financed a beauty parlor for her friend Maiko. In addition to that,
Claire was a talented seamstress and sewing teacher.

Everyone admired Toshio for sending eight children away to college, but permission to go, choosing the school, and finding a way to get
them there was orchestrated by Claire. While Toshio struggled to keep
up with the needs of his large family, never once did Claire tell her children that a university was out of their financial reach.

When the children were small, she brought in girls from other
islands to do all the things she was too busy to do. They would baby-
sit, cook the meals, and clean the house in exchange for sewing lessons
and a place to stay.

However, when the Souka girls were old enough, they took over the
work. Very early on, Jane was planning menus, cooking, and ironing.
Taking a nap was such a pleasure, she felt guilty even considering it. In
contrast, the sons in the family began each day free from domestic
responsibilities.

*When I was about seven, the volcano erupted on the big island. Everyone
was talking about it, and I listened to every word, imagining as well as I
could this amazing event.*

*When my mother suddenly announced that she was sending us over
to see the smoke and lava for ourselves, I was shocked and thrilled. She
understood that an important opportunity had presented itself to her children, and she wouldn't let us miss out.*

*I thought it was sad that she wasn't going, too. You can tell me all
about it, she said when I asked her. Just then, I had to control my impulse
to run and throw myself into her arms.*

*Later, I would remember that moment and wonder if she wanted to
hug me, too. But hugging and touching wasn't her way, just as it hadn't
been the way of her mother, and her mother's mother, and so on. The ticket to the big island to see the volcano—that was her way.*

In Kahului, during the forties, it wasn't unusual for a Japanese family to have eight children. All of them were expected to achieve greatness in school. They were not expected to talk when they were around adults; when they didn't agree, it remained a private thought.

Even while she felt the burden of high expectations bearing down on her, Jane never thought to rebel. She wanted more than anything for her mother and father to be pleased with her.

When I got my first "D" at the University of Michigan, I was completely devastated. Alexander remembers. It was like somebody in the family had died. It was that bad.

You have to understand. I knew how important it was to keep shame from visiting our family. It was important to all the families I knew. As children, we understood without ever talking about it.

Honor and shame—I never used those words with our kids. But I felt them anyway. I think they live in the walls of every Japanese house.

When Jane was in the fourth grade, her grandfather became very sick. Jane was given the responsibility of feeding him, shaving his head, and washing his clothes. This situation overwhelmed her with a sense of great injustice, but she said nothing.

Jane was afraid that one day she would go in to wake her grandfather and find him dead. That never happened, but toward the end, what she sometimes found in his room was much more terrible than a decaying corpse: Her grandfather had soiled his pants.

This was more than Jane could take. Entering his room each day to clean him up and carry his clothes out to be washed was like living in her own personal nightmare. Finally one morning, she brought a stick with her; leveling her eyes and closing off her nostrils to the stench, she poked at the soiled clothes until they were hoisted up and out of the room. Gradually, this system was perfected, and the discomfort lessened somewhat. When he died, Jane felt guilty that she had treated him so disrespectfully.

Through the beginning of my married years, I had nightmares that I had forgotten to feed Grandfather. In the dream, he'd fallen down and was yelling for help and nobody came and I pretended not to hear him. I still hate filth. My bathrooms are always spotless. When I had my first baby, Alexander had to change all the diapers.

When Glen was dying, though, I did everything I could for him without any thought at all. Guy would say to me, Mom, you have to have a life of your own, why are you sitting with Glen? You can't cater to his every whim, you can't be his friend, his mother, and his nurse.

But I sat down in the den, watching TV with him, being his companion. I have no regrets. I don't know if Al has regrets, because he said he couldn't watch the programs Glen wanted to watch. I didn't care. Even when he was sleeping, I was down there.

Whatever it takes, I thought. I didn't want to have any nightmares like I did with my grandfather.

The Souka children went to Japanese-language school, but they spoke pidgin English at home. This was not an accent but a language, common with the people in Hawaii, a combination of English and several other languages and difficult for haoles to understand.

Taught by her parents, Jane came to believe that all things American were the keys to success. Fitting in was the right thing to do. Meanwhile, denial of self became like a mutant gene, passed on from generation to generation.

By the time Jane was in high school, she was pretty and popular. One Christmas she went to a dance with a Chinese boy, Frank Ching. Frank was popular, too, and intelligent; he was on the honor roll. Jane had heard it said, "Chinese is Chinese, Japanese is Japanese," but she thought that was silly. The dance seemed like it would be fun, and after all, it was just a date.

All around her, the many races of people who made up the island population lived their lives as she did, walking quietly with eyes straight ahead, on the streets of Kahului and in her father's market, in the schools that she and her sisters and brothers attended, aware of each other, yet staying firmly to one's own path. With the other Japanese children, Jane memorized the lines of separation.

I learned to be afraid of people I didn't know or whose ways weren't familiar to me, and never to speak of them. Therefore, my fear of homosexuals was a secret, silent terror.

I was brought up in an environment where gays were thought to be disgusting, and we had absolutely no connection with them or even the idea of them. They were unnameable. And yet, I knew gays were out there, and I was afraid. It's not right to feel this way, but the fear and aversion settled into the deepest part of me, and I have had to struggle hard to let them go.

It was all very clear and unchallenged: Some people were to be avoided. Also to be avoided was any sort of disruption of what was expected. I learned to make everything all right.

I emerged from childhood with my own understanding of the Japanese way. Don't talk about anything. Whatever can't be understood will probably go away. Whatever you do, don't cry. Don't touch or hug or kiss. Even as an adult, I was uncomfortable when someone did any of these things to me.

Until Greg died. My father was at home in Wailuku when Greg was killed. I told him not to come to California. We would bring Greg to Maui to be buried. On the other end of the phone, I knew he was crying. He did not say anything, or make even the slightest sound, but I knew. I had never felt so close to him.

There may be those who don't understand how I've lived through all of this. In order to survive, I needed to forget the traditional way. I had to clean out the room where I kept that way of life. If I hadn't talked and cried and touched and hugged, if I had avoided all the things I didn't understand, I would have died with Greg. Who would have sat with Glen and Guy? Some things are meant to be forsaken.

· · · ·

Alexander boarded the plane for Michigan carrying his ROTC medals in his bag. He was nineteen years old, and leaving for a faraway land. He held his bag tightly.

He first noticed the pretty Japanese girl on the plane to the mainland. She was sitting with a friend, chatting and laughing, and Alexander thought she was by far the more attractive of the two. He simply took note of them, making absolutely no move to be noticed in return.

The plane first stopped in San Francisco, and then he had to change planes in Chicago. Those sixty-five minutes in Chicago, Al would recall, were the loneliest of his life. He left the plane with the Chicago-bound passengers and for a moment imagined that someone might greet him at the end of the ramp. He bought a Coke at the snack bar near the gate, watching happy reunions, people calling out to each other and embracing. He thought about what he had left behind in Hawaii. It was as if none of that counted; he would have to start again as nobody.

When he arrived at the campus in Ann Arbor, he went to the International Center. He was able to find the center because a man who was picking up the trash noticed his look of bewilderment and kindly offered to help him. Alexander was so startled to see a Caucasian man performing such a task, he had to ask him to repeat the directions.

The second person he spoke with was a classmate from Hawaii named Warren. He was standing on the stairs of the center, also looking lost, and to Alexander a gorgeous sight. For the first few months, Alexander and Warren spent every moment they weren't in class or sleeping in the dorm in conference, huddled together in the dining room of the International Center or in the hallway outside one of their rooms, deciphering college life.

Alexander had left a girlfriend behind in Hawaii. Myra was soft-spoken and fragile, very feminine, and she didn't demand anything at all, which was just enough for him. When he arrived at Michigan, he was a bit preoccupied with her and wrote to her often. By January, the girl he had kissed four times, five if he counted the peck on the cheek that was his initial effort, had been re-created somewhat for Warren, who began to refer to his friend as "Dr. Love."

Then suddenly things changed. The Japanese-from-Hawaii students began to find each other, and Alexander and Warren joined in their gatherings at the International Center. It was from these new friends that Alexander heard about a beautiful freshman girl named Jane.

The first time he saw her, he was marching around the ROTC field, and she was walking with a student Alexander recognized as Harold from his psychology class. As it turned out, Jane was the pretty girl from the plane.

Harold was from the Big Island, which made him, in Alexander's estimation, rather small-town, like Jane. Harold was really infatuated with Jane, and he befriended Alexander so that he would have someone to guide him in his pursuit. For the first semester, Al encouraged Harold. Alexander could think a good game, he could advise and comment, and he could imagine himself to be the greatest lover in the world, so long as it was to help poor Harold.

Meanwhile, Harold took slow steps to get close to Jane and reported back his progress. He told Alexander about the ten o'clock curfew at the dorm, where you bring your date back, chit-chat, and finally go for the good-night kiss. He described it all to Alexander in excited detail, because Alexander wasn't part of that scene, not yet. Unfortunately, neither was Harold.

"Why don't you just go ahead?" Alexander urged him, tired of Harold's inaction.

"You think I should? Do you think she'd want to, with all those people standing around?"

"From what you've told me, nobody would be looking."

So Harold did it, just once. Shortly after that, things were not going well for Harold; Jane was ignoring him. It was clear to Alexander that Jane was the girl of the hour with almost every male member of the Japanese-from-Hawaii club, but that when it came to actually connecting with her, they were collectively inept. He knew this because Warren told everyone that if they wanted to know how to get a girl, they should talk to Alexander.

In a moment of courage unparalleled in his lifetime to date, Alexander announced to several would-be suitors that he would give them a one-month head start, and if nobody ended up with her by then, he would give it a try.

The weeks passed, and Alexander looked for the right moment to make his move. Then one day he heard that Jane was failing a course and panicking. Suddenly, he had an official reason to make human contact. He could go over and console her, let her cry, offer to help. He was older. He was in.

Next up on the agenda was an actual date. Alexander had a friend, Richard, who liked Jane's friend Gloria. Since they were both social cowards, they decided to double date to a bowling alley, which, as they predicted, created a certain light atmosphere and made conversation easy. But the key to the success of the date was that it was still winter in Michigan. On the way back to the dorm, Alexander had the occasion to put his arm around her, and that's how it all began.

Later, he asked her about Harold. Her face immediately took on a look of disgust as she related her version of their kiss, which had ended with her running into the dorm to brush her teeth. Alexander felt truly blessed, because whenever he kissed Jane, she didn't run anywhere.

On the whole, Jane and I hit it off really well. We had a good beginning. But the four years between the time we first cared about each other until we got married held some difficult times for Jane. I had a terrible temper. Sometimes just waiting in line at the movie theater sent me into a rage. Jane didn't appreciate my moods, but for some reason she stayed with me.

Alexander and Jane were married on December 17, 1960. After the ceremony, their family and friends wished them well, raising their glasses in the traditional Japanese toast, *Banzai, Banzai, Banzai!* They drank to their happiness, to long lives and well-being.

I remember seeing Alexander on the plane. My friend who was riding with me that day was very interested in him. So during the semester he was on my mind, and when he asked me out I was very excited, thrilled to be with him. I remember that bowling was fun, and that when Alexander put his arm around me, he acted like he knew what he was doing. Perhaps I acted that way, too, but actually, neither of us knew anything at all.

There were times during the four years when his moods really upset me. I even thought about breaking up, but I didn't. I had many more positive feelings about him than negative.

I remember our wedding, that it was a happy day, and that inside I was glad when no one said a word about us starting a family, like they often do at weddings.

I think about this a lot. If we had known what was ahead for us, would we have run from each other? Did our particular union produce this terrible future? If only we had given more attention to small annoyances, or been intolerant of peculiarities . . .

And yet, we, too, had a right to our illusions. We were no different than any other couple who assume some measure of happiness and good fortune. No one ever believes they will be on the plane that goes down, leaving no survivors.

Even worse, to be the only two survivors and to count all your children among the dead. Parenting is over for us. It's strange, because we have gone backward. When Glen was born, people said we were starting a family, and I agree, children make a family, and I don't know what that makes the two of us now.

Many people say our chances of staying together, considering the circumstances, are almost zero. And when I think of the tension and the fights and all the turmoil . . . And yet, in the darkest night, we still cling to each other. It's a mystery.

THE AMERICAN WAY

Each time Jane Nakatani delivered a son, she had been hoping for a daughter. She knew so much more about girls, because she had helped raise her sisters. To Jane, girls were safer.

Both Alexander and Jane believed that children should be encouraged to be independent. Alexander insisted that for him, growing up alone had been character building, and he adopted a similar attitude toward his own sons. Jane's mother had presented her babies to the family and immediately moved away from them, and it was this model that Jane dragged with her into motherhood. For both, success was measured by separation, and by the honor brought to the family by self-directed children.

Despite their apparent agreement on a hands-off approach, Alexander and Jane quietly critiqued each other as parents. Alexander saw his wife, whom he believed to be a warm and loving human being, show more warmth and love toward her nieces and nephews than her own sons, while Jane saw Al as a stern, demanding disciplinarian, whose expectations for his children soared way out of reach. Jane should enjoy her children more, Alexander thought, while his wife wished that he expect less of them.

As it happens with many families, these tensions were never

45

confronted, masked by the pressures of daily life and the demands of two occupations. By 1963, Alexander had arrived, as planned, at the Veterans Administration in Palo Alto and begun his career as a clinical social worker. He expected things to go well and that shortly he would have the high regard of his peers. Jane, meanwhile, immersed herself in her role as an elementary school teacher. They felt they were fitting in well in California.

Once in a while, however, something happened that separated them from the mainstream. When they wanted to buy their first house near San Jose, the real estate agent refused to take them by the newly built homes, showing them instead houses that had been repossessed. Alexander and Jane found someone else to help them, and soon they found a house.

The day after they moved in, the woman who lived next door rang their bell. Jane invited her into the kitchen, pleased to be meeting her neighbors. When Jane offered her coffee, the woman seemed surprised. "I would have thought you'd drink tea," she said.

As she was leaving, the woman asked Jane when she would be starting her garden. "Oh," Jane laughed, "teachers don't have time for gardens."

When Jane reported the visit to Alexander that night, her husband dismissed the comments as insignificant. But he recalled the real estate agent, and his mother's incessant warnings about appearing too Japanese. How does one appear only a little Japanese? he had wondered. In any case, the incidents were never mentioned again.

Even as the children began to arrive, Jane tenaciously embraced her career. For a woman who held only bitter memories of being made to baby-sit her siblings day after day, becoming a teacher might have been a curious choice. But by all accounts, she was a wonderful teacher. Beloved, respected, often in demand, her parents thanked her endlessly, and each June her students didn't want to let her go.

I often dreamed about being a teacher when I was little. Teaching is very different from baby-sitting, when you have to feed and bathe them.

Alexander did those kinds of things for our babies, along with the diapering. It was just all too familiar.

It takes a while to work with a child. I develop a personal relationship with each of them. If academics are a problem, I give them less to do. The first three weeks, I reward them for everything. I have little chips and marbles, and every time they do what I want them to do, I put one in a container. After a while, when the container is full, they get more free time or pizza or a little prize. Once I think I have them in the palm of my hand, I start weaning them off the marbles. Sometimes they say, why aren't you rewarding us as much anymore? I just smile.

Parents ask me, why are they trying to do all this for a marble? Teaching is so much easier than parenting.

Glen Takeo Nakatani was born on October 23, 1961 and, to honor the father's side first, named after his step-grandfather. Greg Toshio came on March 29, 1963, and was named after his maternal grandfather. Five years later, on November 25, 1967, Guy Toshiro arrived and was named after a Japanese movie star.

It was a prophetic naming. From the very beginning, the third and last son of Alexander and Jane Nakatani took his place in the spotlight, a place he would strive to keep. He could engage an audience even from his crib, and as a toddle, delighted his family and neighbors with consistently adorable antics.

The ease with which Guy assumed command of the people around him could perhaps be attributed to a certain relaxation on the part of his parents. Seven years after Glen's birth propelled them into the parental role, Alexander and Jane were tired. They were ready for a child they couldn't control, even if they wanted to. They got one.

I raised Glen and Greg the way I was raised growing up in Wailuku. They would be well disciplined. If I told them to sit there, they did, and everyone—baby-sitters, friends, relatives—thought that was unreal. Alexander and I were both stern. We didn't touch or cuddle much, although I noticed that it was easier for my husband. When Guy climbed into the shower with him every night for years, Al didn't seem to mind. But we weren't very loving.

I felt really bitter about having kids, trapped, angry at myself for relinquishing so easily the freedom I had briefly found. I felt like I baby-sat all my life until I got married. But Al said, if we have children now, when they're independent we'll still be young enough to enjoy life.

I just acquiesced to pregnancy. We were married in December; Glen was born in October. I was very upset. Then I was upset when Greg came. Alexander didn't know how I felt.

I tried to nurse Glen, but after two weeks I quit. I suffered for that, but I said I don't care how good they say it is, I can't stand it. I worked so hard to feed him, and when it was finally over it was time to start again. I couldn't take the endlessness of it all.

And nobody else could help me. I was brought up with brothers who were given everything the way our father was given everything—and his father before him. I promised myself I would never marry anyone raised like that. I was going to have help and not cater to him. So obviously, I couldn't breast-feed.

One of the ways I coped with the demands of two little babies was by maintaining an orderly and immaculate house. The cleanest rooms, by far, were the bathrooms. I remember little Glen running in from kinder-garten, a terrified look on his face, barely making it to our bathroom in time. When I asked him why he didn't use the toilets at school, he told me they weren't clean enough. It took a lot of convincing for him to go at school.

I guess it was hard work, being this uptight. By the time Guy was born, I was ready to enjoy. Of course, Guy got everyone's attention imme-diately. In a way, the other two began to take a backseat.

By the time he was ten, Guy was the baby-sitter of choice for his cousins. They marveled at him; he was hardly older than they were. Guy could do anything a mother could do: He fixed their meals, gave them baths, put them to bed. If they ever started to cry, he would tick-le them until they were laughing instead.

Guy organized the neighborhood. He wrote, directed, and produced their backyard shows, always charged admission, which those attending always paid. When they played follow the leader, he was always the leader, because he was the most fun and interesting. Cousins, friends, even the adults agreed: No one could compare to Guy.

Greg, who was five years older, didn't know what to make of his little brother. Not only was Guy out of his control, he seemed to be out of his parents' control, which was a noteworthy development. To Greg, he was amusing, pesky, and useful whenever Greg needed a slave. Getting Guy to do what he wanted sometimes took cunning on Greg's part, but more often than not Guy was eager to give in to his older brother.

Greg took care of me. He sure did. We would have some nasty fights, but that was part of the bond.

Once I was sick and my mom was working, so after school Greg was going to watch me. He said, when I come home today, I'll bring you some licorice. I thought, wow, that he would go to the store and spend his own money and get me licorice because I wasn't feeling very good. I remember that day. It was just him and me.

Whenever we walked together, Greg waited for me. Younger brother. That's what he called me. Not bratty brother, or my brother I don't really like or I have to live with, but younger brother. Most people don't talk about their brothers and sisters, really, because they're trying to find their own identities. But Greg talked about me.

Even so, I used to wish that I was an only child, so all the attention would be on me. When Greg left for college, and Glen had already been gone for a long time, I thought, this is going to be great. But within a week, I hated it. I just hated that Greg was gone. He wrote to me once a month. God, it meant so much to me that he would take the time to write.

Childhood would have been scary without Greg. I think of him and get a huge rush of feelings. He is my connection to something wonderful that's gone now. The worst of it is, I got my wish. What I said I didn't mean. I didn't mean it at all.

When Greg was a baby, he was, in the estimation of his mother, the most rebellious. Jane worried about the way Alexander scolded him, trying to bring him into line. To Jane, a sign of what was to come was Greg's first haircut. Along with everyone who came to see him, Jane delighted in her baby's long, thick "Japanese hair." When, at the age of two months, Alexander had it trimmed to a crew cut, Jane felt uncontrollably sad.

Greg was an active, lively child, not at all like Glen, who spent a lot of time alone in his room or quietly observing everyone else's activities. Greg didn't need nurturing, which Alexander saw as a sign of proper development. When Greg reached high school, his father started to notice his achievements, and they developed a special relationship. Until then, Jane felt that Greg got the least attention.

The middle brother went to school, played on the tennis team, and like his friends worked hard at maintaining a macho image. Once when Greg was about ten, he was bullied by a boy down the street. Pacing back and forth in the Nakatani front yard, he listened to the taunts from four doors down while Alexander washed the car and kept an eye on his son.

"He's calling me names," Greg seethed, continuing to talk to himself while he wore a path across the lawn.

They heard, "Hey sissy!" and with that, Greg turned to his father, as if waiting for permission to go berserk. Alexander's annoyance had also grown. They were a deadly pair.

"All right," he said to Greg. Father and son squared off, legs spread, hands on hips. "What do you think? Do you think you can take him?"

Greg turned a gleaming eye toward the boy, who had ventured a few steps down the sidewalk. "Yeah," said Greg. "No problem."

In my mind, I was programming the attack. I thought, if I give him license to fight, I have to make sure things don't get out of hand. I got all that set in my head, and finally I said, okay, go get him. Things got out of hand quickly.

Greg took off. Alexander panicked. "Wait, wait!" he yelled as he ran to catch up with his son. "Don't run, Greg. Take your time. I don't want you to be all tired out when you get there."

Greg strolled down the street, Alexander trailing nonchalantly behind. When Greg was within two yards of the enemy, he took a flying leap and leveled him, beginning to flail away with his fists. The boy recovered and was able to get back up, but was hardly a match for Greg. Alexander stood nearby, watching each blow carefully, like a referee at a prize fight.

"Okay, that's it," he announced when Greg was sitting on top of his opponent. "You've achieved the dominant position."

From the ground, the boy looked at Alexander strangely, but with some amount of gratitude. "You can apologize now," Alexander directed.

"Thanks, Dad," said Greg as they took their victory walk back down the block.

"You're welcome, son. But that's not something you want to try very often." Greg grinned at his father, patting him on the back.

Greg tried to show his parents he was tough and nothing bothered him, but actually many things bothered him. He got very high marks in school, but told Guy not to strive for that because once you did, you'd never be allowed to achieve any less.

Greg felt himself to be surrounded, by a younger brother who was the most charming child in the universe, and by an older brother who was the model eldest son. Guy was a nuisance, but Greg could handle him. Glen, on the other hand, was puzzling.

Every other summer, Alexander and Jane would return to Hawaii to visit Al's parents, Harriet and Takeo, and the large number of Souka relatives—grandparents, aunts, uncles, and cousins. Glen was Harriet's favorite—he always got more money in his birthday envelope than Greg and Guy, a detail that didn't go unnoticed. And Greg seemed to be favored by Takeo. Guy pouted about not being anybody's favorite.

It may have been that there just weren't enough grandparents to go around, or perhaps to Harriet and Takeo, Guy didn't need an advocate. They remember Guy fixing his own breakfast at the age of four, starting a business selling Puka shells to tourists, and taking over a local gym to practice his gymnastics while audiences of leotard-clad children and curious passersby clapped and cheered.

In the end, it was Harriet and Glen who developed something of a lasting relationship. Much later, during the ten years he exiled himself from home, Glen often lived with his grandparents in Hawaii. During those times, he worked as an assistant manager at a fast-food restaurant, and every morning Harriet fixed his breakfast and they had a little conversation. Glen didn't say much, but then neither did Harriet. It was just right for both of them.

The young man who would ultimately find refuge with his paternal grandparents had been a quiet child, a gentle little being. Alexander remembers carrying Glen around, cuddling him, warming to his softness. Alexander understood that this was not the Japanese way. But somehow, Glen drew his father to him.

Alexander cherished this little baby and spent more time with him than any of the others. But even then, Al was demanding. He wanted Glen to drink all his milk from the bottle and became angry when he didn't. He wouldn't spank him, but he would speak to him with frightening firmness.

Alexander taught his son as he had been taught, not to exhibit any signs of weakness. Emotion was weakness. Crying was unacceptable. Glen never cried.

Glen grew up privately, never voicing a need or claiming a feeling. And to Alexander, he was the ideal child, hardly needing to be disciplined. For the first eight years of his life, the eldest son fit in beautifully and upheld the honor of his family.

Except for once. Alexander came home to discover his three-year-old son with his hair in curlers, thanks to the creativity of a visiting six year old. The father could not contain his fury.

"No son of mine will be a sissy and wear these girl things," he screamed, standing over the two culprits. Glen's accomplice started to cry and crossed her legs so she wouldn't wet her pants. Little Glen was not so fortunate. As the wetness spread over his trousers and dripped onto the rug, he pulled at the curlers, his hands shaking, unable to get them out without extracting hunks of soft, dark hair along with them. As was his way, he retreated to a corner, remaining silent and still for a long time. Early on, Glen had learned how to disappear from a room; on that day, his mother talked with a neighbor about the curlers and all the funny little things Glen did, forgetting that he was there.

If I had a favorite, it was Glen. In the Japanese culture, the firstborn means something special to the father, the one who sets the example for the rest. For the longest time, I really loved that kid, the way he was soft and reflective. In my social worker's mind, I thought he would become a well-rounded man.

At some point, I became aware that certain things were troubling him. He seemed more preoccupied, more disconnected than you would expect of a child. He could stay in his room for two or three hours, and we didn't know what he was doing. We made some attempt to address this, but we didn't want to pry. Do you want to come down, get out, join us?

When Glen didn't turn out to be the son I expected, my feelings for him changed. And I let it happen. God, how I regret that. He closed up, and I wasn't sensitive or knowledgeable enough of these things to call him back.

I held fast to my ethic. The boys would develop on their own, taking responsibility and initiative, and bearing the consequences of their actions. They would need me less and less.

I felt they were being launched. I told them that the only real thing you can count on is your mind and your education. Although I was probably feeding the stereotype about Asians having brains, I told them there was no level playing field out there for us. It wasn't enough to be equal— you had to be perceptively better.

I kept to my narrow view: They were behaving, doing well in school, and even later, when Glen began to give us problems, I still clung to his academic success. I missed the point. He was doing everything on his own, slowly, I've come to realize, preparing to exit from the family.

...e summer before junior high school, Glen spent a week
.ocience camp. He had been home only a few days when his parents
got an agitated call from his counselor.

She had discovered a pornographic magazine under his cot and
had written them a note about it. Had Glen given them the note? Glen
insisted he never received a note. In the discussions that followed,
Alexander and Jane forgot about the magazine while they interrogat-
ed their son about the note. Why would the counselor make this up?
Was he sure he never got the note?

Alexander was angry, and, unexpectedly, Glen was reduced to
tears. Eventually, Glen won them over to his version of the truth, to the
point where even the counselor believed Glen didn't have the note.

Several years later, when Glen moved out and Jane was cleaning
his room, she found the note from the counselor; it had been a gay
pornographic magazine. So much had happened since then, she hardly blinked an eye. Alexander commented that at the time Glen's lie had
been effective. He had thrown them off the trail.

Glen began the seventh grade and became more and more with-
drawn, silent, private; he developed a facial tick. After a few weeks,
Alexander and Jane received a call from the school. Glen refused to
shower after P.E. Alexander and Jane talked to him about it, but he
couldn't explain why he didn't want to shower, he simply insisted that
he wouldn't. His parents said he had to shower. Glen maintained he
would not.

Jane went to talk with the teacher, who said he was failing the class
and that he had a psychological problem and should see somebody.
Jane came home and told Alexander, and both of them immediately
went on the defensive. Jane declared that this was a time when all kids
were self-conscious about their bodies. Alexander responded that men
were conditioned to be together and that eventually Glen would be
ready to be one of the guys, joking around, enjoying the camaraderie
of the shower. He was just shy. Obviously, the P.E. teacher had a problem. Perhaps he should see somebody.

The three of them stood up to the teacher. In the end, it was a negotiated truce, and Glen was allowed to shower alone, after everyone else left the locker room.

It got so whenever Jane and I tried to talk to Glen about anything, it did not go well. I remember our discussion about showering after P.E. He was not communicating much, and I was trying to tell him he had to shower for health reasons, because it was a school requirement, and the fact that they were going to flunk him. I tried to gain his understanding. I was upset he was going to fail simply because he wouldn't take a shower.

So I did a very bad thing at that point. I told him he was going to shower with Greg for a week. I said there was nothing wrong with his body and he would get used to it. I remember Greg didn't say anything. Thank God.

It got to be a power thing. Showering or not showering. There was some resolution, but from then on, the tension around Glen only increased. He was obstinate, sullen, secretive. He never told us anything; he just did it his way.

By the time he was thirteen, he was living two lives. One life was biding his time, working around us, surviving. But all the time he was carrying on all alone, planning a future away from us.

Glen's double life began in earnest. He fooled everyone—teachers, counselors, employers, everyone who was part of his life. At the age of thirteen, he obtained false identification that afforded him many privileges, including a job at Jack in the Box. At fourteen, he had a credit card. When he was fifteen and a sophomore, he took classes at a nearby junior college, and that spring he took the G.E.D. exam and was out of school. Jane and Alexander never knew any of what was going on. He would say anything to anyone to satisfy them, to hold them off.

Much later, they went to the manager of Jack in the Box. "What are you doing," they asked, "hiring someone who is underage?" The manager assured them that Glen had produced the proper identification. Their son, he reminded them, was quite creative.

Around this time, Alexander was unfairly passed over for a

promotion at work. He had thought the job of assistant chief of social work was his, the next step in his plan. The present assistant chief seemed to be on his side. To this day, he keeps safely tucked away copies of personnel documents that support his contention that he was victimized by those who controlled who would be favored.

Slowly, the confidence which had befriended Alexander since his first success as a high-school ROTC cadet slipped away. In his mind, he paced back and forth like a caged animal, casting dark, resentful eyes on the world outside. He indicted his boss, but he blamed his family. If they had been willing to move, a promotion would have come easily. But Jane didn't want to move to Texas. That would be the last straw, she declared.

Inside, I was thinking terrible thoughts. My family had become a liability. If I had exercised my male prerogative, taken control of my own destiny and said, come with me, I would have reached my fullest potential.

I feared my own anger then, as I had my whole life. I realized that if I made Jane and the children move, it would devalue her somehow, and it would be out of anger.

Soon after, I left Palo Alto to accept a dead-end position in San Francisco. For all practical purposes, my career was over.

Alexander distanced himself from his family, brooding over his inadequacies and his fate. Jane complained that Al was never there. They were growing apart, and although both of them wanted to make things right, neither of them had any energy at all to look past the struggle and the bitterness.

And then Glen left.

To say that I had been preoccupied with my own troubles would be putting it mildly. Besides my bitterness toward my family, I was in a state of rage, living with the reality of being professionally violated. Worse perhaps was my decision to cop out, as I did not fight what I knew to be a discriminatory decision.

Meanwhile, the problem of Glen wouldn't go away. He was the first-born son and he was not acting honorably, nor was he setting the standard for the family. He had become quite devious. The social worker in me began to worry that he was going to be a criminal. He was hurting his mother, disturbing the other boys. Everything began to crash in on me. My anger took hold and directed itself toward my son. He was an easy target.

Then one day I came home from work, and he was gone.

Neither Jane nor Alexander can recall the exact events that precipitated the departure of their oldest son during the spring of 1977. Jane remembers sadly that it was just one more incident, no worse than some of the others. But Guy, who was nine years old, seems to remember his mother and his brother arguing about money and a forged check. An angry confrontation, a slight move by Glen in Jane's direction, sudden silence, and then he didn't live there anymore.

When Alexander came home that night, he made some attempt, through his wrath, to comfort his wife and failed to notice his two younger sons, huddled together on the stairs, wondering what would happen next. What happened next was that all of Glen's pictures came down off the wall and the eldest son was officially dismissed.

"I have no son!" Alexander seethed.

Jane was inconsolable. "Yes, you do," she sobbed, but her husband wasn't listening.

I have no son. The remaining sons heard the father's words, registering them in their minds, inscribing them in their memories. *We have no brother.*

Later that night, Greg and Guy made a pact. Never again would either of them do anything to cause their parents pain. They would be model sons and solve their problems on their own. Greg would take over as the oldest. Guy would fit in properly. They would make up for the shame of Glen.

When I took down the pictures, I may have been acting out some ancient ritual. I don't know. I wanted to dismiss him from my mind and not have to invest any more thoughts or feelings.

Eventually, the pictures went back up. I'm convinced now that Glen left as much out of sparing us his turmoil as being angry at us. He didn't know what else to do. The answer to all of his questions was obviously not in our house, so he went away to find them elsewhere.

I thought that he was choosing against living up to the code of the oldest son. I never challenged the code or considered the distress of my eldest cadet.

I can be very harsh when my expectations aren't met. At some point, the message hit home that my kids were frightened of me. What I had to do was modify my approach, lower my expectations. It's a process. How do we help our children get where we want them to go—independent, strong?

Jane was always better at communicating about the difficult things. I was the bad guy. I was like the guard on the prisoner march, ready to punish the stumbling inmate but demanding he walk unaided.

I needed to change. I remember when Glen was born, I changed. No one had cuddled me as a child, but from the moment I looked at Glen I just couldn't help it. I did what came naturally. I touched him. One of my favorite pictures is Glen as an infant sleeping on me. I should have taken it from there.

THE THINGS
WE DEMAND OF A MAN

Jane and Alexander were, in the end, no different than any other parents who had watched the furious flight of a troubled child. Initially, anger flowed easily over the other things—the sense of failure, the mark of shame, and in the middle of the night the terrible emptiness. As those harsh feelings receded, they asked themselves, What did we do? And they turned to their remaining sons and tried to forget what they had lost.

Where a place had once been set for three sons, the two who remained spread out their lives, offering no resistance, stepping carefully. The tension gone, Alexander and Jane often remarked to each other that Greg and Guy seemed to be thriving.

Greg began high school and immediately excelled at everything he did. Guy was exhibiting more and more confidence, constantly on the move, reigning over the neighborhood, bringing home from school his special collection of friends. For Guy, school was not a classroom but the neighborhood bar, a sort of educational lounge with plenty of action. It was interesting to him, not because he hungered for knowledge but because it offered the possibility of companions, associates, and contacts, a place for him to preside as social chairman.

He was still in grammar school.

Guy was cute and in my experience unusually affectionate, which I remember mentioning to Jane more than once. He came right up and touched me whenever he wanted to. I suppose I decided he was doing just fine, but of course he was still a little boy.

He couldn't stand for anyone to turn him away. I remember when I was growing up I figured that 50 percent of the people would like you, and 50 percent wouldn't. But I had a son who only understood 100 percent. His personality was: You've gotta love me. I'm lovable. And you did. And he was.

Glen had been Guy's hero until he started hurting us, and then Guy really looked up to Greg after Glen left. Greg made a very good model, excelling at school, taking care of himself, being strong. My feelings for him began to grow, and I started looking forward to coming home and finding out what noteworthy things Greg had done that day.

Jane and I both remember the day he graduated from high school— our pride over his achievements, of course, but more for what happened after the ceremony. He came up and hugged us. There were tears in his eyes. I realized then that Greg was truly a wonder.

When Greg went off to California State University at San Luis Obispo, Guy settled down into his role of center of the universe. He missed Greg, but never talked about it.

Junior high school was an auspicious step in social opportunity for Guy. Every morning started with the same focus, the same question: "What should I wear?"

"I can't believe I have a son who's a clothes horse," Jane told a fellow teacher. Early on, it was clear to Guy that his allowance fell far short of his apparel needs. He made a list of services he would perform—baby-sitting, pet-sitting, mowing lawns, and washing cars—and took them around the neighborhood. Soon his schoolwork had to contend with both shopping and employment to support shopping.

Alexander didn't take Guy's obsession with appearance too seriously. He had taught his sons to present themselves well, and Guy did that beautifully. However, one night when Alexander took his son to the movies with some friends, he commented, "You can't be all flash, Guy. You've got to have substance."

"I know that, Dad." What does he think I'm doing, thought the son. Guy had a purpose for every move he made, and the two goals he had set for himself in September, when he began the seventh grade, had been fulfilled by the following May. First, he was popular, by any standard. But more important to him, the most beautiful girl in the school had just agreed to become his girlfriend.

The summer began gloriously for Guy and Melanie. They spent every moment together, pouring out their secrets, exploring a new world of emotional and physical intimacy.

The summer ended and Melanie told her mother that she'd had sex with Guy. Guy knew that Melanie's parents would tell his parents, so in order to circumvent any problems that might cause, Guy wrote a letter explaining the relationship and gave it to his father.

August 28, 1981

Dear Dad,

I know that Mrs. Arturo has probably told you by now that Melanie and I made love. I'm calling it that, Dad, because that's what it is. We love each other, and I believe we have a very mature relationship. I do not want you to worry about this. We did not have sex right away. We respect each other and we talked about making love for six months before actually doing it.

I believe it is possible to love somebody when you are thirteen (Mel is already fourteen!) because the love I have for her is wonderful and good. I think that many people don't understand what love really is, even when they're old. I feel that I have been very responsible about sex, and we have taken precautions every time, if you know what I mean.

I just wanted to let you and Mom know that everything is okay. Please don't worry! I know what I'm doing.

Love, Guy

Neither Alexander, Jane, nor their son remember much about what happened next. The recollection of whether a fight ensued or an ulti-matum was issued seemed to have dimmed with the passing of the years. In any case, when Melanie went to high school and Guy was still in eighth grade, they broke up. Jane and Al felt relieved. Guy felt prepared.

While Guy was conquering high school and Greg was becoming an engineer, Alexander moved past his personal career disappointment and began to enjoy work again. Jane found it easier to be a teacher and a mother, now that the boys were older and the tension of Glen was gone. Their oldest son was now just an infrequent visitor in their lives.

Glen's aptitude for financial creativity continued. He began his self-imposed exile with some acquaintances in an old house not far from home. His roommates put him in charge of the utilities and tele-phone, which were under his name. When Glen found himself left with all the bills, he simply left the house.

He was able to get credit at will, used college loans to live in Hawaii, and received a steady stream of welfare checks for years. If something went wrong, he could maneuver himself out of any predicament. Unfortunately, his schemes often involved his parents, and whenever Jane or Alexander received a call from a bank or a creditor or the wel-fare department, embarrassment, anger, and massive anxiety ensued. After a while, "wrong number" became their standard reply to being found by some victim of their son's ingenuity. They simply didn't want to know.

Once, when he was living in San Francisco, Jane and Alexander dis-covered during a telephone call that Glen was ill. Al offered to bring his son home until he felt better, and Glen didn't object. Alexander wouldn't allow Jane to come with him to retrieve Glen, afraid of what he might find.

He found his son living in a run-down apartment house in a seedy part of the city. His tiny room held a bed, a little television, lots of dirt and clutter. Glen was so sick that Alexander had to assist him to the car. His parents nursed him back to health, and Al tried to reconcile with his son, suggesting that he stay with them for a while. But Glen already had other plans and another room he could move to when he was well.

His new place was a lovely apartment near Nob Hill, and his new roommate was friendly and polite. Alexander simply observed this development, not asking questions. At least he would have something hopeful to report to Jane. But within a month, Glen had moved again.

On one occasion, Jane resorted to tough love. Glen forged his mother's name on a one-hundred-dollar check and took off for Hawaii, using a credit card he would never pay off. Jane exploded, her frustration and rage for all his devious actions coming to rest on a hundred dollars. She reported to the bank that her check had been forged, and the bank warned her that when Glen came back, he would face consequences, maybe even jail. Jane told the bank that jail might be what her son needed. Later, when her anger turned down to simmer, she wondered about herself. The person at the bank, she concluded, must have thought she was a monster.

A year later, Alexander offered to pay for a semester of college if Glen would come and live at home. Glen came back and enrolled in school, and things went beautifully for a while. He attended class, studied, and brought home the highest grades possible.

But then the second semester started, and his attitude seemed to change. He asked if two friends could move in for a few days. A few days became a week, then a month. His parents told Glen they had to leave, and in the dispute that followed, Alexander pointed out that his so-called friends were taking them all for a ride. Jane said simply that they were scum. Glen responded bitterly that he would leave with his friends. The day that Glen was to move out, Jane discovered that the tuition check for the second semester had been diverted to Glen's per- · sonal account, and Glen admitted smugly that he had used it for going to bars.

Alexander's anger was ferocious. Glen grabbed his few belongings, the fury between them trailing out the door after him. Jane followed her son and her husband onto the driveway, wondering if whatever brittle strands of relationship that still existed between them had finally snapped. As they walked silently back into the house, she left the door ajar. He was their son, no matter what, and the door must always be open to him.

Everyone is looking for relationship. When you start out as a young person, it's more intense. I'm sure that my son Glen was desperate. In his shoes, I would have been desperate.

Jane and I worried about his unhealthy relationships. There were big clues: Matchbooks from strange places, casual liasons that probably meant multiple sex partners, and Quaaludes—nothing much harder I don't think, like poppers. He was going to bathhouses, but at the time, my concern was not as much for his body as for his gentle, fragile spirit. Nevertheless, when he came home with scabies, I know he could feel our revulsion. He informed us quietly that he was leaving, so that he wouldn't give it to all of us.

On another of his visits, we found negligees and panties in the trunk of his car. It seemed as good a time as any, so Jane asked him, are you gay? And he said yes.

I suppose Glen had what you might call stereotypical gay traits. He was much more feminine than I thought a boy would be. He liked dolls and didn't like sports. I had been trained that these qualities exist in both girls and boys. You don't assume that since a boy is effeminate he must be gay. You don't make that leap.

I remember when Guy was in high school and whining about one thing or another, I told him to stop acting like a girl. It was just something you said as a parent. Now, with two sons dead and another dying, I realize that we hadn't understood. The leap is fine. It's the landing we couldn't handle.

Glen was left on his own—the child, feeling insecure to address these issues, and the parents being ignorant, totally unaware. I can say with confidence that as uncomfortable as the revelations would have been coming earlier, and as badly as we might have handled them, we would have stuck by our children. But they had heard the words come out of our mouths: faggot, queer. They had drawn other conclusions.

Guy graduated from high school in June 1986. For his parents, commencement exercises were just another occasion to witness their son's soaring popularity and social prowess. He had done well in school yet below his potential, which bothered his father. We have three smart kids, Alexander comforted himself, as others in Guy's class carried away the academic honors.

Still, Guy seemed happy. However, his frantic social schedule was of some concern to his parents; he was always partying, except when he was organizing the next party.

There had been one or two more girlfriends early in high school, but since then, no one special—he went to every dance with the prettiest girl of the moment on his arm. Alexander noted that he never dated anyone Japanese, and when he asked his son about it, Guy replied that someday he would marry a blond, blue-eyed beauty, because that combination would produce gorgeous babies.

His parents watched Guy's careful construction of an image with fascination; he molded and remolded himself until everything was perfect. They laughed at some of his efforts. The permed hair was interesting. He did, indeed, present himself differently than other young Japanese men—the designer clothes, the professional photographs of him modeling the designer clothes, the perfect accessories. But the blue contacts looked plain silly. Who was he kidding?

About this time, he chose his first disciple. Anne Takeuchi was a year younger than Guy and eager to follow him. Soon she, too, was modeling clothes, changing her hair, finding a photographer. Guy would prepare a daily sermon on the decorum of utter coolness, and Anne memorized his every word.

Anne loved being Guy's "best bud," as they called each other. She was startled when one of her friends remarked that she was Guy's shadow. "I'm not his shadow," she retorted angrily. "I'm his best friend."

"Okay, okay," the other girl admitted. "How about sidekick?"

With Anne at his side, Guy could more efficiently organize the social lives of their ever-widening circle of friends. Once in a while, there was a glitch. When Alexander found a case of liquor in Guy's car, he wrote his son a letter expressing his concern over Guy's safety. Guy appreciated the mature way his father had handled the discovery. Many other fathers would have come unglued, he mentioned to Anne. Instead, they all had a calm discussion. After that, Guy and Anne were more careful where they stashed the beer.

For the most part, this was a peaceful time for the Nakatanis. Jane was especially enjoying Greg, who wanted to do things with the family. He had moved to San Diego, where he'd begun a master's program in engineering at the University of California. Alexander and Jane looked forward to their visits with him. He had saved his money and bought a nice little truck and, with his parents' help, put a down payment on a townhouse.

The only part of Greg's life that was not in order was his love life. Greg's dates in high school had been limited to a few dances and parties. He hadn't planned on going to his senior prom, until Jane intervened, encouraging him to go, because there would never be another time like this for him. So he'd asked a girl he didn't really know very well who had just broken up with her boyfriend. From that moment on, Beth was the center of his life.

Greg and I went together for almost five years. He tried so hard to be macho, and sometimes it got him into trouble. Once we went to a bar in San Luis Obispo called Boomers and stood in line, trying to convince the bouncer to let us in. We weren't having much luck when a huge guy, who must have been a football player, cut in front of us and waved his obviously fake I.D. at the bouncer, giving him a wink, like he was just too cool to be carded.

Greg was 5'7", maybe 140 pounds. This animal was 6'3", at least 250 pounds. Greg puffs up right in front of the guy and says, hey, buddy, if they didn't let me in, they sure as hell aren't going to let you in.

I thought Greg was going to get his head ripped off, so I jumped between them and grabbed Greg by the hand. He gets a little crazy when he drinks, I said to the football dude. And the guy started to laugh that his girlfriend would hurry in to save him, I guess. I led Greg away. He wasn't mad at me. He was too stunned.

Greg Nakatani was warm and caring underneath all that bravado. No one in my life has ever believed in me the way he did. He told me, set out your goals, and then you only have to take them one at the time. He was right.

Greg was also very controlling. I could never have a separate time or a separate friend for myself. When I broke up with him, I missed his family, especially Guy. But I also felt like I'd lost a hundred pounds.

Later, I visited Greg, just to make sure he was all right, because when we parted, he was a mess. But the one who does the heartbreaking can't be the one to mend it. I didn't see him after that.

Beth ended their relationship just before Greg started graduate school in San Diego. To make matters worse, she began to date Greg's roommate. Greg called home, inconsolable, barely able to get the story out to his mother, who cried with him until Alexander got on the phone. Greg told his father that he couldn't study, couldn't concentrate. Would it be okay if he didn't go to school for a semester? Al told his son to come home, of course, to take a rest. To this day, Alexander takes great pride in that conversation, in the caring for the heart over the mind, in the emotional freedom that swept them all away.

When Greg and Beth were going together, they felt free to retire to the privacy of Greg's room in front of the whole family. Talk about liberation. Jane and I never even had to discuss it.

Jane wondered if Beth's mother was uncomfortable with Greg being Japanese. Beth wasn't Japanese. I didn't think it mattered, because Greg was Greg.

Although Beth made Greg very happy, it is difficult to forget his grief over her. When it happened, I recalled an incident in the fifth grade, when he became the object of a racist remark. Some kid was full of hatred—the dirty Japs, we deserved the bomb—the whole thing. It really troubled Greg. I had to explain to him that kids were like that because their parents were like that. The kids weren't really evil. But my son was still very, very hurt.

Greg was ten when he was denigrated by a classmate. He was twenty-one when he was rejected by Beth. Of course, his later pain was much greater, and I've thought a great deal about this, but besides those incidents, I can't remember another time when we really shared, emotionally.

Greg grew up questioning whether we loved him. Just to go about your daily tasks, doing what you're doing, meeting certain expectations—that was the business of living in this family. When we said he could come home after Beth left, we weren't evaluating his progress. We were telling him we loved him.

I always appreciated Glen for being so gentle. With Greg, his soft side was hidden beneath all the things we demand of a man. I feel very bad about that. It was a clue that might have saved us all.

One Saturday morning in June 1986, shortly after Guy's graduation, Jane sat at her kitchen table, thinking about her sons. Greg called her nearly every Friday night, and his call the night before had reassured her, somewhat, that he was finally getting over Beth. He has so many other things going for him, she said to herself. If only she could feel the same way about Glen.

In actuality, Alexander and Jane had agreed that Glen was showing signs of getting his life together. He had joined the Air Force earlier that year and was stationed on the island of Oahu.

"If that doesn't do it, nothing will" was Alexander's comment upon hearing the news. And so on that Saturday morning, Jane reminded herself that Glen was still her son, despite everything, and that she wanted what was best for him.

I wasn't like Al. I didn't deal with Glen being gay, because I didn't deal with Glen. With my oldest son, it was out of sight, out of mind. He was someplace, we were never sure where, living his life in ways I couldn't imagine, much less understand. Once in a while I felt like I might lose him, and I imagined getting a phone call that he was sick or that he was dead in the trunk of someone's car.

Whenever he reappeared and I sensed that he was reluctant to tell me what he had been doing or show me where he was living, my concern would heighten. I remember once when he was home for a couple of weeks, Guy and I asked him if he wanted to come with us to pick plums at a neighbor's house. I don't think he knew I was watching him; he was so skinny, and his hair was greasy and stuck under a beanie. He looked sick and not like any of the rest of us.

But then he would disappear again, and with it the burden of constant worry—almost like he was somebody else's son.

On the other hand, nothing separated me from Greg and Guy. I looked forward to Greg's weekly calls, and I worried about what he was eating and how he was feeling, as if he was here with me and not far away in San Diego. And Guy, well, I really had to run to keep up with him. Even though I raised an eyebrow at his constant shenanigans, I loved the fact that we were still living in the same house, and he was too poor to move out very soon.

Suddenly, Jane remembered that she had to go upstairs and awaken Guy. Even though his friend Derek, who lately had been spending a lot of time with the family, had stayed overnight, Guy had asked her to make sure he was up in time for his gymnastics workout.

Jane opened the door and saw that Guy's bed hadn't been slept in. She looked down and saw Guy and Derek on the floor, their bodies fit snugly together in a perfect S.

My first thought was, why would Guy be on the floor with Derek if he has a bed? My second thought was, how could I have two gay sons?

I flew back down the stairs, and I don't really remember but I probably started shouting things like I have no son and you can't live here anymore. Guy was at my side instantly, trying to calm me down. I just screamed at him that he was turning out just like Glen and for him and Derek to get out. They both left. Guy went down the street to a neighbor. I don't know where Derek went. I never saw him again.

I know I did a terrible thing. I just never suspected that Guy was gay. He had acted like such a stud. When he brought Derek home, I was

69

gracious to him. He even went with us to visit our friends. He started to sleep over all the time. I kept thinking about how I'd treated Derek like my own son, and I felt like an accomplice, as if my making dinner for Derek helped Guy to be gay.

I was a crazy woman. I wanted to call Greg. I wanted him to go through what I had gone through, and when I imagined him reacting the way I did, it made me feel better. I would cry to him and thank him for being normal.

When Alexander came home from his golf game, Jane greeted him with the news that Greg was the only real son they had left.

"What the hell are you talking about?" he demanded. When he finally understood, Alexander gripped his internal controls tightly and allowed the waves of shock and anger to run through him, directing the explosion of emotion to his mind. Determined to appear calm, he found Guy at a neighbor's house down the street and asked him to come home.

Alexander and Jane assured him that he was still their son, that he could stay, but Jane added the condition that none of his gay friends could come into their home.

Alexander paced back and forth. "We still love you," he said, and then he said it again and again. Jane stood frozen in place, irritated by her husband's refrain.

Of course I still loved Guy. But it was as if that feeling was being crowded by so many others—anger, disappointment, confusion, fear, and, worst of all, shame. I couldn't help but think of how others would react. Only a few people in my family knew or suspected the truth about Glen, and even that bothered me. I couldn't imagine telling anyone about Guy. First of all, who would believe it? I'm not sure I believed it, certainly not in those first bitter hours.

I watched my husband, desperate to convince our son of our love for him, and I wanted him to be quiet. How could I, his own mother, claim to love him and not accept him? I remember thinking then that this had to be the worst day of my life.

Alexander didn't sleep that night, turning the new information over and over in his mind. From the start, he had designated Derek a shady character. But a sexual relationship with Guy?

Never in my wildest dreams.

I tossed and turned, planning what I would say in the morning. I would explain to Guy that Derek wasn't a good person, and that being gay had nothing to do with it. I would reassure him that Jane had overreacted and that his friends would be welcome here. But even I couldn't reconcile how Jane and I were going to relate primarily to gay people.

I needed all night to calm down. I intended to say just the right thing, without emotion, without judgment. The merit of my argument must not be lost because my son perceived I was angry.

Alexander found Guy in his room the next morning, hunched over his desk. A book was open in front of him, and Guy was fingering one of the pages, staring at it with still, empty eyes. For a fleeting moment, Alexander wondered if they had driven the life from him.

"We're sorry, Guy. Your mother's sorry. She was just surprised."

Guy's hand dropped into his lap, but he didn't look up.

"You know, son, I realize you must be searching for friends, I mean, others who feel the way you do. I'm just not sure Derek's the one—gay or straight."

The empty eyes rose slowly to meet his father's. "Don't worry," he said without a hint of emotion. "Derek won't be back."

Alexander simply nodded. When Guy didn't say anything more, Al went on, feeling the distance between them widen, losing confidence in the words he had prepared, as if he had in his hands a poorly written script that still had to be read.

"Uh, I know you've heard about AIDS. Are you, you know, taking precautions?"

The dull gaze coming from his son held steady. "I'm not going to get AIDS."

"But you know what to do . . ."

"I'm not really that sexually active."

Again, Alexander nodded, helpless to respond differently. He felt the push of fear, the disturbing sense that something precious was missing or, worse, still present but dying, and he could not save it or even discern the danger. He struggled to turn away from his confusion and finish what he had begun, to make things right with his son.

The father cleared his throat and began again. He reaffirmed their love for him, but the words sounded hollow as they came from his mouth, as if he was making an argument that was too thin and common to convey to his son any depth of understanding. So he tried to communicate his profound concern over the heartache involved in being gay; the unbending perceptions of society would curse every day of his life. As he spoke, he had to stifle a wave of panic—his personable young son, so eager to please, so delighted with life's comforts, having to face what was surely ahead for him. He didn't share the most fundamental of his fears: This will destroy him.

Alexander finished and awaited Guy's response.

"Yeah, Dad," he said finally, leaning his chair back on two legs and assuming a more casual pose. "I appreciate your concern. I'll be all right."

Alexander realized he had been dismissed. He moved to the door, dissatisfied, and it came to him that this might be his last chance to make things turn out differently. In the end, a forbidden hope betrayed him.

"Maybe you're not gay, Guy. Lots of young people experiment. People get confused. Think about talking to somebody."

From the doorway, Alexander saw the slight smile and the brown eyes lose their focus.

· · · ·

The following Friday, Jane informed Greg that he had another gay brother. Greg reacted with disgust and anger, disowned Guy forever, and slammed down the phone.

Alexander called him back. "Yes, Greg, you do have a brother." They talked it over, and Greg was much calmer. He's so like me, Alexander reflected, quick to rage and back again. Al thought about calling Glen too, and decided later that what kept him from doing it was not a reluctance to share the news, but a reluctance in that moment to face, even over the phone, his eldest son.

Greg never replayed those first feelings for Guy. Instead, he wrote his younger brother a letter telling him that he could still be all that he wanted to be, but that he would probably have to try harder than others. Guy kept the letter under his pillow for weeks.

In August of that year, all the Nakatani family, except for Glen, reunited in San Diego. Alexander and Jane went first, and Guy joined them several days later. Guy was nervous about seeing his brother for the first time since the scene with Derek and was grateful when Greg acted as if nothing had changed.

In the short time between their discovery of Guy's sexuality and the visit to San Diego, Jane and Al had spoken often of the reality of their situation and the recomposition of their family. Greg was now their only hope for grandchildren, the only child who would go through life with an uncluttered chance to succeed, the only one who might find relationship without stigma and ridicule. To Alexander, Greg was the son who would rescue the family honor. To Jane, who glanced around her and feared the worst, Greg was their last claim to normalcy.

Some parents never experience the closeness we had on that trip to San Diego. I kept saying to Alexander, how in the world could we ever have a son who wanted to fulfill our dreams and be so close to our goals? It was almost too good to be true.

One night before Guy arrived, Al got sick. We had all gone for a walk on the beach. Greg and I teased him about being a wimp, and we felt bad when he made us stop at a drugstore for a thermometer so he could prove to us he had a fever.

Greg and I decided to go to a movie by ourselves, and it was so wonderful because he took me to his favorite place, a taco stand not far from his house, and he said I could have whatever I wanted, burritos or whatever, and that it was his treat.

We took our dinner down to the beach that was a special place for him. He told me that often he would pack up his truck and come here to see the sunset. We had a nice talk, just the two of us, sitting on the beach and eating our burritos, being careful not to get sand in the little container of hot sauce we had between us. He told me that he was worried about Dad not getting enough exercise. He said that he sets up goals before he does things, and he was anxious about Alexander just going out and doing things and not having goals. He said I should encourage him, because golf was not enough.

And then Greg shared his own goals. I think he was very proud and excited about them. He would work at General Dynamics for a year. He would get his master's, and he'd be so good that his professor would want him to be his associate. He had it all planned.

Imagine how I felt, listening to him. It was all a parent could want, so many years more mature than his colleagues. He was sacrificing now to get his townhouse, but in a few years he would be able to lead a comfortable life. He was getting where he wanted to go.

I have never been more aware of the specialness of a moment. It was as if we were making up for years of intimacy that had been missed. I was surprised at the strength of my feelings. Sometimes I wondered if what I was experiencing was real, because it was all so amazing.

When we were leaving, I said to myself, you know, I just have to hold on to him a little while longer. He didn't like to be hugged or kissed, and there were only certain times that he would allow us to do it. I wanted to hug him then; I wanted to very much. But I respected him, so I didn't.

On the way home, Al and I talked about how when we retired, we would move to San Diego. The climate and the beaches there reminded us of our childhood home, and Greg loved it so much. Greg had said, when you retire, you can buy my townhouse. Al laughed at that, because he already owned most of it. But it didn't matter, because Greg was telling us he wouldn't mind having us around.

One Saturday morning a month later, Alexander and Jane awoke, wondering why Greg hadn't made his usual Friday night call. When the phone rang, Alexander answered.

"Yes," Alexander said into the phone, "he's my son."

Jane watched her husband's face contort with pain. "What?" he exclaimed, pleading, denying. "He's dead?"

Jane bolted from the bed and grabbed Alexander's arm. "Who's dead?" she shouted. "Who's dead?"

While her husband struggled to have some kind of conversation with whomever was on the phone, Jane began to shake, grasping at Alexander, who had turned away from her.

"It's Glen, isn't it?" she screamed. "Glen's dead, it's Glen!"

The seconds slowed to an agonizing halt as she waited for Alexander to acknowledge her. In the frozen time, Jane saw the sweet face of her beautiful firstborn baby boy and knew that her worst nightmare had come true.

"Glen, Glen, Glen," she repeated, sobbing and gasping for air between the words, pulling Alexander around to face her and gripping his face with her hands.

"Please wait, Jane," Alexander whispered.

Sinking down onto the bed, Jane began to wail. Alexander lowered the phone and knelt down to put his face next to hers.

"No, Jane, it's not Glen. It's Greg."

WEDDINGS AND
GRANDCHILDREN

I'm killing her.

Alexander put the phone back to his ear and tried to listen to the San Diego County coroner, but his son was dead and his wife was surely dying.

It was Saturday. The morgue would be closed until Monday morning. They could come anytime after nine, but the body must be claimed no later than Tuesday.

Alexander's mind fought wildly to persist in his old reality: There was a problem; they would go to San Diego and stay with Greg and wait for Monday morning. But without mercy, the new, terrible truth shoved him along, and he looked back to see the world he had lived in just an hour ago grow faint and small, until it vanished altogether.

He wondered what was happening to Jane. She should still be on the bed, he imagined, his words having killed her. But she was no longer in the room, and in the distance he could hear her screams.

Eventually, the coroner said everything he needed to say. Alexander hung up and went to find his wife. He found her standing over Guy, who lay huddled in the fetal position on the floor next to his bed.

Jane was still screaming, trying, apparently, to make Guy understand. Alexander pulled Jane away from Guy and into his arms, where she collapsed into wrenching sobs. He held her there, waiting for time to pass, some fragment of his training instructing him to get past the initial, ravaging shock. Over Jane's shoulder, he could see that Guy hadn't moved. Suddenly, Jane seemed to pull herself together.

"Oh, my God, Al," she cried. "I came in here and I was screaming, and Guy was asleep. He woke up and then he crawled over the side of the bed. He hasn't said anything. He hasn't moved."

The father gathered up his son into his lap and spoke gently to him, rousing him out of his stupor. Guy opened his eyes and began to cry. Alexander gave Guy to his mother, and together they entered grief's first chamber, where the darkness is still incomprehensible.

September 20, 1986. That's when all of this began for my mom and dad, and for me, too, I guess.

When my dog Bambi died, I was the one who found him in the backyard. I was so much more devastated than Glen and Greg. I couldn't function for three months. The issue wasn't death, really, it was that Bambi had gone away from me. The idea of never, ever seeing Bambi again was something I just couldn't accept.

When they called my dad that Saturday morning, they asked him normal questions. Are you Alexander Nakatani? Are you related to Greg Nakatani? My dad didn't know, at first, that it was the coroner on the other end of the line.

I woke up to my mother's face and her screaming, "Greg's dead! Greg's dead!" I can remember every inch of her skin, the lines on her face. When I opened my eyes, her face filled up all the space in front of me. I couldn't get away. And the sound. I can't stand to be awakened by a loud voice anymore.

The next thing I remember is that they left for San Diego. I thought, I'm going to try to deal with this the best I can and take care of the house while they are gone. I would take care of everything. I would fix it all up.

When Bambi died, I knew eventually my grief would get to my mother and produce a new dog. But I could never have another Greg, and the idea of never, ever seeing him again was something I just couldn't accept.

Jane and Alexander arrived in San Diego early Saturday afternoon. Using their key to Greg's townhouse, they let themselves in. The lights were on and the sliding glass door to the bedroom had been left open a little. His ticket to fly home at Thanksgiving was being held onto the refrigerator by a magnet that read *San Diego Scuba.*

Abalone shells were everywhere. On his desk, an immense shell held his phone bill and a picture of Greg with Guy, clowning on the beach just a few weeks before. Alexander removed the bill and the photo and cradled the shell for a moment.

"He's a man of the ocean, Jane," he commented. "Did he get to start his sailing lessons?"

"I hope so," Jane whispered. She stood rigidly in the middle of the room, her arms wrapped tightly around her chest, shielding herself from the memories that lie waiting all around her, poised to strike. She feared the pain would be excruciating. I'll disintegrate, she thought. And after a while, that idea didn't seem so bad. All the molecules that are me, she concluded, will simply float away.

There were no messages on the answering machine. Alexander popped up the top and tapped *Announcement.*

"Hi. You've reached Greg Nakatani. If you leave your name and number, I'll return your call as soon as possible." They sat down next to the phone and listened to their son's voice over and over again.

After a while, Al brought in their luggage, and they began to move around the rooms, arranging themselves amid the memories. Jane cried and cried, but surprisingly she didn't come apart. They slept in Greg's bed, ate whatever was in his kitchen. They did his wash, put away his dishes. They would touch everything he had touched and remember the feel of him forever.

After I felt assured that I wasn't going to lose Jane and Guy too, I called Jane's cousin, and she was there in less than ten minutes. I called the airline. More people started to arrive, and each time someone walked in, everyone would get very upset all over again. Except for me. I found things to do. We wouldn't be home for a couple of days, so I watered the plants and straightened up the house for Jane. She was doing all the grieving at that point.

Finally, I got our suitcases and carried them up to our bedroom. I opened my drawers and the closet and started pulling things out of them to pack for San Diego. And then I stopped, and it came to me. Oh, shit, I said. I was looking at the drawers, and the open closet, and I couldn't stop crying.

On Saturday night, Greg's friend David, who had been with Greg when he was killed, came to the townhouse. He sat next to Jane at Greg's kitchen table, his own shock and pain still fresh, the story he struggled to tell laced with guilt and recrimination. Jane gave him tissues and tried to comfort him. Alexander stood brooding by the sink, needing the facts desperately but not wanting to get too close to this young man who was the last link to their son. How is it decided, he wondered, who lives and who dies?

Shakily, David began. They were at the taco stand where Greg had taken his mother on their last trip to San Diego. Sitting on the stone wall that surrounded a little patio in front of the stand, they had just starting to eat their burritos.

Suddenly an old, dented yellow Mustang pulled in too close to Greg's truck. When the driver flung open his door, the ugly crunching sound of metal against metal caused several diners to look up.

"Hey," Greg said, standing and taking a step or two toward the driver and his passenger, who stood fifteen feet away, still poised by the doors of the Mustang. "What are you doing?"

As a proud father, I could list Greg's accomplishments whenever called upon. One of them was that Greg spoke fluent Spanish. He had a very good friend from Mexico named Jorge, who had been an exchange student at Greg's high school. They kept in touch through college. One summer, Greg had spent two months with Jorge at his home in Mexico City.

If nothing else, Greg was macho. Greg asked Jorge how to be macho in Spanish, and Jorge told him that there was one expression he should never say to a Mexican. Knowing my son, Greg needled him until he shared it, but he told Greg never, never to say it. It would be a license to kill you, Jorge had warned him.

But Greg put the expression in the back of his brain, waiting for an occasion to use it. When you're macho, you test your manhood by taking chances.

A few angry words were exchanged. From somewhere in Greg's memory, a weapon was unleashed.

"*Chinga tu madre,*" he snarled at the driver. Greg never saw it coming. The passenger reached into the car and pulled out a pistol from under the seat. Five shots rang out; one struck Greg in the heart. The witnesses—David, the taco stand owner who knew Greg, and the other customers—all ducked, and then watched in horror as the two jumped back in the Mustang and sped away.

"But that door already had a dent in it," Alexander later explained to the police. It seemed ironic to him that Greg would die over a truck, a simple scratch on a less than perfect piece of metal.

Jane kept asking David, did Greg do this, did Greg do that, trying to make the ending of his story come out differently.

"I couldn't believe what was happening, Mrs. Nakatani. Greg was lying there, and there was a lot of blood on his shirt." David broke down, his tears splashing onto Greg's kitchen table, his hands trembling as he tried to wipe them away.

"I asked him if he had been shot. And he said yes."

"He was alive?" Jane cried. "He spoke to you?"

"Yes, I think so. I heard him say something, but then everyone was around us, and I started to yell to call 9-1-1. He didn't talk anymore after that."

All day Sunday, Jane comforted herself with her disbelief. Greg had been alive and speaking to his friend. If the door was already dented, why would Greg force a confrontation? Greg wouldn't bother with that door, she insisted to Alexander. She indulged in all sorts of fantasies that spared her son—it wasn't Greg, someone borrowed Greg's truck or stole it, David had made a mistake. Her son was simply away, still alive and ignorant of all this commotion.

Alexander, too, tormented himself by pushing back the clock in his imagination, watching his son glance up at the yellow Mustang, curse under his breath, sense the danger of a confrontation, and wisely let it go. But he woke up from his fantasy knowing the truth. The son of Alexander Nakatani would demand his rights. The father had taught the son to be strong and stand up for himself.

On Monday morning, Alexander and Jane went to the coroner's office. They were led to a room, white-walled and sterile, furnished only with a little table and several chairs. A policeman came in with Greg's belongings: his clothing, bloody and shredded from the hospital's efforts to revive him, his watch, and a plastic bag marked, "Nakatani, Greg T." He poured out the contents of Greg's pockets onto the table.

Alexander was staring straight ahead. He couldn't look at the table. He could feel the last particles of his control leaving him, evaporating in the air dry room, the imminent disclosure of his raw emotions momentarily terrifying him. Most of all, he couldn't look at Jane.

He heard a gasp, her breath letting out slowly, and finally her voice, uttering a single, desperate sound.

"Oh."

She picked up her son's wallet and examined it, tenderly fingering his driver's license and his credit cards and each of his photos, piling them neatly on the table. The last of her illusions quietly slipped away.

"I want to see him," she said.

"I'm sorry, Mrs. Nakatani, but you can't see him. You have to call a mortuary, and they will prepare him for viewing."

"I don't want any viewing except to see him right now. I have to see him one last time."

Alexander asked if they could have a moment. Left alone in the room with Greg's things, they decided, finally, to remember him as he had been on that last, perfect visit to San Diego.

They arranged to have his body cremated that evening. The next day, they would find an urn, reclaim the truck, and pick up the death certificate. On Wednesday, Jane would fly home and Alexander would drive Greg's truck home, carrying the urn beside him. They would return to San Diego later to take care of the townhouse and become involved in the prosecution of Greg's killer.

On that last night, Al and I got into Greg's bed, but we weren't sleeping. Pretty soon he got up and went in the other room, and I was alone. I buried my head in Greg's pillow and breathed in as deeply as I could. I moved my hands and touched the places on his sheets where he had lain, simply sleeping, just four nights before. Why did he have to go to the taco stand? How could a young man so full of life and potential be so unlucky?

I closed my eyes and saw him, a perfect little boy, warm and alive, running happily across my mind. Down at the mortuary, his body would be consumed quickly by the intense heat. I didn't want to believe Greg didn't need it anymore, and I panicked.

There's a Japanese tradition that the spirit leaves the body in a fireball, and I had always imagined a spectacular moment of separation when the spirit bursts out and flies free into the heavens. I tried hard to remember that now, to calm myself as I thought about what was happening to Greg.

Alexander came back to bed, and I was crying and telling him about the fireball, and I thought he would say that he didn't really believe in those things. But instead he said, yes, I know, I just saw it. And he told me about how he had been standing outside on Greg's little patio, and he had seen the fireball streaking across the sky. Like a rocket to heaven, he said.

And then, something even stranger happened. He reached over to hold me, and his hand ran across my body. But he drew it back quickly, and he said, Jane, your stomach is burning up.

And so it was. I cradled the womb that had held my son, and it was hot, almost too hot to touch. Alexander stroked it too, and we were crying together, scared, I suppose, but grateful. After a little while, the heat went away, and I knew my son's spirit was free.

I slept off and on during the night. It was very early in the morning, still dark, and I decided to get up so I threw back the covers. That awakened Al, and he turned on the light. Scattered on the sheet between us were small gray flakes, and I picked them up and rubbed them between my fingers. Ashes. Alexander picked them up too. There were a handful there, beneath me and beside me. I might not have believed, but we both saw them, and we both touched them, and nothing can change the wonders of that night.

On Wednesday morning, Alexander packed his son's personal belongings carefully in the back of the truck, concentrating on his task so that he could simply accomplish it, rather than turn it into some kind of sad processional between house and vehicle. But when only the urn was left, sitting by itself on the kitchen counter, Alexander sensed the powerful approach of his emotions.

"Come with me, son," he said out loud, pushing through the moment, snatching up his son's ashes and hurrying to the door. "I'm taking you home."

For the first hour, they rode together in silence—the father with his son in his urn on the seat beside him. After a while, Alexander could feel the thin threads of control around his feelings unraveling. They were alone. It was their time. They must talk.

"I'm really angry about what happened to you, son," Alexander began. The tears came quickly, violently. "Oh, my God, Greg, how could this have happened?

"Was it me? Did I teach you too well to be righteous and strong? Did I reward you too often for your masculinity?" Alexander gripped the wheel, his body pulsing with self-recrimination, his eyes straining to see the road through relentless tears.

"What were you thinking, Greg?" And then the thought came to him, on the attack, and he shook his head violently. "My God," he whispered, "was it me who was in your last thought, encouraging you to say such a thing and get yourself killed?"

Alexander wept uncontrollably, his plaintive moans escaping as he gulped for air, his torment protected by the walls of the little truck. "I'm sorry, Greg, I'm so sorry," he chanted, until the feelings released him and his mind began to clear. Exhausted and spent, he fingered his son's urn tenderly. "I'm taking you home," he began again, "I'm taking you home."

When I arrived home with Greg's ashes, Glen was already there. We had spoken to him from San Diego, and he cried on the phone. He tried not to, but I knew.

I had picked out a special place for Greg—a little table next to the computer. That was where he was going to be, on that table. I brought the urn in and put it there, and I said their names, Glen and Guy, and invited them to come over and talk to their brother. This is Greg now, I said. This is all we have.

Guy was fairly free with his feelings. But poor Glen had a hard time. He tried not to break down. But I was crying so hard, how could he not know it was all right? I kept repeating, he's home. Greg's home.

I already had it in my mind that Greg would not be buried on California soil. I just felt that the way he died, it would be alien earth for him. We would bury him in Hawaii. Then I could say to him, you're safe.

I had been so proud, so sure of him. To be proud is a risk. To be sure of anything is madness.

At Greg's memorial service, Glen and Guy each had a little part to play. Guy was sure that Glen wouldn't be able to do it, but in the end it was Glen who had to support Guy.

The family witnessed this lapse in Guy's control from their place in the front pew of the Methodist church where the service was held. They had filed in silently, after the rest of the mourners, Alexander, Jane and Guy, Harriet and Takeo, and Glen, standing apart at the end of the row, like he was not part of the family. An old friend of Greg's, Sam, gave the eulogy, a humorous recollection of their friendship and Greg's achievements.

"When you think about Greg," Sam concluded, "consider yourself lucky to have been part of his life."

Alexander nodded while Jane wept quietly into her handkerchief. As the sounds of the rock group Bread filled the chapel, Guy and Glen rose and strode purposely toward the altar. Guy waited while Glen placed a white carnation next to his brother's ashes. Then it was Guy's turn, and Jane touched her husband's arm when she saw her youngest son falter. After a long moment, Guy took a deep breath and walked forward, his hand gripping the carnation and coming down hard next to the urn. When Guy's head dropped down and his body began to slump, Glen reached for him quickly, putting his arm around his little brother and gently assisting him back to his seat.

During the next months, Alexander transformed what had once been Greg's room into a shrine, the walls papered with news clippings about Greg's death and the investigation into his murder, and his desk piled high with police reports and testimony from the hearings. On the little table next to the computer, Greg's urn stood watch. Burying Greg in Hawaii would have to wait; the least a father could do was make sure that the murderer of his son was brought to justice.

And to that end, Alexander became obsessed. The driver of the Mustang was arrested, but the killer slipped back into Mexico. Alexander fumed that the two were undocumented persons, and blamed the border patrol, the San Diego police, and the district attorney's office for allowing the killer to disappear into the dark underworld of Tijuana. He sat in the courtroom, his rage an ulcer gnawing at his soul, while the driver, the murderer's accomplice, was questioned and set free for lack of evidence.

He hired a lawyer, and a private detective was assigned to pursue the case further. He called the governor of California, who took on the case as a blatant example of the legal system gone awry. This high-level involvement earned Alexander the attention of local media, who presented the story to the public as a grieving father's relentless pursuit of justice. Eventually, the accomplice was brought back to the courtroom and convicted of his crime. As the driver of the yellow Mustang was led away, Al turned to his wife and declared their mission officially over.

But the father of Greg Takeo Nakatani felt that he, too, had been sentenced, to a lifetime of anger and irresolution. Yet his rage eventually dissipated, his mind instructing him to stay rational, to construct an explanation, to calculate a new future.

What was still to come, however, was not reasonable. He would have to feel his way through.

After Greg died, I spent a lot of time thinking about why things happen the way they do. I wondered, was Greg taken away so Jane and I wouldn't be able to abandon the sons who remained?

With Greg went a lot of dreams. That just one of our children might live his life with less difficulty, not having to hide, prospering and carrying our name into the future—that thought had so comforted us. Greg made it possible to speak of weddings and grandchildren, just like everyone else. We had carefully balanced the scale of our illusions between the promise of Greg and the burden of Glen and Guy, as if Greg made up for everything.

I feared we were being punished for thinking these things. I was astonished by our sins—our giving up on Glen and Guy, and our failure to imagine them as our future the way we had so thoroughly honored Greg. Emotions that truly frightened me followed me around for weeks, ghosts of the past that I knew were there but couldn't quite recognize. I made deals with my surviving sons that they would never hear and prepared myself for a lifetime of being haunted.

It's crazy, all the thoughts that go through your head.

FULL-BLOWN

Greg's accomplishments had, indeed, masked the rest of the family realities—one gay son who left home at fifteen and would live alone, often impoverished and sometimes dangerously, for ten years, another gay son who until three months prior had been parading around as a flaming straight. Jane, still painfully homophobic. Alexander, caught up in his analysis of their situation, grappling with his ignorance. Greg's death seemed to uncover everything at once, leaving them unprotected from their confusion and raw, relentless pain.

The seed of their survival, however, was planted the first Saturday after Greg's death. Sleeping fitfully and awakening early, Alexander and Jane talked and cried together in their bed, reliving the nightmare of the week before. Their shared grief became a weekly ceremony in Greg's honor, a Saturday morning liturgy of whispered conversation and tears that would go on for years, ultimately sustaining them through all that was to follow.

In his room across the hall, Guy could hear the murmur, starting very early and sometimes continuing for hours. The sound comforted him, and he began to listen for it every Saturday. Soon the talking and grieving spilled out into other mornings, becoming a necessary ritual that made the rest of the day possible.

For Alexander, each day was a slow, deliberate turn toward Glen and Guy. His old plan having self-destructed, he faced his two surviving sons and started to make his way into their territory, reasoning that it was his only choice. He would not lose any more children.

Jane simply carried on, immersing herself in her young students, making it through the day. She told her friends at school not to mention Greg, that she would give them a sign if she wanted to talk. She couldn't handle her own sadness, much less theirs.

In the beginning, I coped with Greg's death by pretending he was away on a trip. I said, he's away from San Diego, but he's still alive. When we went to the coroner's office to get his things, I knew he wasn't away on a trip. Yet even after that, I could pretend if I had to.

Greg's ashes sat on Al's computer table for a year. We couldn't seem to put him to rest. The first anniversary of his death went by in a fog. We were still so sad, and the regret—I thought it would kill me too. We were grieving constantly, and that was good, I suppose. But instead of talking less about Greg, we talked more and more, while we were driving somewhere, even at dinner. I was always crying.

Finally, I said to Alexander, this has to stop. We had to go on. The urn had to go.

Alexander, Jane, and Guy carried Greg's ashes to Maui and buried them in the family plot. They met Glen on Oahu at the time of the Obon festival, where Buddhists join in remembrance and celebration of the dead. During the Obon, the spirits revisit their loved ones and are sent back to sea in little boats during a ceremony called Toranagashi. In Haleiwa, a picturesque town by the ocean, the surviving members of the Nakatani family waited with the other mourners to light a candle lantern on the cardboard boat they had ordered from a nearby temple.

Alexander and I do not practice Buddhism, and yet, I think it is in our souls, because it has always been around us. According to the belief of our ancestors, the spirit stays around the house for forty-nine days, and on the forty-ninth day, it leaves to go to heaven. I had been to the Buddhist service for many of my relatives, including my mother, and had been comforted by the chanting and a sense that the spirit was at peace.

Although some of my relatives inquired, we didn't celebrate the forty-ninth day for Greg. It was too soon to let him go. But when we buried him, the time seemed right to say good-bye. We were lucky to be in Haleiwa at the time of Toranagashi.

It was Glen who took our boat to the water. He had been carrying it around with him, pants rolled up, not saying anything, but making it clear that he would be the one to do it. When it came time, he knelt down, lit the candle, and gave the little boat a gentle shove. It was so beautiful, hundreds of sparkling lights, bobbing up and down, moving away together into the sea. I felt happy and relieved. Greg was free, and not alone.

For Alexander and Jane, small surprises began to enliven them and gave them new hope. Alexander observed that the loss of Greg had motivated Glen to do something with his life. More often now, Glen communicated with them in letters, where he spoke of his life at the Air Force base in Tacoma, Washington, of completing his college degree and making a future for himself in business.

Glen wrote to Guy too. The first letter came only a month after Greg's death.

17 October 1986

Dear Guy,

I hope everything is going well with you and Mom and Dad. I've met a few people from the base at the bar here in Tacoma. Maybe I'll go out there next week, to celebrate my birthday.

I asked Mom to send me a picture of Greg for my room. Maybe you could help her decide which one? I want an 8 by 10. I went to the mall to look for a nice frame tonight, but didn't find one I liked. I thought it should be oak. Didn't Greg like oak? Or since it's my room and I have to look at it, I could get something that isn't oak and Greg wouldn't mind.

I hope you are doing all right. As for me, I guess I'm okay. I haven't been around Greg very much, so it still doesn't seem real to me that he is gone. So most of the time I'm all right, its just every so often things start to seem real, and then it gets rough.

I wish I could be home with you now, but I'll see you at Thanksgiving! I'd welcome a letter letting me know what's going on with you. When I come home maybe I could help you choose your college courses. I know you said college has been a drag so far but don't give up.

Let me tell you, for me it's been a long process of ups and downs. Come Christmas, you'll have a brother with his bachelor's degree, but you don't want to try the nine-year plan, like I did. Not fun, my friend.

I'm sure you have better things to do than read all of this. Take care of yourself, and remember that you're going to be everything for Mom and Dad that I couldn't be.

Glen

"Well, at least you got one thing right," Guy muttered as he stuffed Glen's letter into a drawer. "I'm not you."

Guy had a new toy and a new playmate. He had inherited Greg's truck and christened it with a personalized license plate that read: YNGR BRO. "Where did that come from?" his friends asked, and he explained that his older brother had helped him acquire it. Guy drove it lovingly, usually accompanied by a tape with the songs from Greg's memorial service.

When Anne went away to college, a new young woman, Catherine Tamura, who was a freshman at UCLA, became his favored friend. Again, his parents couldn't help but enjoy the tales of their adventures that Guy chose to share. They noted, but never discussed, that Catherine was Japanese and straight. Guy took classes at San Jose State and taught gymnastics at a nearby gym, but, once again, it was his social life and his monthly rendezvous with Cat that stimulated his genius for planning the perfect party.

I didn't grieve right away for Greg. My grieving happened a year later, when we buried him on Maui. I started feeling pretty bad then, but I didn't talk about it all the time, like my parents. And I didn't grieve with them. I grieved through my friends.

I missed Annie when she went to Davis for college. For a while, I would sit by myself at our favorite coffeehouse and write long letters to her and my other friends. But it wasn't like me to be lonely.

I met Cat at a party—what else? She was so easy to be with, and we were so alike. No worries. Nothing serious. It felt really good. I remember one gathering I planned just for her. It was a bring-an-exotic-booze party, and we had a contest to see who could come up with the weirdest liquor. Believe me, there were some wild entries like Tahitian Orgasmic Rum. So how is a Tahitian orgasm different than a normal one? I'm sure I don't know. Anyway, we ended up outside, holding on to each other, throwing up in the bushes and then laughing so hard we both peed in our pants.

She said that parties were my calling. Thank God for Cat. I could grieve on the inside and still be happy on the outside. I just couldn't talk to Mom and Dad. Glen had hurt them so much, and Greg's death nearly killed them. I didn't know how much more they could take.

Glen came home for Christmas in 1987, and, for the first time, Alexander and Jane couldn't wait for his visit. He seemed to be thriving in the Air Force; in his most recent letter, he had spoken with enthusiasm about his new goal of becoming a pilot. For Al, it was a comforting development. His son Glen would never have a family, but he would pursue his father's abandoned dream. Amid their heartaches, something finally made sense.

Fifteen months after Greg's death, the holidays were almost back to normal: The house filled with family members, Jane and her sisters gossiped in the kitchen, Guy couldn't control himself and spoiled almost all the secrets that sat under the tree. Glen was typically quiet, standing off from the festivities, but seemingly content to be with his family. He said nothing that would indicate that he was in terrible trouble.

Shortly after Christmas, Glen called home, asking for his father.

Alexander hurried to the phone, pleased to hear from his son. Things were so much better.

Glen got right to the point.

"Well, Dad, I'm HIV-positive."

I struggled to comprehend what he was telling me. We hadn't worried that because Glen was gay, he would become infected. We had acted like any parent, putting the risk way back in our minds. This would not happen to our son.

We had been in denial on every front.

"Are you sure?"

"Yes. I'm full-blown."

"How do they know?"

"I don't know. I guess I don't have very many t-cells."

Full-blown. T-cells. The terminology of AIDS. Alexander felt himself falling into some new darkness. He had lost one son and, somehow, barely, he had survived. Another one was too much. Clearly unsurvivable.

As was his way now, he rapidly collected his emotions and covered them with calm. He must have the facts. He must understand what he was dealing with.

"What happened, son?" he asked. "Please tell me."

The memory of that Christmas he spent with us was still fresh. It was a really great Christmas. But typical of Glen, he came and went without allowing us into his life.

He already knew. He had tested positive for HIV in early December. He already knew that after the holidays he was being sent to Texas for a medical exam to determine if he was fit for duty. But he told us he was being moved from Seattle to Texas for temporary duty, creating the impression that this was just normal Air Force reassignment.

The tests took two weeks, and then they told him he was being discharged. He denied being gay. He had to. This was the military. He was given temporary disability retirement and full benefits, even with the HIV diagnosis. Unbelievably, they told him that if he was unable to come back in five years, he would be put on permanent disability. In 1987, when they looked up HIV in the Air Force manual, they didn't find much.

I asked him what he was going to do. He said he was going to find a job in Seattle. He liked the area. And then, without asking Jane or even thinking, I just said it: "You're welcome to come home."

No questions. His terms. The kid was sick, he'd had it pretty rough, we would take care of him. He didn't have anybody else.

A month went by without a word. For his family, it was as if his illness wasn't real—he wasn't there, he wasn't sick. But then, his things started to arrive at their house. From the first package, the father understood that the eldest son was coming home.

Alexander piled the boxes in a corner of the bedroom that had belonged to Glen a lifetime ago and called the Veteran's Medical Center in Palo Alto to inform them that his HIV-positive son would be arriving soon. He asked them to send information on AIDS. When it came, Jane cried. They waited.

Glen came home on March 20, 1988, exactly a year and a half after Greg's death. Immediately, he set out to find a job. He searched ardently, really pushing, filling out applications, taking tests. The first bout with pneumocystis came a month later.

Alexander and Jane could tell something was happening. Glen was very ill, running fevers.

"How do you feel, Glen?" Jane asked him.

"Not too bad" was his stock answer.

Then one day Glen couldn't breathe. He was clearly in distress, and Al rushed him to the hospital in Palo Alto, fearful that they had waited too long.

By the time we arrived at the hospital, I was frantic. I went in first to get him admitted and, immediately, I ran into a big problem. They questioned his eligibility. I was furious. They told me they couldn't deal with his eligibility, and my son, who I didn't realize was on the verge of death, walked in. No wheelchair. It's unbelievable to me now, thinking about what he went through.

So I said, screw you. We got back in the car, and I drove like a bat out of hell to Letterman's Hospital in San Francisco. Now this was a classy operation. Before I knew it, they were examining Glen. He had to have a chest x-ray, and again he walked from the examining room to the x-ray room. He gave me a little smile as he went by.

"He can't be that critical," Alexander reasoned, muttering to himself from his chair in the hallway.

At that moment, the doctor who had been examining Glen appeared in front of him. "I'm afraid I have some bad news, Mr. Nakatani."

As Alexander stood up to meet the young doctor's look of concern, he entertained a single, bitter thought: You have no idea.

"You have a very sick boy in there."

Al sighed. "What does that mean?"

"The next six hours are critical. He could die."

I was shocked. He was walking around, for Christ's sake. I thought, oh, Jesus.

Alexander hurried along, barely keeping up with the orderly who was now rushing Glen to intensive care on a gurney. He watched anxiously as his son was put on oxygen and hooked up to a variety of machines. He dreaded the next step—he would have to call Jane.

Another phone call about a dying son. How much can one mother take? I'm a professional healthcare worker. I have the resources to keep my emotions in check in these dire situations. But she wasn't prepared. It was the middle of the night, and I wouldn't be there to help her. I had to force myself to walk to the phone.

"He has pneumocystis. It's like pneumonia, only worse. It's typical of AIDS patients."

Jane was unusually quiet during Alexander's explanation. Encouraged by her calm, he cautiously continued. "They say the next six hours are critical." Al paused. Had she heard what he said? He panicked, imagining the slow dawning of understanding on the other end of the line.

He rushed on, steering her away from the truth. "After that, they'll know better how he's going to respond to the treatment."

"Oh," she said. Good, Alexander thought. Let her think about treatment. She was listening now. He could direct the action.

"Jane, it's just six hours of waiting. There's no sense in scrambling up here. Wait to hear from me, and then maybe your cousin can run you up." He wondered if she would accept his directions. An uneasy silence floated between them until finally she spoke.

"Is he going to die?"

Whatever small measure of control Alexander had wrestled from their situation turned as sour as the stale hospital corridor. What terrified him even more than Glen's condition was the memory of Jane's face, twisted in unimaginable torment. She's not strong enough to go through this again, he thought frantically, and I'm not strong enough to watch.

"I don't think so. Listen to this. He walked by himself from the car into the emergency room, and from there to the x-ray room."

"Oh." A moment went by. "You'll call me then?"

Alexander exhaled. "Yes, I'll call. Try to get some sleep."

He sweated out the next six hours alone. By the time Jane and Guy arrived the next day, Glen could smile at them from beneath the tubes. While they sat outside the intensive care unit, waiting for their ten minutes of visiting time, Jane talked about how caring the intensive care nurses seemed.

"They don't seem afraid of AIDS," she commented to Alexander.

"They see it all the time, and they understand what the public doesn't about the disease," he told her.

"They're just all so nice."

Sitting beside her, Guy noted that most of them were probably gay men, but he didn't mention it to his mother. Toward the end of the day, Al sent them down to the cafeteria for dinner while he stayed with Glen. In the elevator, mother and son had a moment alone.

"Promise me, Guy," said Jane. He turned to her. "Promise me you won't get this. Promise me you won't do anything to get this."

"I promise," Guy replied quickly, solemnly. "I promise you I will never do anything risky. I never have. You don't have to worry."

When Mom and Dad told me Glen had AIDS, my thought was, well, we kind of expected it. It didn't affect me. When he came home, things didn't change all that much, except that we had a stranger in the house.

I don't think Glen was all that surprised by the diagnosis. If he was, he was really, really stupid. I don't think he took it very seriously. He was still thinking of doing all the stuff he had planned on doing and ho-hum nothing was going to change.

When he came home after Letterman, my mother became his companion. That made me angry, because she was spending a lot less time with me. I felt Glen was taking advantage of her. He let her do things he could have done himself.

It wasn't jealousy. I had a relationship with my mother that Glen would never have, because he hadn't been around. When it comes to Glen, I can't tell you that much. Because I separated my life from his, and I know only a little of what he did, and nothing of what he felt.

Glen survived, but he stayed in the hospital for six weeks, fighting the aftereffects of the deadly pneumocystis. By June, when he was finally released, his already slight frame had lost an additional twenty pounds. The next month was spent resting, gaining weight, and preparing to look for a job. He bought a computer and spent many contented hours applying his considerable technical aptitude to getting to know his new love.

Glen seemed happy to be home. He was part of the family—comfortable. His father regretted that they knew nothing of Glen's feelings, but the uneasiness of living under the same roof had all but vanished.

Glen's first illness demanded that as a father I take note of the way my son operated. No matter how badly he felt, he probably wouldn't tell us. I would have to make up for all that time he had been away from us, developing into a separate, grown-up person. In order to better care for him, I would have to learn who my son was, quickly, and without intruding.

By August 1988, Glen's health had improved to the point that he spent each morning job-hunting, returning in the afternoon visibly tired but never complaining. The emergency had passed and Alexander and Jane relaxed a little. Where the urgency of Glen's condition had preoccupied them for two months, they now looked back out on the world and found a moment here and there to enjoy themselves.

They didn't need to look very far for entertainment. Guy continued to live life outrageously, and his parents, without energy to analyze his activities, simply watched their youngest son whiz by.

"He'll be all right," they often told each other. Although his passion for partying meant occasionally overdoing it, they considered both his intelligence and his self-absorption, and they were sure he simply valued himself too highly to risk injury to any part of his body or mind.

"And he doesn't act gay," Jane would always conclude these conversations, holding fast to her secret belief that Guy would someday announce his foray into sexual deviation concluded, his "normal" life reclaimed, and his marriage to a gorgeous blond, imminent. To his mother, this was a scenario that reeked of logic and inevitability. But it was not to be.

I remember that day in August. It was very hot, and even though I know how much my husband loves golf, I still thought it was strange that he was out there playing in that heat. But I was out in it, too, shopping or something, I don't remember. I couldn't wait to get into the air-conditioned house. Guy was home by himself.

Jane pushed open the front door and quickly abandoned her packages and her sandals. "God, it's sweltering," she exclaimed, expecting to hear Guy somewhere in the house, eager to join her in a good round of complaining about the heat.

"Guy," she called out, walking toward the kitchen and the stairs down to the den. A noise, something like a cough, came from the living room and she turned back, finding her son slumped in a chair.

"Why are you sitting like that, Guy? You look funny."

Guy raised his eyebrows to get a view of his mother, but his head remained in an awkward position, slightly tilted and sagging down toward his chest.

The voice that answered her was that of an old man, a sorry rasp that stilled everything else around them.

"It's the only way I can breathe."

His voice scared me, and I had this quick, strange thought that he had rigged up a tape recorder and was playing some sick joke. I started to laugh, because he looked so weird. But then he said that maybe he ought to go to the doctor. He asked me to back his car out of the garage and angle it up toward the front door. Are you kidding? I asked him. He wasn't kidding. So I brought the car around. He could hardly stand up, much less make it to the car.

They admitted him immediately.

Guy had been in the hospital for twenty-four hours when his doctor met with Alexander and Jane in Guy's room. "I'm afraid your son has pneumocystis. And his blood test was positive."

Alexander stood motionless at the end of Guy's bed. Jane began to cry, sobbing against Al's shoulder, the blue of his shirt staining quickly with her tears. In his hospital bed, Guy fingered the tube that protruded from the top of his right hand, saying nothing.

"This can't be," Jane whispered. Her face, gutted with pain and disbelief, slowly turned to Guy. He returned her gaze desperately, as if he knew what was coming.

"Guy, you promised. You promised me."

I didn't suspect HIV at first. It was the farthest thing from my mind. I thought I had the flu, except one day I got up and my feet were blue. And then I had to hold my head a certain way in order to breathe.

At the hospital they started to do some tests. When they checked the oxygen level in my blood, I knew that's what they'd done to Glen, and I guess that bothered me.

I felt so awful I couldn't think clearly. I remember losing it with the person doing the blood-gas test. When you're really sick, your veins aren't as strong as they should be. She kept poking and poking. I yelled at her that I was tired of being poked. Then they did a lung culture. They tried to make me swallow a tube, which is impossible, by the way, and it scratched my throat going down. I was miserable.

After that, they put me in intensive care. I wondered if I was being quarantined, and I knew then what it might be. Of course I didn't want to think about it.

Then the doctor came in: It's HIV. I thought, oh shit, what am I going to do? What's going to happen? I remember my mother, saying over and over again, no, no, no.

While I was in the hospital, I tried not to complain. That was to protect my parents, and myself, because I couldn't take it—the idea that I had hurt them, too. And when my mom reminded me of my promise, I knew I was no different.

Jane got home from the hospital and sat by herself in the living room. She closed her eyes, and the dark lines that had given her face such stinging definition gave way to a smooth visage—ghostly white, the nothingness of resignation. The air-conditioner came on, and Jane remembered the weather outside. Just two days ago, she thought, she had been concerned about the heat.

It was fun to complain, you know, as if Greg was still there, and Glen wasn't sick, and all I had to think about was the damn heat. For two years I had imagined time backing up and everything turning out differently. Then one day I just let things be, it was me again, hot and tired, coming

99

home to Guy, who was living with us in some timeless, untainted space.

Before, I had allowed myself these fantasies of turning back time. Alexander wouldn't have approved. He would have said it wasn't healthy. But it soothed me sometimes, and besides I still had Guy. Dreaming is all right, so long as there's still some reason to come back.

Now even my fantasies were dead. There was nowhere I could go to escape the pain. Why bother imagining anything different when it was just all so unbelievable anyway?

That night, Jane came into the kitchen where Glen and Alexander sat together at the table. She stood in the middle of the room, not sure why she was there, aware of the sounds of normalcy—the ice machine, Rocky, the dog, nosing his metal dish around the patio to get their attention. The light on their answering machine was blinking. She touched the message button.

It was Anne. She knew Guy hadn't been feeling well.

"Hi, Guy," her voice said with its usual enthusiasm. "Are you dead yet? Call me."

Jane picked up the phone. Her husband and oldest son listened while she reported to Anne without emotion that Guy was in the hospital, and perhaps she should go visit him. Alexander imagined Anne's response—guilt over her flippant message, remorse that would go on for days. Jane didn't mention the diagnosis, nor did she give Guy's friend a kind word. She hung up and joined them at the table.

"Guy can tell her. I just can't."

Rocky bounded up onto the deck and stood at attention, tail wagging furiously, watching them through the sliding door.

"Hi, boy," Alexander said absently, making no move to let him in. "He probably hasn't been fed." Slowly, he stood up.

"Dad." Glen's voice was very quiet.

"Yes, son?"

"It's too bad about Guy."

Glen stood up and left. Alexander went outside to feed Rocky. Jane sat alone in the kitchen, empty of dreams.

Measure of Success

Two years before, in September 1986, Guy had been bored during his first year at San Jose State University—his social life no longer depending on school corridors. The one plus of going to college was that if he arranged his classes carefully, an excess of daytime hours remained for shopping. His favorite store was Nordstrom, the most popular, most upscale department store in northern California. The Nordstrom closest to Guy was in Rockridge Mall, a shopping center not far from his house. His favorite department was The Brass Rail, which catered to cool, casual, young men.

Everyone in "The Rail" knew Guy, including the manager, Yvonne, who offered him a job during the summer of 1987. The choice to leave school came easily. He would work part-time at Nordstrom and keep his weekend job as a gymnastics instructor. Just as easily, he gave up the idea of going to the Olympics. Too much work. Too many missed evenings of opportunity.

"I'm only taking a break. It would be good to get out in the business world for a while," he told everyone.

During my elementary school years, I dressed in hand-me-downs. My clothes were all right; they just weren't what I visualized for myself. I learned early that people are judged on how they look, how they talk, what they wear. These things became important to me, because they were the things I could control. I couldn't change, for instance, the fact that I was Japanese.

When I took Anne shopping, I would explain to her that comfort was not an issue. I'd say, it doesn't matter that those shoes hurt, as long as they look good. You are what you appear to be—that was my motto until quite recently. Now I tend to think you are what you feel.

One year later, in June 1988, Guy was ready to give up coaching and make Nordstrom his career. He had found a friend in the department manager at Rockridge, and he begged Yvonne to take him with her when she moved to the Woodside store, which was a bigger, busier, Nordstrom branch. She offered him a full-time position in The Brass Rail at Woodside, effective August 1.

But on that day, Guy Nakatani was in the hospital, hearing the news that he had full-blown AIDS.

I was out for six weeks. When I finally started in September, I went up to personnel to check on the status of my employee benefits. Now that I was full-time, I was entitled to full benefits and long-term disability. When I think about it now, I'm amazed that I was thinking about this. Some little voice inside of me told me to protect myself, and more importantly, my parents.

No, I didn't tell Nordstrom I had AIDS. They didn't ask, and I didn't feel I needed to. I wouldn't be putting anybody at risk. My disease would not affect my performance. And, although I was worried, I wasn't without hope. I believed I might beat it.

I got in just in time. During the next few years, things changed. Too many people in the industry had come down with the disease.

Guy was Yvonne's best employee at Woodside, which didn't go unnoticed by the people on the third floor. By November, he had been promoted to manager of The Brass Connection, which sold clothes to young boys—or, rather, to their mothers.

Suddenly, Guy couldn't relate to his customers. He was used to The Rail, where teenagers made their own decisions or the twenty-to-thirty crowd were easily guided and hardly ever brought anything back. He hated having to entertain tired, whining children while their mothers picked out their clothes. His crew of three wasn't very much help.

The department, the crew, even the customers—everything was too small. I wanted to be where I could function with people my own age, really help them put together a wardrobe. And those mothers! Women shoppers are harder to work with and are higher returners than men, which is a disaster because the success of any department depends on things staying sold. Men come in for a reason. Women come in to pass time. The men took my suggestions. The women had acquired tastes, which made them think they knew more than I did about what looks good. Yeah, right.

Guy wasn't happy in The Brass Connection. He went to Yvonne and asked to be demoted.

"This is quite unusual, Guy."

"Yes, I know. But I've been manager of The Connection for three months, and I haven't come before now because I wanted you to see what I'm like. I'm good. I'm organized. I know that people usually step down at the end of their careers when they don't want to try anymore. That's not me. I don't want to ruin future management positions; it's just that I feel I could produce more for Nordstrom in another department."

When she still appeared hesitant, Guy told her he was sick and wanted to be happy with what he did for the rest of his life. She agreed to the switch.

From then on, Guy's career blossomed steadily. He made more money as a salesperson in The Rail than he had as a manager in The Brass Connection. He could suggest, persuade, and sell. He gave everything he had to his job. His doctor warned him about stress, long hours, poor diet, and uneven rest; his was an opportunistic virus waiting to happen. And in August 1989, Guy's immune system faltered once again.

He was depressed. It was only the second time he'd shown symptoms of the disease, although not as severely as the year before, when he was diagnosed. He worried about what was happening in The Rail during his absence.

Still coughing and considerably thinner, Guy returned three weeks later. Yvonne had been transferred back to Rockridge, so she wasn't there to greet him. The new Woodside store manager saw him walk through the door.

"My God! What are you doing here? You look awful."

"Thanks," said Guy grimly as he marched past.

By February 1990, Guy had been promoted to manager of Men's Sportswear. It was a promotion, because the department had more inventory and higher prices, but for the long term, it wasn't what Guy wanted. In the fall, a new store would be opening in Oakville, and the idea of being the first-ever manager of a brand-new department sent Guy's heart, and his imagination, soaring.

I believed in Nordstrom. The company attracted people who wanted the best for themselves, and that's what I wanted. I was the ideal employee: dedicated, ambitious, creative. Nordstrom's philosophy, which has proved enormously successful, is that the customer is unconditionally right. Their employees can grumble and complain all they want outside the store, but inside, courtesy and professionalism are strictly demanded.

And I loved to demand! I modeled my department after my own closet, every item that wasn't hanging folded just right, sized, colorized, or fanned out to perfection, my crew would do over again until I was satisfied. Yet I never left the store before they did. Whoever took over for me in the morning found a wonderful, clean floor. No one ever claimed to have done Guy Nakatani's job for him.

I wanted so badly to be transferred to the new store. Handling the inventory, helping to choose new merchandise, creating a beautiful department—I could taste it. But the management at Woodside blocked the move. I didn't know why, but I could take a guess.

A call came in from my old friend Yvonne at Rockridge, wanting to know if I was available; I heard about it because I knew somebody who knew somebody who knew the Woodside store manager's secretary. But again, he wouldn't approve it. He didn't like me, but he didn't want anybody else to have me, either.

I was driven to succeed in Men's Sportswear. I figured if I had enough power, he'd have to let me go. What could I do, I wondered, to make this happen?

I did something really stupid.

On the last day of June 1990, Guy was only three hundred dollars away from reaching a monthly target figure for Men's Sportswear—an incredible amount of money that would make him the talk of the store.

It was 8:30 at night; the store closed at nine. Guy buzzed around the department. "If there's anything you need, buy it now," he hummed to his employees. His prodding wasn't unusual for a manager; to say to the crew—we're this close, we're that close—it was done all the time. A young woman on his crew offered to buy a leather jacket, provided she could bring it back later. Keeping his expression steady, Guy maneuvered her out of earshot of the other employees. He told her to return it after a few days, when the purchase had been safely credited to the department.

However, the strain of four hundred dollars on her VISA bill proved too much for her. She returned the jacket the next day to a Nordstrom store in San Francisco.

It was big news, because I was one of the top managers. And the irony of the whole thing was that while all this was going down, the Woodside store manager was transferred, and the new manager loved me. I know she did, because she didn't fire me. I couldn't believe it. I told her I would probably have fired me.

Instead, she asked me where I would like to work—as a lowly salesperson, of course. I chose Fashion Fair which, next to Woodside, was the hottest Nordstrom around, and located in San Jose.

It had been an ultrastupid move on my part. I had everything to lose, not only my position, but my benefits! I had been in charge, and now I would have to do what somebody else said to do, knowing I could do it better my way. I don't know what was I thinking.

Guy had been a salesperson at Fashion Fair barely two months when he began his climb back up the corporate ladder. He was made the assistant manager of Men's Sportswear. He loathed being an assistant anything, but he knew it wouldn't last. To make things more difficult, he didn't get along with the head of the department. For the first time in his life, Guy woke up in the morning dreading the day ahead.

He began to take more time off, telling everyone he needed to grieve for his sick brother. After only a few weeks, he was named manager of The Brass Rail. He was back where he had started, and on top again.

· · · ·

Throughout the summer of 1990, Glen was in denial. Determined to continue at San Jose State University in September, he marked registration day on the calendar and announced quietly that in the fall he would be taking an accounting class as part of the master's program. It was, Alexander told Jane, as if he planned to live forever.

Since Glen's return home two and a half years previously, the disease had slowly yet decisively weakened him. But also during that time, he had become an auditor for the State of California, mastered every computer he touched, formed new relationships at work, where his friends spoke of him with affection and admiration, revitalized his wardrobe, and earned enough money to buy, among other things, a beautiful leather briefcase and a BMW. He consulted a financial adviser, listed his assets on his computer, checked the stock market every day. The future was on.

Alexander and Jane enjoyed the new Glen, but Guy, in a rare moment of interest, was incredulous. "My brother's a yuppie," he sniffed.

*At the time Glen was coming out, most gays were losers. To be accept-
ed in the gay community, you had to party constantly, take drugs to last
all night. There were times when my brother would go three days—party,
recuperate, party, recuperate. You can't hold a steady job or have goals and
focus if you live that kind of lifestyle.*

*He'd go to gay bars where he'd meet sleazy people. It's very hard to
begin a relationship in a gay bar because everyone you find there is still
trying to find himself. Even in a straight pick-up joint, you're not going to
find the big professional or, very rarely, people who have goals and their
lives in order. And I don't know how he could take some of those people. I
still tell Anne, stop me if I flame.*

*Still, we have an advantage, living in an area that is at the forefront
of and acceptance of homosexuality. I'd hate to be somewhere else.*

Although Glen loved his computer, he loved his car even more.
Alexander shared his son's satisfaction. It was a symbol of his surprising success, his final achievements, and, his father suspected, of being
accepted into the world that surrounded him.

By August, Glen's condition began to deteriorate rapidly. His days
at work became so sporadic that he decided to give up his position, at
least temporarily. He would rest and become stronger, continuing with
school so that when he did return to work, he would be ahead.

Alexander began to drive Glen, always in Glen's car, to his appoint-
ments at the hospital or anywhere his son wanted to go. "You can drive
today, Dad," he would say, as if tomorrow he'd feel up to it. Glen had no
intention of dying—he was simply allowing his father to drive. More
and more, it was a struggle just to open the door, maneuver himself
into the passenger seat, and pull the door closed behind him. Al
watched the procedure, agonizing, but certain that his son would not
appreciate his help.

He worried about his son's state of mind—was Glen preparing at
all for dying? Alexander wanted to bring up the subject. Later, he would
smile when he imagined embarking on such a conversation with his
son. "What," Glen would have said, "you think I'm gonna die?"

When the day came to register for his class, Glen was too weak to drive. Alexander offered to register for him and was glad when Glen accepted, although he knew that meant his son was sicker than any of them, especially Glen, would admit. Glen began the class, which met two nights a week. By October, he could no longer lift his heavy binder, so he took out the pages he needed and carried them to class with his pencil.

Through the summer, his trips to the hospital as an outpatient had been monthly. Now they were weekly, sometimes requiring him to be admitted. On nights when he was forced to stay at the hospital, he would check himself out, drive to his class, and then drive himself back to the hospital later that night. It was an act that made Jane weep uncontrollably. Alexander's grief was just as desolate, but as usual he held fast to his emotions.

We went through this terrible routine—Glen trying to live his life normally, but then he'd be too sick, and he would have to go in to the hospital. I remember one of the last times. We were getting in his car, and he said he wanted to drive. It was agony for him. He had pancreatitis, and I could see him grimace when he shifted gears or put on the brake.

As it turned out, he wanted to drive his car one last time. On the way home, he gave it over to me. It was like, okay, I've done it. I felt just awful for him. But I couldn't tell him. All I could do was put my hand on his knee and try to communicate that I knew something of what he was feeling. He looked over, and we looked at each other. That was the nature of our relationship, just a look.

The truth is, I was afraid to say a word. I didn't know what the hell would happen to me if I lost my composure. I'd seen what happened to Jane, and I felt I had to stay strong for the duration. That's what they taught me in the military—no matter what, you've got to be in position to take care of it. Somebody has to keep going.

• • • •

Jane avoided any conversation about children, particularly the dreaded question: How many children do you have? With one son dead, one dying, and another terminally ill, she felt sorry for the poor person who asked. Alexander suggested she direct these conversations toward Guy.

"But then they want to know all about him, Al. All roads lead to disaster."

Alexander couldn't understand why she did this to herself. All roads simply led to the truth. She didn't want to deal with the truth.

"The truth is tragic," she declared.

Which of our tragedies, he wondered, are you referring to? Alexander believed that his wife didn't want to talk about having two gay sons. They had learned of Glen's homosexuality in 1978. Ten years and one more gay son later, Alexander could hardly remember a conversation about their sexual orientation, except for the one explosive morning in June 1986.

There were a few exceptions. Jane had discussed it with one of her sisters, who immediately scouted out a good-looking, "decent" man for Glen. "She keeps telling me what a nice guy he is, and that he doesn't look gay," Jane told her husband, who didn't comment.

But Jane, too, was bothered by this line of thinking. "Nobody should have to go through life alone."

"No, Jane," Al finally replied. "In that respect, Glen's no different than anyone else."

When their oldest son was diagnosed in 1988, there was a series of urgent discussions about what to tell the world. Glen had a heart problem, lung cancer, leukemia, tuberculosis—anything but AIDS, Jane would later recall.

As Glen neared death, Alexander moved nearer to the truth. He told their dentist, who was also close to the family, ostensibly because Glen needed care. He started telling their closest friends. With Jane, he clamored for honesty.

"What about Ryan White?" Jane repeated what she believed to be her strongest argument. Ryan White had brought the country's ignorance about AIDS to the forefront of the news when he was kept from attending his local elementary school by a group of hysterical parents. She had nightmares about that happening at her school.

But Alexander was ready to put Ryan White and all of Jane's other excuses to rest. "First of all, that's an old argument. Where have you been for the past five years? There's been a lot of educating going on.

"And, second, we need to tell the truth. We're dishonoring our sons by lying."

"We're not dishonoring them. We're protecting them."

"And, finally, these are our friends, Jane. People who love you, who love Glen and Guy. You've been so worried about how they would react. Haven't you noticed? The ones who know have been wonderful. They want to help. Let them."

Jane broke down and Alexander softened, feeling his persistent need, despite the conflict she was causing, to shield her from further pain.

"Besides," he said quietly, holding her close, "I want to know if there's somebody out there who wouldn't want to be around us anymore. I mean, if that's the way they feel, then . . ."

"Screw 'em," came a tiny voice. Al was impressed.

The comments people made were so insensitive. I would go to lunch with my friends, the ones who didn't know, and a gay person would wait on us. And one of them would remark, I wonder if they sterilized this cup. They would say they couldn't imagine having a gay kid. They'd say whatever they wanted to.

Even so, I realized that Alexander was right. Our closest friends would want to be there for us; I would have felt that way if it were them. I would say, I don't want you to be too shocked. Of course they were really shocked, when I finally told one or two of them about Guy.

Later on, I could accept the idea of Guy and James, but for the longest time I didn't tell anyone that James was living with us. It's the way I was raised. I know that must sound silly, but whenever I tried to deal with these feelings, this sense of dread would come back to me, without me wanting it to. It's difficult to overcome fear.

. . . .

By November, Glen had lost volumes of weight; the doctors announced he was suffering from wasting syndrome. On the seventeenth of that month, he was admitted to the hospital for the last time. Alexander and Jane took turns sitting with him, engaging in quiet conversations, watching him sleep, helping with his care.

One night Alexander asked Jane if he could talk to her in the corridor outside Glen's room. "You know, I've been thinking about the terribly difficult life our son has had."

"So have I," said Jane. The circles under her eyes were prominent now, and her voice always trembled a little under the permanent strain of her grieving. "And now, just when he seemed to have gotten his life together, he's losing it." She struggled for control. "I just want him to have a good death. Not like Greg." She shook her head violently, as if engaged in dire combat with terrifying images of what was to come.

Alexander reached over and, for an instant, touched her face with such tenderness that her breath caught and she was still, gazing into his eyes. He smiled at her warmly.

"I had an amazing conversation with Glen just now," he said, his voice almost a whisper. "He told me about a man he was involved with in Hawaii." Alexander hesitated. "He was married, but because of—you know—his relationship with Glen, he and his wife ended up divorcing."

A look of portentous distress came racing back across Jane's face. "I don't think I want to hear this, Al."

"Oh, I know, I know, you're thinking that he wrecked a marriage. Of course that crossed my mind too. And from the few things he shared, the marriage hadn't been right for a long time. Imagine the pain and anger for everyone involved. Glen and his friend were under enormous pressure."

"Of course there was pain and anger," Jane began, her voice rising. She couldn't understand her husband's attitude. Was he condoning this behavior? "What did they expect . . ."

"Jane!" Alexander stopped her and then repeated, more gently, "Jane." She watched him, trying to be patient.

"You're right, I mean, maybe you're right. We don't know anything about this couple. But that's not why I wanted to tell you this."

He sighed deeply. "Jane, our son loved this man, and he loved Glen. He told me, not in those words exactly, but I could tell that's what he was trying to say."

Right there, in the middle of the busy hospital corridor, Alexander Nakatani put his arm around his wife and pulled her to him. He didn't care. He wanted her to feel it, too, a single moment of hope in this cavern of confusion and despair.

"To experience love. That's what we'd hoped for our children, isn't it?"

Jane wept silent tears in her husband's arms. And they remained that way, together, motionless, while others moved around them.

No Comparison

Preparations for Guy's twenty-third birthday were part of an annual ritual that had begun two years previously, when Guy decided that if his life was going to be short, each celebration of his birth might as well be a doozy. This particular bash would repeat some of the sentimental favorites from 1988 and 1989; on November 25, 1990, the party would again be held in the Sycamore Suite at the Doubletree Inn, the drink of choice was beer, the menu pizza, the music loud selections from Guy's extensive collection. Guests could spend the night in the bedroom or the living room, but Guy would be first in line for a bed.

The invitations were created by Guy, an elaborate collage of pictures from GQ: gorgeous men with designer clothes and tan, shiny bodies. "Come Party with the Big Boys," the invitation read. Anne was sent to photocopy the page when Guy finished it; she remembers lamenting the fact that after all his work, the black-and-white copies didn't look nearly as glamorous as the colorful original.

Anne also remembers being nervous about this party. For the first time, Guy had invited some of his Nordstrom coworkers, who weren't old friends or family, and therefore, Anne fretted, not as likely to show up. Including the family was out—everyone was caught up with Glen, and many of Guy's usual buddies were out of town or unable to make the trip from southern California. Guy, too, may have been concerned about the success of this year's bash, but when Catherine called to say she was coming, he pronounced the event on track and ready to be launched.

"Cat will be here, Annie, and now everything's purr-fect!" Guy fairly sang to Anne over the phone several days before Thanksgiving.

"Yeah, Guy, great." Anne had a bad feeling. First, Cat's presence seemed to be the barometer for the party's success. Since when did she make the difference? Then, Guy invited those people from work. "They're flaky, Guy," she protested, which only seemed to bolster Guy's enthusiasm.

"They're fun, Nastasia. Don't worry, they'll show."

And finally, while all this was going on, Guy was getting closer and closer to being an only child. Anne couldn't believe Guy's single-mindedness. When it was announced that Glen would be home from the hospital for Thanksgiving, she hoped it meant that his death was not imminent.

While Guy was planning, I was thinking, are you crazy? Of course I didn't say anything. Glen was dying and Al and Jane were running back and forth to the hospital, but it was like there was a glass cover over what was happening. You could see it, but you couldn't get to it. And Guy, well, he was dancing around on top of the glass. He knew his brother was there, but he just kept on dancing, and no one told him to stop.

The morning of the party, Guy went to pick Cat up at the airport. He was so excited. It was going to be a great day, a great night, a real blast. He had something special planned, but he wouldn't tell anyone what it was, not even me. I asked him if he was going to tell Cat, and he got this funny look on his face and said no, he didn't think he'd tell Cat. Whatever that meant.

All along, Cat was a toy and I was a chore. Chores are something you have to do to keep everything okay. Guy could stop to play with her whenever he wanted to; that's why she seemed like so much fun. I was fun, too, but I was around all the time, mixed in with real life. Guy's favorite game was not the one he played every day. It was the one he saved for special occasions.

When Glen arrived at the house for Thanksgiving, his gaunt face bore a slight smile that never disappeared all day. He allowed his mother to fuss over him, cut his turkey, unfold his napkin. Sitting in the middle of a den full of relatives, he watched attentively as people talked, laughed at his brother's party plans, and took a long nap on the couch after dinner. No one who was there that day can testify to the amount of pain he was suffering; no one remembers a single grimace or moan. He was frail and weak, sinking into the cushions of the couch and almost disappearing under his blanket. But never, Alexander would reflect later, had his eldest son seemed more sure of his membership in the family and desirous of their company.

Jane agrees with me that, at the end, Glen was almost noble about the disease. He never complained, never asked for anything.

But things never got talked out, either. I felt I had to translate the few words Glen uttered into what he needed or how he was feeling. I would ask a question, try to get a reading. If I misread him and made a mistake, he was very gracious about it. Not like Guy, who expected so much more and made demands on everyone. But at least he talked.

When Glen returned to his hospital bed that night, the nurses teased him. Had he eaten too much? They hoped so. For a few hours, he slept well, contentedly. It was as if he was gathering his energy for one last try at living.

Glen awoke at midnight, sitting up straight and gasping for air, drenched in sweat, struggling to talk between gasps. On her chair next to the bed, Jane stirred instantly and tried to calm her son, retrieving his oxygen mask and fighting with him to allow her to put it back on his face.

"Lie down, Glen, take some breaths." She bent over him and

caressed his face, holding the mask with one hand and slipping the thin straps back around one ear and then the other. Her face very close to his, she whispered to him an ancient mantra of comfort: "Don't be afraid. I'm here. Don't be afraid. I'm here."

His hand trembled as he reached for the mask.

"Don't try to talk, Glen," she urged him. But he pulled at it, uncovering his mouth finally, a few tears escaping down his cheeks as he met his mother's eyes.

"I'm afraid, Mom."

"I know, Glen. So am I." She moved onto the bed next to him, stroking his face and his forehead, continuing her protective chant. His mother's breath seemed to join his as he worked hard to take in air, and his fear grew, until Jane could feel it filling the room, threatening to choke them. She held her son desperately, powerless against the terrors menacing her child, vigilant in her watch for the angel of death, who would snatch Glen away, should she sleep. Just after dawn, Jane wept into the phone to her husband.

"He's really, really fearful, Al. And I'm not sure I can bear it."

"I spoke to the doctor, Jane. Glen is stable. He'll make it through the day."

"I won't," Jane snapped. Alexander hung up and drove to the hospital.

Friday dragged on. Glen's abdominal pain became more acute, his breathing problems continued. He couldn't eat; he didn't have the strength to move from the bed to the bathroom. He moaned in his sleep, but when he was awake, he did not speak of his obvious pain. The doctor increased his dosage of morphine, and Glen slept, fitfully, yet more consistently Friday night, while Alexander kept watch and Jane made a futile attempt to sleep on an empty bed in the room next door. Jane finally dozed off in a chair next to Glen's bed around 5:00 A.M.

At 6:15, she jolted awake. Glen was awake, too. Alexander was gone.

"Hi, Mom," he greeted her with his familiar lopsided grin. Relief rushed through her, threatening to topple her fragile composure.

But the smile she returned to him was calm, confident.

"Good morning, Glen. You've been busy while I was sleeping— you've gotten much better."

Glen looked away, but the grin remained. "Where's Dad?"

"He went for some coffee. Ellen's coming, you know."

Ellen was Glen's longtime friend, a young woman he'd met in Hawaii when they were children. The thought of Ellen's arrival pleased Jane; where most of the windows into Glen's personal life had remained closed to them, Ellen was someone through whom they'd seen a glimpse of Glen as others saw him: a good man, connected to others, worthy of friendship. She would be arriving in an hour.

"I have to get ready." To Jane's amazement, Glen pulled himself up and shifted his legs over the side of the bed.

"Where are you going?" she managed to ask.

"Gotta take a shower."

Alexander walked through the door in time to see his son stand up, wobble a little, and begin a slow shuffle toward the bathroom. Neither parent moved, sharing an urgent prayer that he wouldn't collapse onto the floor. But they knew their son. What, you think I'm gonna die?

"Wow," said Alexander softly, as the bathroom door swung closed behind him. Only the day before, Jane had to bring a bowl and a towel and bathe him—gingerly. A few friends from work had come to visit, but Glen didn't have the energy to talk to them. Yet that morning Ellen came, he got up by himself, showered, and washed his own hair. They could hardly believe it.

Glen's room had been relatively crowded that morning—three teachers Jane worked with, some cousins, and Alexander's parents, Harriet and Takeo, had all stopped by. Glen didn't seem to notice. He sat with his hands folded in his lap, motionless behind his little smile. Ellen was coming. He had been waiting for her.

When she arrived, the last of the visitors filed out into the waiting room, giving Jane a knowing look, as if Glen might have some deep dark secret to tell Ellen before he died. Jane almost laughed; after years of caring what people thought, she was feeling recklessly unconcerned.

She suspected it was because she hadn't had any sleep, and went in search of an empty hospital couch, leaving Glen alone with his friend.

I waited by the door for everyone to leave Glen's room. Then I climbed onto the bed next to him and put my arm around his shoulders.

He was skin and bones. I remembered him healthy. I remembered when he came to visit, and we went to a little Italian restaurant, just the two of us. We sat eating artichokes, looking at each other, talking a little. We were very comfortable doing that, and other things, such as playing Japanese cards. We were so good together.

We were each other's only childhood friend. I felt close enough to say to him, you knew what was going on out there, why weren't you careful? He said he hadn't thought about it, that he hadn't been afraid to "really live." I don't think he cared if he got infected. He would rather be free.

For a long time, I just held him. He was fully awake. Guess what, he said to me, my father bought tickets for the Nutcracker Suite. He couldn't wait to go. It was going to be at Christmastime. Glen loved Christmas.

The first time I saw Glen after he was sick, I told him I would think about him every day at twelve o'clock. I believed if I thought about him, he would get well. Of course I didn't do it every single day, and now I knew there was no turning back—he would die soon, and I felt guilty. But of course Glen reassured me. Ellen, he said, no one could have saved me from this disease.

There was something magical about Glen. Other than dying, he saved himself from everything else.

After close to an hour, Ellen came out and said Glen was tired. Jane gave her a long hug. She was glad Ellen had come, but Jane knew her son would die now. There was no one else to wait for.

• • • •

Friday evening, Guy, Anne, and Catherine arrived at the Doubletree Inn an hour early. Guy checked into the suite and kept the reservation desk busy while his friends carried in ten cases of beer, several gallons of red wine, and enough tortilla chips and crackers to keep most of northern California nourished for a week. Guy personally took care of moving his stereo.

Inside the suite, they set up the bar and set out the food. Guy chose the tapes that would be played and lined them up in order—mood music to begin, move to dance tunes, save the best for last. Under Guy's direction, they rearranged the furniture. At 7:50, he pronounced the room ready.

"Let the games begin," he mumbled. Anne and Cat exchanged a glance. Try as he might, Guy just wasn't himself.

. . . .

Jane and Alexander were trying to quiet Glen. As his mother suspected, Ellen's departure marked the beginning of a rapid decline in their son's condition. The evening wore on, and Glen's agonizing battle to breathe, and his unfettered fear, nearly broke them apart. They didn't want him to die this way, struggling and frightened. There had already been one incident where Glen turned blue, prompting a flurry of activity from the staff and sending Jane to the brink of hysteria. Then only an hour ago, they had to pump his stomach, and Alexander was sure Glen would pass out from the pain.

"Why don't you lie back, Glen," Alexander pleaded with him. "You need to rest."

But as soon as he tried to relax, he would jerk up again, calling out in panic, "Dad, Dad! I can't breathe!" Terrified, he gasped for air, moaning between breaths, the pain in his abdomen exacerbated by the harsh motion of his body pitching forward, his lungs struggling to inflate.

Alexander felt his control waning. With each passing minute, Glen's torture slowly increased, along with their dread. There would be no relief for their son, short of death. It was too much for a parent to behold.

"We need to increase his morphine," Al demanded of a nurse as he followed her down the hall.

"That could cause respiratory failure, Mr. Nakatani. We have to be careful."

"But it could decrease his pain and calm him down." Al could feel himself breaking apart. "Please, my wife and I, I'm not sure we can watch this much longer."

She paged Glen's doctor, who hurried in to adjust the morphine drip. They brought more pillows and urged Glen gently to sit back, to try to relax. His eyes darting back and forth fearfully, Glen lowered his body slightly, testing the position, his hands clutching at the sheets.

"Dad," Glen murmured, and his father moved close. "I didn't think it would be like this." Finally, Alexander's tears would not be denied.

I remember that moment vividly. You didn't think what would be like this, Glen? Death? This horrible, horrible disease? Or maybe he was refer-
ring to life. I didn't think life would turn out this way, Dad.
Neither did I.

Eventually, Jane saw her son take a deep breath and close his eyes.

His doctor drew them away from the bed. "He might be able to rest now, but I'm afraid his breathing difficulties are only going to get worse. That's the nature of pneumocystis, I'm afraid, his lungs . . ."

"We know," Alexander cut him off. Glen's lungs were filling up; eventually, he could suffocate.

The doctor turned off the light over Glen's bed, and the shadows in the room softened. He put his hand on Alexander's shoulder as he moved through the door. "One of you could get some sleep—the room next to us is still empty." He paused, his eyes heavy with kindness. "But I wouldn't go far."

Alexander and Jane had no intention of leaving their oldest son. Jane sat on the bed, stroking his arm, weeping quietly, a pile of tissues spilling off her lap onto the floor. Glen winced in his sleep, and his already labored breathing quickened. Al stood up and leaned over his wife.

"It's probably going to be tonight," he whispered. "I should call Guy." Jane could only nod.

The call took only a minute. The desk at the Doubletree Inn quick-ly transferred him to Guy's suite.

In the background, Alexander heard shouting and laughter and music raging. A thought fluttered across his mind that the television must be on. It took a moment for him to register the sounds. Oh, yes, the party.

"Hello?"

Alexander decided that the voice on the other end must belong to his son. "Your brother's very, very bad. He's probably not going to make it through the night, Guy. Do you want to come?"

Someone picked up the extension, and a blurry voice interrupted, "Hello? Hello? Who's there?"

Guy finally spoke. "I'm on the phone in here."

"Sorry." It took several loud tries before the receiver made its way back on the hook.

"Do you want to come, son?" Alexander repeated. "I think this is it."

"No, Dad."

For Alexander, the noisy background faded away while the phone became an echo chamber for Guy's words. *No, no, no.*

"I mean, what can I do?"

"Nothing." Alexander answered dutifully. "There's nothing anyone can do now." He listened to the sound of his own voice—measured, strange. He couldn't quite comprehend the conversation they were having.

"So you aren't going to come?"

"No." The echo again, getting louder and louder until Alexander wanted to push the phone away.

"Okay, son." Thankfully, the line was quiet. Was there anything left to say? Then he remembered. "Happy birthday."

I felt I had said my good-byes at Thanksgiving. It was my birthday, and Glen wasn't going to ruin it.

Standing next to Guy, Anne picked up the gist of his conversation with his father and began to run around the suite, frantically searching for someone who was sober.

"Okay, Guy," she reappeared at the doorway to the bedroom, dragging her volunteer behind her. "I've found someone who can drive you to the hospital."

"I'm not going," Guy said pleasantly. "And besides, it's time for my surprise."

Anne could do nothing but follow Guy into the living room, where he was directing someone to turn off the stereo. She saw him motion to Catherine. He stood on a coffee table, his hand on Cat's shoulder.

"I have an announcement to make," he exclaimed, his free hand brandishing a wineglass above the gathering.

"This is not just my birthday party. This is an engagement party!" Without a doubt, he had their attention. Guy swept the room with a look of gleaming delight.

"Cat and I are getting married!"

He received the expected response, as a whoop went up and drinks flowed anew. Chaos swirling around her, Anne stood paralyzed with disbelief.

Ditto Cat.

. . . .

By eleven o'clock, exhaustion overtook Alexander. Jane urged him to try to sleep next door. He touched his wife's arm and brushed his lips across his son's forehead. "I'll be right here," he told them several times as he backed out of the room.

For the moment, Glen was calm and awake, but he didn't respond to Jane's simple questions: Do you want some water? Do you need another blanket? His mother watched him beneath his oxygen mask and wondered where he'd gone.

When Glen was still at home, spending endless hours on the family room couch, he developed a daily ritual with his hair. It was falling out, and whenever he got up he would find handfuls of it on his pillow. Methodically, taking care not to miss any, he would brush the hair with one hand into the other and then drop it slowly into the wastebasket, watching it slip from his fingers, rubbing them together gently until every strand had fallen.

Now Jane looked on with fascination as a long, thin arm rose up from out of the recesses of the sheets to touch his face, his bony fingers lingering there momentarily, catching imaginary strands of hair in his fingertips, drawing them away carefully toward the side of the bed. Feebly, Glen dusted his fingers against each other until he concluded the hair was gone. His arm dropped back down to the sheet, where it rested until he began again.

"Glen?" Jane asked after this had gone on for a while. She moved a little closer. "Where are you, Glen? Can you see Greg?"

His arm stopped mid-air.

Jane too froze. If her son had entered the spiritual dimension, she didn't want to interfere. "Glen," she whispered reverently, "can you see Grandma? Can you see Uncle Ted?"

She waited breathlessly. Glen's arm flopped down to his side. He turned to her and wrinkled up his face. Jane giggled.

I'm not dead yet.

After that he seemed to be in the present, in his hospital bed, understanding what was happening to him, and Jane continued to watch his every move. What she saw next made her stifle a scream in her throat while she grasped the sides of the chair and calculated how long it would take Alexander and the nurses to get to her should she need them, which appeared to be momentarily.

Glen had yanked off his oxygen mask. He took long deep breaths, exhaled slowly, and then closed his eyes, waiting. He's trying to die, Jane realized, panic stampeding through every part of her being. But she sat motionless, crouched on the edge of her chair, a battle over Glen's last moments being waged inside of her.

He's going to die right now, one part of her offered. Jane looked at Glen, and then at the oxygen mask next to him. *Put it back, Glen, put it back!* she heard herself begging him silently. But another voice crowded her thoughts: *He wants to be in control. One last act of his own. He deserves that much.*

So she waited with her son. It wasn't long, though, before Glen began to gulp for air, his eyes wide with terror, which gave her permission to help him retrieve the oxygen mask, adjusting the straps over his ears, her fingers, numbed by her fear, moving over his cheeks to his temples to feel the reassuring warmth of his skin.

"I don't think it's time yet, Glen," her words tumbled out like dice on soft felt. *Please, please.*

And he gazed up at her and saw it. Love, unconditional, denying even fate.

ELDEST SON

Alexander had dropped into a deep sleep. In the distance, he could hear sounds, terrible sounds fit only for nightmares, uttered by creatures from the darkest night. Alexander started to feel his terror, and then he was running, but the sounds got louder, closing in on him. His conscious mind came to rescue him, demanding, Is this a dream? And even as the darkness lifted, he grew suspicious of waking. Better to stay where he was and wrestle with imaginary monsters.

When he awoke, Jane was screaming.

Alexander was asleep and here I was, witnessing this awful moment over and over again, my son trying to die and then becoming so frightened, struggling to get the oxygen mask back on. He was tired of the terrible pain. He wanted to go, and he thought he'd go sooner that way. I couldn't believe what was happening.

I was glad when the nurse came in, even though she looked very young and inexperienced. I had been afraid to move, even to breathe. I told her what Glen was doing. I was really upset.

And then she did the strangest thing. She said she needed his vital signs and she was going to take his temperature. She put a thermometer in his mouth.

I wondered how long she would keep it there. Glen's eyes were open. He was looking at me, questioning. He couldn't breathe at all, much less with his mouth closed. Just when I was going to say something, he bit down.

Jane heard the deadly crunching sound.

"Oh, my God," she screamed, "he's going to swallow the thermometer!" Glen's arms were flailing around, and then suddenly he was still.

Jane stared at her son in horror. Her voice, first a low moan, rose quickly into a peel of hysteria.

"Glen! No, Glen!" she cried, reaching for him, touching his arms and his chest frantically, calling his name. But he was gone, the thermometer still dangling from his mouth.

She turned on the nurse, her rage—pure, ancient, limitless—bearing down on the woman. "Why did you do that?" She moved toward her steadily. "Why did you leave it in so long? He swallowed the thermometer!"

The nurse was feeling for a pulse, watching uneasily as Jane approached.

"What do you think you're looking for?" Jane demanded. The nurse turned and headed for the door. Jane followed her down the hall to the nurses' station. "He's dead! You know he's dead, because you killed him with the thermometer!"

"Please calm down, Mrs. Nakatani," the young woman began, backing into the counter where three other nurses stood motionless, watching the scene. "Let's get your husband. It appears that your son has died."

"Because you killed him!" she shrieked.

A door flew open and Alexander rushed out. Jane stood alone in the middle of the hall, her body heaving up and down with each desolate wail. No one moved to comfort her. Struggling to get his bearings, Alexander stepped to his wife's side and encircled her with his arms. He turned to the group at the nurses' station.

"What happened?" he asked calmly, stroking Jane's hair and keeping her firmly within his embrace. After a brief moment, a faceless voice answered him from behind the counter.

"Your son has passed away, Mr. Nakatani."

Alexander took a deep, quavering breath. Jane stirred in his arms.

"Glen's dead, Al," she sobbed. "Glen's dead, and she killed him," she pointed to the nurse who was still pressed against the counter, her youthful face filled with a raw anguish that made Alexander want to hold her too.

"You killed him! You killed my son! How could you be so stupid?" Jane threw herself against her husband furiously, clawing at his shirt, her face contorted into a quivering mass of grief and rage. For the second time in four years, he had lost a son and was afraid he would lose his wife too.

The nurse bolted away from the nurses' station and disappeared into Glen's room. Alexander wanted desperately to follow her. Glen was in there, still warm, Alexander imagined, yearning to touch his son while life still lingered around him. But Jane's distress was frightening.

The remarkable thing was that after everything we'd been through, Jane and I, we'd come to understand each other in our grief and our pain. Just when I thought she was beyond comfort, she came back to me, sensing, I guess, that she was scaring me.

"I'm okay," she whispered, and she allowed me to lead her down the hall to the empty room next to Glen's. She was shaking, so I took her inside, and we sat down on the bed where we had been trying to sleep when Glen was still alive. I still hadn't seen my son, but I knew I had to tend to the living.

Alexander continued to hold his wife, entreating her quietly to tell him what had happened. Somehow, the mother related the story of the death of her child.

She was still shivering and Alexander was still holding her when the young nurse returned several minutes later, her expression rigid, clasping her composure around her like a thin coat in a blizzard. An older woman, who had trailed in behind her, spoke to them quietly.

"Mr. Nakatani, perhaps your wife would be more comfortable out in the hallway."

Jane peered over Alexander's shoulder to glare at the supervisor.

"I don't think you want her out in the hallway," Al remarked.

They huddled around the bed. In voices just above a whisper, the women tried to reason with Jane. But she was relentless. "She killed him, Al. I was there. He bit down on the thermometer. He must have choked on it."

"Oh, God," her wail rose up again, "I didn't want him to die this way. Not again. Not again."

The nurse who had taken Glen's temperature left the room quickly, her resolve shattered. Moving very slowly, the older nurse stepped to Jane's side and knelt down beside her.

"No mother should have to go through what you have, Mrs. Nakatani. But I can tell you for sure that Glen is at peace now."

Jane glanced at her sharply. "If you had been there, you wouldn't think he was at peace."

"My nurses are well trained. I'm sure that taking your son's vital signs had nothing to do with his death. Of course, you became upset when your son died. It would be natural to want to blame someone."

As quickly as Jane stood up, Alexander was with her, his hand on her arm.

"No," he said firmly, holding the older woman steadily in his gaze as she slowly rose to her feet. "That's not what happened. What happened is that a young and perhaps inexperienced nurse made a very poor decision to take the vital signs of a dying man in obvious respiratory distress. Please do not make matters worse by dismissing this incident as an overreaction on the part of my wife. Please," Alexander's voice was clear and even. "Do not disrespect us in that way."

After a moment, she turned and walked away, hesitating when she got to the door.

"Mr. Nakatani," she began, but Alexander raised a hand to silence her.

"Our son was dying. Your staff acted inappropriately, but we will not hold you or anyone responsible for his death. That would be foolish on our part, and we are not fools." Alexander looked at his wife. "We are simply grieving parents, who have to say good-bye to another child."

She was gone quickly. Jane was strangely silent. Al wondered if she was going to argue with him. He knew she would never forgive the nurse. She could be very stubborn.

He reached for her. "Let's go see Glen."

"I don't know," Jane said faintly, sitting back down on the bed.

"Okay, why don't you think about it. I won't be long."

Jane nodded. As much as he wanted to be with his son, Alexander's hands were shaking as he pushed open the door. Oh, God, he prayed, closing his eyes momentarily, please don't let him look like his last moments were spent in agony.

Inside, he found the young nurse hovering over Glen, fixing his blanket, relating to him as if he was still alive.

"Leave him alone," Alexander said to her without anger. "You don't have to do anything. He's dead." The nurse pulled back from Glen's bed, touching one hand to her flushed face. "Leave us, please."

Wordlessly, she disappeared.

His face was serene. His eyes were closed, his skin brilliantly clear, his mouth, his father noticed right away, turned up in the hint of a grin. Alexander moved to his son's side and sat down on the bed.

"Glen," he murmured, holding on, knowing there was something he must do for Jane. He reached into the box of sterile gloves on Glen's tray and put one on. Carefully, he put his finger between his son's lips and opened his mouth.

Alexander gave a great sigh. There it was, an inch-long piece of the thermometer, its mercury tip intact, resting on Glen's tongue. He took it out and put it on the tray, removed the glove, and tenderly closed his son's mouth.

Across the room, the door was opening.

"He's at peace, Jane. Come look." He brought her to their son's side.

"Oh," Jane breathed as she gazed at him, "you're right." She touched Glen's face, now unburdened with the mask. "He looks wonderful," she said, trembling just a little, her weeping softened with relief.

She heard the sound first, a deep moan, and turned to see the violent shuddering of her husband's body as he fell heavily across his son. Jane leaned over him, laying against his back, pressing her spirit to his. What meager powers remained between them were entwined. She would survive, and he would finally give in to his own profound, unspeakable grief.

· · · ·

Shortly after midnight, the phone rang again in the Sycamore Suite of the Doubletree Inn.

"May I speak to Guy, please?" said the voice on the other end.

"Who?" Even though hotel management had called in two complaints, the noise level at the party had risen far above being able to decipher a phone call.

"Guy Nakatani," the voice insisted.

"Uh, he's kinda drunk." Laughter. "Just a minute."

"Yes?" Guy said into the phone, spilling his beer into the receiver.

"It's Dad. Glen's gone. About an hour ago."

"Oh. Okay." Guy made a serious effort not to slur his words. "Thanks for calling, Dad."

"Do you want to see him one last time?"

Guy concentrated hard. "Uh, I don't think so. I want to remember the way he was. Not dead."

Guy waited for his father to say something else. He wanted to say something else. He wished hard for something to come to him.

"Dad! Don't hang up."

"Yes?"

"Tell Mom I love her."

"Okay."

Guy chugged the rest of his beer and looked around for Anne and Catherine. He found them cuddled up on one of the beds. It's only midnight, he thought, and already they're sleeping. He crawled in beside them and closed his eyes, and darkness came quickly and mercifully.

I felt very sad about what Guy did that night. But I agreed with Al that we couldn't pressure him. He was aware of the fact that his brother was going to die within hours. All we could do was ask one more time, do you want to come? But we knew he had no intention of coming.

I suppose it sounds strange, but Guy was the only one who could do the eulogy. I mean, he was the only one who could make it through without breaking down. I worried about what he would say. I kept reminding him that a eulogy is in praise of a person. I know, I know, he said. Don't worry.

I worried anyway. I knew how he felt. He would say it often after that, Glen died on my birthday, as if Glen had spoiled it.

But at the service, Guy was wonderful. He talked all about Glen, his accomplishments, how Glen had held him up at Greg's funeral. He said that what he had thought to be pig-headedness was really determination. He said Glen had shown people around him the meaning of love.

I don't know how much Guy believed what he said, but he said it well. I looked up at Glen's blue marble urn, and I hoped it was all right with him. Knowing Glen, it was.

Jane stoically endured the scene at the house after Glen's funeral. She didn't want to break down, but she also hated hearing that she was "so strong." She didn't want anyone thinking she was over it.

"It will never be okay," she told Alexander. "I'll never stop grieving. I just don't want to talk about it."

So her cousin put out the word to the family that Jane didn't want to talk. About anything—Greg, Glen, Guy's HIV.

In January 1991, Jane returned to her classroom. Guy insisted on accompanying her on her first day and stood next to her in the faculty room while they accepted condolences from her friends. Then he set forth the rules.

"My mother doesn't want to cry," he explained to the startled group that stood before them. "But if she does, it is not a sign of weakness. Treat her normally. This is neither the time nor place to be feeling sorry for her. It's fine to give her a hug and a smile, but that wimpy, pitiful look is definitely out."

Jane appreciated Guy's help and the careful compliance of her fellow teachers. But as the days went by, her grief gave way to agitation.

Something was wrong, unfinished. I thought about Glen, and immediately I felt bad, you know, something different than sadness. It was as if he was following me around. I wanted to turn and ask him what he wanted.

But Glen was never one to let us know. Okay, I told him. I'll figure it out for myself.

A week had gone by when Jane asked Laura, her principal and good friend, to call a meeting of the faculty; she had something to tell them. The superintendent of the district was also invited, but he did not come.

Without shedding a tear, Jane announced to the teachers and staff of Robert F. Kennedy Elementary School that her son Glen had died of AIDS. When Greg was killed, the superintendent had been one of the most consoling of all Jane's colleagues. Several days after her disclosure about Glen, Jane asked the principal if Mr. Harris had heard the news.

"Yes, Jane. I called him personally."

Jane did not hear from him. She next saw him at a meeting three weeks later. He was cold and distant. She was furious.

Later that day, one of her fourth graders called his classmate a faggot and felt the wrath of his teacher descend upon him.

I decided that I wanted everyone to know the truth. And, for a moment, I felt better.

Something had happened to me during those last days, when Glen was dying and I was sitting with him. I remembered holding him in the hospital when he was born, thinking my secret thoughts—that he was a little stranger and I didn't know what I was going to do with him.

And, too, I remembered when Glen was so sick at Letterman in 1988, and Guy and I actually said that maybe it might be better for him to die there. I never dreamed Glen's health would improve or that he would find happiness. But in the next two years, there were so many happy moments for him. I will always be thankful that I was around to see them.

Now we were back in the hospital, and I was holding him again. And I realized he wasn't a stranger anymore, not at all. He was my son, and I knew exactly what I was going to do with him. I would be with him every minute and help him die.

And just briefly, I felt better, about Glen, and about me.

Jane settled into a routine. From her friends: no looks, no questions. She cherished her classroom; the children rescued her from her "other life" for eight precious hours a day. It seemed that she should be breaking down all the time, and she was amazed that her students could make her forget.

"If this weren't happening to us," she would tell Alexander during one of their early-morning talks, "I wouldn't believe it was possible." She marveled that she could still walk around, eat lunch, go shopping. She congratulated herself when she went a whole day without weeping.

Still, her vulnerability lingered, leaving her constantly on guard. Once in a while, the enemy would find her, and she would be caught by a flood of feelings that left her gasping, drowning in grief, deep and endless, until she doubted she could survive.

It happened quite unexpectedly one spring day about six months after Glen died. She had become very close to one of her parents, Pam Dunnett, a mother of three daughters, two of them grown, the youngest whom she had taught several years before. It was her first visit to Pam's house.

Jane was enchanted by their home. The antiques, the wood, the warm, intimate atmosphere—all of it surrounded Jane with good feelings and the suggestion that love had happened there.

"Would you like to see Katie's room?" Pam asked. Jane's old student was now a busy teenager. Pam led Jane up a staircase to the second-story loft. At the landing, a little paradise had been created for their daughters. "This was a playroom, and now it's home for all of Katie's friends."

"I think I'll come live here, too," Jane laughed, noting the big-screen television, the stereo system, a table cluttered with books and games, and huge colorful pillows all over the floor.

They stood at the door of Katie's room. Later, Jane would say that it didn't hit her right away—she was too caught up in the sights. Before her stretched the most charming, most magical bedroom she had ever seen. The braided rug, the antique desk, the wall of shelves filled with stuffed animals and books and framed memories. Tucked under the alcove formed by the sloping roof, a brass trundle bed was covered with a thick down comforter that matched the curtains and the wallpaper. A crumpled pastel afghan was falling off a cozy window seat that looked out on the grass and pine trees surrounding the house. How safe, Jane thought.

She felt it coming when she began to read the walls. "Kate the Great" one poster proclaimed, a blown-up photo of a very small Katie and a very large tennis trophy. Beside the bed, an old computer print-out, faded but still readable, remembered a happy occasion: "Happy Birthday to My Best Girl from her Best Mother!" And above her desk, a bulletin board was covered with at least a hundred slips of paper of various sizes, each held with its own thumbtack. Jane moved closer.

"What's this?"

"Oh, that's Katie's collection of lunch notes. Every day her dad writes her a note and puts it in her lunch bag. He's been doing it for years."

Jane winced, sensing the presence of raw emotion about to over-take her.

Pam didn't notice. "Just to make her feel special, I suppose."

Special. Each of Pam's children was made to feel special. Jane's sudden, violent tears surprised Pam, but she was able to catch Jane when she stumbled, running toward the door.

"Jane, Jane, what's wrong?" she cried, easing her onto Katie's bed.

But Jane couldn't respond. She cried bitterly, uncontrollably, her wrenching sobs filling up the pretty little bedroom until the air was saturated with sorrow.

"You made her feel so special," she finally got the words out. Her friend stared at her, tears of helplessness running down her own cheeks, trying to understand. Jane was in anguish so profound, so complete, Pam dared not imagine it.

Inside Jane, the abyss opened up and swallowed her, sadness and regret rushing by and pooling infinitely, waiting to greet her at the bottom of her emptiness.

THE OYSTER CLUB

Early Saturday evening, December 15, 1990, Sterling James Martin was preparing for a night of dancing at the Oyster and considering his circumstances. He had been living with Danny since July and had come to the conclusion that his roommate was a compulsive liar and a little hussy who spent time lurking at roadside rest stops. Once Danny called him because his car was impounded—he had been picked up at one of those places.

"He's practically a prostitute," James fretted as he combed and recombed his hair, "except he doesn't get paid for it."

James met Danny at The Oyster Club, an upscale, comfortable bar in the restaurant circle of downtown San Jose, well known to the gay scene and not totally understood by anyone else. A month later, Danny moved in. But since then, it had been no different than other relationships for James—less than satisfying.

I heard later that Danny tested positive. I'm not surprised. God only knows what he did and who he did it with. But for a lot of reasons, I wasn't worried. I didn't pick up people in bars and have sex on the first night. It was a rule for my self-esteem. If you have sex the first night, there's nothing to build on later. Lovemaking is so personal, and doing it can give away too much. I always said I hated sex. But it was just that I didn't want to be known.

James grew up thinking the life he shared in the trailer with his mother and younger brother was normal. Her constant unhappiness and her drinking, which began early and continued late, the teasing he received at school, his brother's scorn—it was simply the way he lived.

By the time he got to junior high school, his mother was rarely there. Every month, James went to the same drugstore to cash her welfare check. Then he and his brother bought food and necessities, although they did this separately, never trusting an alliance that might make their singular struggles to survive any easier. Accordingly, electricity and water were often extras.

James can't remember ever hearing a guideline for life. There were no values, no rules, no limitations. There were only needs and ways to fulfill them. There was his mother's unpredictable behavior and a plan each day to avoid her by disappearing into the neighborhood and its people, who sometimes provided James with secret pleasures.

James felt comfortable, he would later reflect, with just about anything that happened to him that did not include pain. He found himself facing challenges, but never choices. He accepted it all.

When I got to high school, I realized that I was going to have to hide a lot of things in order to survive. All through my childhood, I was teased about effeminate behavior. I never had any interest in what my brother did—I wanted to play house and cook and giggle with the girls. I loved to sing along real loud with every song on the radio. When I hit all the high notes, the ooh-ah stuff, it drove him crazy.

I wanted to touch and be touched by other boys, and all the times that happened, it felt good. I was constantly thinking about men, staring at the bulges in their pants and enjoying the tingle that gave me.

But now that it had been banged into me that none of this was normal, I buried those feelings and decided I would prove them all wrong. I would date women—sleep with them if I had to. And I did those things, hating it more and more, knowing that for me, it wasn't at all normal.

When James was sixteen, he met a woman named Anita. She invited him to a gay coffeehouse called Cafe Decadence. James had just gotten his license, so he drove her there in his mother's car. On the way, Anita talked about being a lesbian, which prompted James to share with her that he thought he was gay, too.

It was an exciting moment for me, like knowing for a long time that there's a present hidden in the closet for your birthday, and you can't tell that you know, and then finally you get to open it. I ripped open the wrapping, and the words came bursting out: I think I'm gay.

As soon as we walked into Cafe Decadence, I knew I had come home. Gay people were everywhere, drinking coffee, talking together. It was as real and ordinary as anything I'd ever seen, and it was wonderful.

From then on, there was a place to go to make friends. To keep my cover, I still slept with women, but I slept with men too. I could get through it with a girl if I could look forward to being with a boy.

James had his first test for HIV in 1989. At the time, he was with Larry. Before that there had been Shaun and a few others, each of whom had been only momentarily promising. Along the way, he experienced several firsts: anal sex, physical abuse, and a broken heart. By then, James knew that sex could mean pain. But one day it dawned on him that now sex could mean death. He didn't tell anyone, even Larry, that he was going to be tested.

I sat in a room at the county HIV and AIDS clinic, thinking about everyone I had ever been with and what I had done with them. There was a difference between fooling around and hard-core sex. I hadn't done much of that. I sat in my chair and considered things like open sores and hidden abrasions and exchange of bodily fluids.

The lady who took my blood had long, jet-black hair and lots of makeup. Her perfume was too strong and when she bent over me it filled my nostrils with a harsh, sweet scent. She had me captured, so in case I wasn't already a goner she gave me a lecture on safe sex. She handed me a paper with a number on it and told me to come back in seven days.

All week James walked around in a fog, terrified of what some unknown, uncaring lab technician was writing next to his number. Finally, he found himself back in the room again, waiting, staring at the cold concrete floors and the people that he decided were seedy and not his crowd.

James lamented the fact that he hadn't brought anyone with him. How was he going to get home if he was HIV-positive? And then what?

What the hell, I thought. I would run to another city and start a new life and live crazy.

They called my number and a man took me into a little room and sat me down on a chair in front of his desk. I was thinking, he knows my results. He had another piece of paper on top of mine so I wouldn't be able to see. I was captured again.

He went through the same routine as the black-haired lady. Did I know how HIV was transmitted? Did I know how to practice safe sex? Finally I said, this has been the worst week of my life and couldn't he just tell me? Negative, he said, and he even smiled a little.

Relief. All I wanted to do is get out of there, but he kept talking. I thought, I know now I'm not going to die, and I don't want to listen to your bullshit. He didn't have any power over me anymore.

He gave me a little packet of safe sex stuff, rubbers and water lubricants and I don't know what else. I was embarrassed to carry it through the hallways and threw it in the first garbage can I could find. I didn't need it because I was never going to have sex again.

James treated himself to fish and chips at Caesar's Fish and Poultry Palace. He lasted several weeks before he had sex again with Danny, but he certainly didn't do anything risky—no anal sex, no exchange of bodily fluids—and as usual he didn't like it all that much anyway. He was tested two more times after that, but he wasn't as nervous.

I knew I was negative, but still I got pretty depressed, watching myself live, knowing it wasn't the movie I wanted to be in. Then I met Guy, and things went from black-and-white to living color. For a brief time, life was so amazing, and I wanted to choose it over and over again forever.

. . . .

When James and Danny strolled into The Oyster Club at about ten o'clock, the dance floor was already full, a loud, gyrating mass of men and women dancing together in no particular arrangement. They made their way to the bar upstairs, ordered drinks, and peered over the balcony at the action below.

"I'm thinking of moving to Hawaii," said Danny.

"Oh?" said James.

After a couple of drinks, we went downstairs. We had just moved onto the floor when I saw him dancing. I remember I stood there staring until Danny said, aren't you going to dance? God, he was gorgeous. I kept maneuvering around Danny so I could watch him. He was a little hotty out there, and could he move that body! I consider myself to be a good dancer, too, so I turned it up, and he noticed me right away. It was electric, just for a moment, and I thought, oh, Lord, you're making me crazy!

Danny and I got off the dance floor and went back up to the top bar to order a drink and sure enough he was right behind us. He walked up and tapped Danny on the shoulder and said something like, hello, how are you? How's it going? They knew each other vaguely, but he was doing that so he could meet me. And of course, I felt like I was going to throw up. I was so nervous, trying to look my best and keep my composure. Just stand there and be cute and don't go all jello over him.

"This is my friend James," said Danny. "We're kind of seeing each other."

James gripped the bar to keep from punching Danny. The beautiful man, however, did not seem to care that Danny and James had ever had any relationship at all. He closed in on James.

"Hi," he breathed into James' face. "I'm Guy Nakatani."

I remember it so vividly, our eyes meeting, locking, some crazy sparks flying. We shook hands, and then he turned back to Danny and they started talking. I stood there holding my beer, scared to death.

After a while, Danny was saying something, I have no idea what, and Guy and I were looking at each other again. It was his smile, the twinkle in his eye—I get excited, remembering. It feels so good to tell it again. It was magic.

Guy drifted down the long bar, his deep brown eyes drinking in everyone he stopped to greet, his hand reaching up to push back thick black bangs that had been carefully styled to flop over onto his forehead. James followed his every move, peering through the crowd, leaning around Danny, who was too interested in what was going on else-where to notice the connection that had been made. Later, when Danny and James were on their way out the door, Guy materialized before them.

"It was nice meeting you," he said, taking the occasion to extend his hand to James, who immediately panicked, hoping his own hand wasn't too clammy.

"I hope to see you again," James stammered, yet meaning every word.

Guy smiled. "Oh, yes," he purred, "we will definitely see each other again."

Oh, oh, oh. That sexy little voice. He was sure we'd see each other again. My heart pounded away.

The next night, I was sitting on the couch watching TV when the phone rang, and of course I ran in there thinking, who can it be?—I love the phone! It was Guy. Hey, what are you up to? Not much, I said, and I started to sweat right there on the phone.

He said he was going to the Oyster with his friend Anne and did we want to go. I said I didn't really want to, but maybe Danny would.

Why did I say that? Playing hard to get, I guess. Or maybe I was scared. I would have to get dressed up, and what was I going to wear? And does my hair look good, and do I have a tan? All of those things.

Guy came and just beeped the horn and Danny left. I was sad but relieved. I wanted to look my best and be up to my highest energy level. You know, no dark circles.

James didn't realize then that Guy had made a decision. James had been moved to the top of the A-list. In fact, there was no longer a list, only James, and Guy would not be deterred.

The next night, he called again. Did we want to go to the movies? I said, who's we? He said, I'm asking if you and Danny want to go with me to the movies. But it was me he wanted. He told me later that Danny was not the kind of person he would hang around with. But Guy was so attracted to me, and he figured he had to ask us both out in order to be with me. I could never thank him enough for doing that.

Danny was surprised at all the sudden attention from Guy.

"Wow," he remarked to James. "We've just seen each other a few times at bars. I didn't think he was interested."

James couldn't believe Danny's stupidity. But at least if Danny came with them to the movies, he wouldn't have to face the daunting prospect of being alone with Guy.

I sat between them. Somehow, it just ended up that way. I was so scared I was going to touch Guy, that our arms would bump on the arm rest, or my leg would hit his when we shifted in our seats. So I leaned toward Danny. Touching Danny didn't do a thing for me anymore.

Later Guy told me that he was fascinated by the way I held Danny's Coke for him. I'm a caring person, and this is something I just did. I would hold it there between us and whenever Danny nudged me, I'd give him a drink. Guy appreciated this intimate little gesture, and he wanted someone who would do those kinds of things for him.

"We saw 'Dances with Wolves' and I had to sit still and act like I was interested in a three-hour movie! I kept looking at Guy out of the corner of my eye—what are you doing over there? It was like a first date, except

that Danny and I were still supposed to be involved. I plotted how to get him out of my life.

Guy was just sitting there watching the movie. I didn't watch one bit of it, because I was in my own little heaven. Afterward, Danny and Guy talked about the movie, which scenes they liked, and I put in my two cents, acting like I knew what they were talking about. I sat in the backseat while Guy drove us home. He was looking at me through the rearview mirror, but every time he caught my eye I looked away. I knew what was happening and I wanted him very much, but he scared me. There were several incidents with speed bumps, because Guy was busy looking at me in the mirror.

Three or four days went by. Guy kept calling; Danny kept going out with Guy and his friends; James kept staying home. Eventually, James couldn't stand it any longer. He mustered his courage, tried on everything in his closet, and joined Guy's entourage for a night of drinking and dancing at The Oyster Club.

The top bar was crowded and loud. Deftly, Guy moved to James' side and bought several rounds of Kamikaze shots and Lemon Drops, until they were both very relaxed.

Later, he tried to tell me I did it. But no way, he did it all. The whole little setup, with Anne and some other girl I didn't know asking Danny to dance so that Guy could be alone with me. I even think they asked me to dance, too, but that last Lemon Drop gave me courage and I said no, I'll stay here. And Guy said, yeah, I'll stay here, too.

We're standing at the bar. Masses of people. We're just totally into each other. I don't remember hearing the music or anyone talking around us. We're flirting like crazy, gazing into each other eyes, looking away.

And then he leaned over and kissed me. His mouth was over mine, and suddenly I was melting. The kiss went on and on, deeper, teasing, like he was saying, there's a lot more where this came from.

To have dreamed of such a moment, imagined it with my whole body and soul—I thought I might start to cry.

But instead I pulled myself together. I thought, what do we do after that? So I reached around and gave him a little pinch, smiling at him and whispering, you're wonderful. I couldn't believe I was that brave, but his kiss made me feel like I was no longer the person I had been only a minute before.

That night when we drove home, he adjusted the rearview mirror so it was pointed directly at me. He didn't care. We were all pretty drunk too, so it's a wonder we got home with Guy never once looking at the road. It was just me smiling at him, and him smiling at me.

The next few weeks were a blur, night after night of dancing at The Oyster Club, Anne pulling Danny out onto the dance floor so that Guy and James could flirt and kiss and hold each other. People came by and asked James about Danny. You two aren't together anymore? And James would smile and say that he and Guy were just good friends.

The next night, they were going out again, and I was staying home. Guy came in wearing this really cute red-and-white striped shirt, with jeans and red Sperry topsiders. He looked as perfect as anyone could look. I was lying on the couch, watching TV in my shorts and shirt and looking like a gross pig. I wasn't too upset, because we had already kissed and only a fool would have doubted the attraction between us.

Danny left the room to brush his teeth, and Guy came right up and leaned over the couch and kissed me, softly at first, and then he drew back just for a moment and the look he gave me wasn't a question, really. He was so sure of himself. I closed my eyes and then his tongue was in my mouth, no holding back this time, and I was thinking, oh, my God, what am I doing? What is going on? Nothing like this had ever happened to me before.

Danny came back from brushing his teeth, and Guy was so smooth, making small talk and acting like we hadn't just been making out on the couch and my whole world hadn't just exploded right there in that room. He walked out behind Danny, but before he closed the door he gave me a wicked little wink. I honestly believe I started to float up off the couch.

They talked every day on the phone, getting to know each other better, remembering how it felt to kiss, wishing Danny would hurry up and move. They found conversation to be comfortable and enchanting. Neither of them wanted to break the spell, so James avoided speaking of the past, and Guy, of the future.

Guy was complimentary and thoughtful, interested in James' job with handicapped adults. "I could never do that," he told James admiringly. "I don't have your patience." *So this is what it's like to be important to somebody,* James rejoiced to himself, cherishing his good fortune and wondering how life could get any better.

When Danny received a plane ticket from his mother in Hawaii, James and Guy graciously offered to help him pack up his things. This was what they had been waiting for.

Everyone was wondering about Guy and me by then, except maybe Danny. How could he not notice what was going on up there by the bar? Honestly, I don't think he cared. He was just using me anyway.

After Guy and I took Danny to the airport, we were going to be alone, so I got all dressed and cute. But don't get me wrong; I was terrified.

We left Danny at the gate. I felt sad and even got a little teary-eyed, because he had been part of my life and I wanted to show Guy that I wasn't the kind of person who just moved without feeling from one relationship to the next. But I don't think Guy noticed. While I was giving Danny a last hug, Guy just stood there with this look of glee on his face. I've got him, it said—he's all mine.

So Danny got on the plane, and we got in the car. Guy put his hand on my leg and said, it's our time now. Oh, God, I thought, what does that mean?

He asked, what do you want to do? I said I wanted to go home. He just laughed. Even then, he was in control.

Guy and James went to a cafe for coffee and gelato. The night was unseasonably warm, and they sat outside for three hours, sharing their stories while, from the other end of their bench, a homeless man listened in.

When he told me about his brothers, I was astonished. I wasn't very close to my brother, but I couldn't imagine him dead. Guy cried when he told me about Greg, and Glen, well, he simply said he didn't really know his other brother.

We talked about what we wanted in a relationship. I said I was looking for someone to give all of my attention to, that I was starving for a relationship, and I would be very loving and loyal toward that person. He said he was looking for someone who was very caring and giving. He said he thought I might be that way, because of how I held Danny's drink for him when we went to the movies.

If this had been an audition, I would have come away sure I'd gotten the part.

Later, James lay in bed and reflected on his change of fortune. Only two months before, he had been stuck in a relationship with a man he couldn't stand, with no prospects for anyone new. Suddenly, Danny was gone. He had a new place and two new roommates who were very nice to him. He had a boyfriend who was almost too good to be true. Dear God, he prayed, please don't let me wake up.

They spent the next week flirting—in little notes they sent to each other, over the phone, in the car, at Guy's house, and in James' apartment, even when his roommates were there.

We were like a couple of fourteen-year-old hormonal wonders. But we hadn't had sex, not yet. I couldn't believe how much I wanted to—I didn't hate it anymore! But I said I wasn't ready, and then he said he wasn't ready either—that's the game we were playing.

I had already decided this was someone I could spend my life with. He was such an interesting character; I knew I would learn a lot from him.

But it wasn't one-sided; he wanted to know about me and he didn't seem to mind hearing about my problems. When you love someone, you

want to know everything about them. When Guy wanted to know every-
thing about me, I began to think amazing thoughts. When he called and
asked if he could come over, that he had something to tell me, it never
crossed my mind that he would say anything but, "James, I'm falling in
love with you."

"I'm HIV-positive."

We had been laughing and giggling, and he was lying on top of me. It
happened in an instant, the sudden change in him, so severe that I felt as
though it was no longer Guy who was staring down at me, his eyes pulled
back in their sockets like he was having trouble focusing.

He had something to tell me. Only a moment before, I couldn't wait
for his surprise. Now I felt fear rising up inside of me. Something was very,
very wrong.

"I'm HIV-positive."

James returned Guy's stare, their faces still only inches apart. As the
words penetrated his consciousness, James flattened his arms on the
couch, suddenly aware of the enormous weight of Guy's body and that
he was in imminent danger of being crushed.

"What?" James managed. Guy rolled off the couch and knelt next
to him.

"They think I might be HIV-positive. I had to tell you before we
went any farther."

James pulled his eyes away from Guy. "So tell me."

"Two and a half years ago, I got sick. I ended up in the hospital and
had one conclusive test. Later, I had another one that wasn't as conclusive. None of the doctors can believe how well I am, and they're doubt-
ing the diagnosis, I know they are. When I first got sick, someone said
it might be Legionnaire's Disease, but do you know what I've been
thinking? I've been thinking it might be some kind of mold growing in
the air-conditioning ducts at Nordstrom or, I don't know, some weird
virus that looks like HIV, but it's really a mutant strain or something."

Guy stopped, because James had started to cry.

Day turned to night. It had been a great dream. Shorter than I would have liked, but at least I can say I had a few carefree, deliriously happy days. I often wonder if ever in my whole life I will feel that way again.

I rejected him, not harshly, I just said I didn't know if I could deal with it. I asked him to leave so I could think.

I cried for a whole day. Guy was gone, and I lay on the couch and bawled. By the time my roommates came home, I had locked myself in the bathroom. They finally broke the door down, because all they could hear was my sobbing and wailing, and when they pounded on the door and called to me, I didn't respond, at least not coherently. Then they held me and said quiet, soothing things, like a mother would, until I managed to crawl to my bed.

The next day, I went to work still crying. A friend of mine asked me what was wrong, and it killed me to tell her. Every morning I had been giving her updates about the new man I was seeing, how wonderful he was, what we'd done the night before—and now I was telling her he's HIV-positive.

What went through my mind? Everything, really—shock, anger, sadness—it all trickled in eventually. I thought, I'm young, I have my whole life ahead of me. Do I really want to put all this energy into someone I know is going to die?

I was so in love. I had been fantasizing about buying a house, getting a dog, planting a garden, being a happy little family. Every few minutes the realization would hit me: It isn't going to happen. And hot, hot tears would be running down my face all over again.

My friend convinced me to go home, and I hid under the covers and listened to music. I don't know exactly when it came to me, but I remember that my head was clear and my decision was final: Life wasn't going to screw me again. I had to be with him.

That evening, Guy called, and James asked him to come over.

"Have you thought about it?" Guy had stepped inside but hadn't moved far from the door.

"Yeah, I've thought about it," said James, walking toward him. "I'm in love with you, Guy. I don't want to lose you. I want to spend my life with you."

It was that simple. He ran into my arms, we both cried. I knew I had made the best decision of my life.

We discussed our situation. He was feeling really good; I said no one would ever believe he was sick. I don't think he was lying about the Legionnaire's Disease and all those other things. He had wanted to soften the blow. He couldn't bring himself to make it so final—for him or for me.

We just started up where we'd left off, getting to know each other, tumbling around in our puppy love. This was going to be the picture-perfect relationship I had been looking for.

We didn't talk about his disease after that day—not for a long time.

Guy and James moved quickly toward consummation of their desire for each other. And as they did, the specter of AIDS faded into the background, and the suggestion of another explanation, the seductive scent of hope, stayed with them.

The first night we made love, I just opened up, and it felt so wonderful. He said I was beautiful. I didn't think I was beautiful—in fact, I made him turn all the lights out. It had to be totally dark, and if he caressed my stomach, I'd push him away and say, don't touch me there, I'm fat.

You're not fat, he would argue, very lovingly. He actually said I was gorgeous. Nothing stopped him, and eventually I was comfortable with the soft light of a candle.

I call it lovemaking because it was the first time in my life I understood what that meant. What we were doing flowed out of our feelings, and it was mutual and gentle. And for a while, it was safe too.

GOING PUBLIC

Alexander and Jane had learned how to deal with Guy's search for love: They watched from afar. His medical condition had produced hardly a flicker on the screen; what they saw was a socially hyperactive young man who happened to be gay and sick, although neither of those facts were readily apparent.

Jane liked James well enough. She was pleased when Guy told her about his special gift with handicapped people. Around Al and Jane, James was very polite and very nervous. He obviously adored Guy. But most important, she had never seen Guy so thoroughly, openly in love.

Three months into their relationship, Guy surprised James with a weekend trip to the Beverly Hills Hilton.

James hated secrets, and I knew it. Every night for a week I taunted him—I've got a big surprise for you. But I wouldn't tell him. Please, please, please, he'd say, and he almost wore me down, but amazingly enough we got all the way to the airport before I blurted it out. I'm better with secrets than he is.

They rented a car and drove around Beverly Hills, taking pictures of each other and asking people to take pictures of the two of them.

Going Public

Guy took me to Rodeo Drive. We bought our first cologne together, Red by Giorgio. Ooh, stop it! I'd say every time I'd smell it on him. We went halves on the bottle, and later we fought over it because he wanted it at his house. So I asked him, when do I get to wear it, if it's at your house? He said I could wear it when I came over.

That night, we got all dressed up and went to Jimmy's. I had to borrow one of his jackets because I didn't have a sports coat. He had bought a tie that almost matched mine so we could be twins.

Guy and James returned to their hotel room after dinner, high from the wine and the foreplay that had been going on throughout the meal. Guy disappeared into the bathroom and left James sitting on the bed. After a while, James heard the water running. Okay, he said to himself, I thought we were clean enough. But then the door opened and a sultry voice said, "Come here, James."

Guy had performed his magic on the bathroom. There were candles everywhere, and with all those twinkling lights reflecting back and forth in the mirrors, I felt like I'd stepped into a starry sky. The bath was so filled with bubbles they were floating over the sides, and next to the tub was a champagne bottle, opened, and two glasses.

"Take off your clothes, James. We're going to take a bath."
James pulled off his shirt and hesitated. "Blow out the candles."
"The candles make it romantic, silly."
"Blow them out, and then we'll light them again when we're in the tub."
"No, James."

Finally, I just undressed and hopped in. Guy had his camera perched by the sink, and he set the timer and climbed in on top of me. The camera took a perfect picture, both of us smiling, covered by bubbles.

It was true romance, like nothing I'd ever seen in the movies, because it's always a man and a woman. I wanted to fulfill him and be fulfilled.

That was the first time we had unprotected sex. I mean, not total all-out everything-goes sex, but something in between that and safe. Guy would pull out, or I would. The idea of ejaculating inside had never appealed to me—I saw that particular area as an exit, not an entrance. We were aware, I think, of fluids and openings, trying to keep them from meeting. But we were playing with fire, as if a single spark couldn't possibly burn down an entire house.

During the night, Guy tossed and turned furiously. It was still dark the next morning when James poked him awake.

"I really could use some sleep, Guy. Could you hold still?"

"I can't believe I let that happen."

"Let what happen?"

Guy reached up and turned on the light. James blinked several times and pulled the sheet over his head.

"James, I didn't even think about a condom last night."

From under the sheet came a few muffled words. "It was the heat of the moment."

"What?"

James lowered the sheet. "The heat of the moment. I'm just as much to blame."

"I wasn't thinking straight."

James considered him for a moment. "Maybe you don't have AIDS."

"Yeah," Guy sighed. "Maybe."

Guy and I had done it once, and that made it easier to do again. If I had been infected during those first months, I couldn't have blamed it on him. It was a mutual thing; I let him do what he did. My judgment had been warped by my love for him and these feelings that were raging out of control. If I got sick, too, we would live the rest of our lives together, and I would meet him in heaven if he went first.

After a few more times, Guy got paranoid I would get it. When I said I didn't care, he was furious. He made me get tested again. I was negative, but he said we had to stop. I thought he meant we had to always use a condom and be extra careful. But I would soon learn that he really wanted to stop. Everything.

. . . .

Jane knew that Guy was spending lots of money on gifts for James, not through any furtive peek into his life, but because he reported to her, with great delight, every single purchase. She understood that he needed to share with someone his new love and the way James made him feel. But Alexander was skeptical. The sweet smell of infatuation, he told his wife, could easily turn sour.

It will probably never be known exactly whose idea it was for James to move in. Guy said he wanted his father to think it was his idea, but that actually it was Guy's idea all along. Jane knew that it could not be her idea. And James claimed he didn't know anything about it.

In any case, when Guy let it be known that he intended to move in with James, Alexander proposed that it be James who moved in with them. He explained his thinking to Jane: First, he wasn't sure the relationship would survive, and he wanted to rule out an impulsive decision on Guy's part. Better to throw James out than haul Guy back in. Second, he worried that if Guy moved in with James, he would no longer be able to live in the manner to which he was accustomed. His son paid no rent, had no worries about food or laundry, and in the event of a medical crisis, would be provided with two free, round-the-clock nurses.

Alexander couldn't believe that Guy hadn't carefully considered his options. "If Guy hasn't figured this out, especially the part about the rent, he's not as cagey as I think he is," he commented.

In the end, James moved in and Al moved over, cleaning out half of the room next to Guy's that he had been using as his office, because Guy said even though he was going to share his bed with James, there was no way he was going to share his closet. Jane started wondering how she was going to explain their new tenant to her friends and relatives.

Actually, I felt it was fine for James to live with us. He was here day and night anyway.

As I spent more and more time with them, Alexander began to feel I'd grown too close to James. I have to admit, James acted like I was his mother. Al said, now James will never leave us. I reassured my husband that I cherished our relationship more than anything. Eventually, James would go back to living his own life. He couldn't stay with us forever.

My son loved James, and I loved Guy. I wanted to spend every moment I could with him. We had fun—James, Guy, and I. They made me laugh.

James moved in on October 30, 1991. The next evening, James gave out Halloween candy for the first time in his life. Each time the doorbell rang, James jumped up immediately, yelling, "I'll get it!" as he ran to open the door. Alexander, Jane, and Guy watched, fascinated.

Before I moved in, Guy would invite me to dinner every night, but I would never go. I said, Guy, I don't sit and have dinner with a family. I've never done that in my life, and I can't see doing it with a family I don't know.

Guy thought I was crazy. He told me he was very family-oriented and if I was going to be part of his life, I would have to start spending time with them.

Of course, after I was living there, it was much harder to avoid dinner. The truth was, I was afraid to let anyone know me. There were things I never really thought about, much less talked about. I know I'm not to blame, but I watched what I said around them anyway.

"James is a project," Alexander commented to Jane one day soon after he moved in. And it was clear that Guy had taken James on. Over the first year of their shared residence, Al and Jane watched while James was remade in the image of Guy.

"Goals," Guy directed James, "you need to get some." Preaching the philosophy of his brother Greg, Guy urged James to create a five-year plan for himself, and then he set about helping his lover make it happen. In November 1991, James began working part-time at Nordstrom—with borrowed visions of a new image, a padded wallet, and even his own department dancing in his head.

Also in November 1991, Guy began to lose sight in his right eye. He took more and more time off from work to receive intravenous treatments for CMV at the hospital, which, luckily enough, was only a five-minute drive from Rockridge. His new store manager accommodated him without question. But other medical problems took their toll, and, quickly, his energy abandoned him.

His last day of work at Nordstrom was January 26, 1992.

That November, I was on top of everything! Nothing slacked. Business in my department was still great.

James had started at Nordstrom, and even though I was constantly having to advise him and calm him down, it was fun having him around.

In January, I told my crew about my illness. Only one of them, it turned out, was concerned—something about the ticketing gun and needles used for alterations. We had a meeting—me and my crew, the regional trainer, and the head of human resources—which turned out to be a seminar on HIV and AIDS. After that, there were no problems with anybody.

I tried so hard. I was walking around with fevers of one hundred four, one hundred five degrees. I had night sweats and woke up soaked through my pajamas, even my mattress. I would roll over onto dry towels.

I had every intention of going back. But I didn't get better. I ended up in the hospital, where I had the operation to put my heart catheter in. Now at least I could take my medicine at home.

They went on without me through February. They did a good job, but business wasn't increasing. At least I quit while I was ahead.

It's almost harder to think about it now than it was then. My job at Nordstrom meant everything to me. When I was there, I had nothing to talk about unless I talked about work. It was my whole life. But I was so sick and so weak, I needed the rest.

While Guy's career was waning, James' was taking off. After Christmas, he took a full-time position at Nordstrom. During the next few weeks, while Guy was commuting between home, the hospital clinic, and Men's Sportswear, James was learning how to sell, sell, sell in The Brass Rail. At night, Guy listened while James announced his daily total.

"James is cocky as shit right now," Guy complained to Anne.

Anne made a weak attempt to sympathize. "It's new for him, Guy. And remember, you were the one who made it happen."

"I'm not jealous," he pouted.

"I didn't say you were." You need some new toys, she thought.

In February 1992, one month after his "retirement," Guy returned to the third floor at Fashion Fair Nordstrom. He had an appointment with Deborah, the regional trainer who had developed an HIV and AIDS seminar for Nordstrom employees.

That morning, Guy told his parents he thought he might like to get involved. "I've never heard of a company that develops seminars on things like sexual harassment and substance abuse and AIDS, and then pays their employees to listen to them."

"At least not a department store," Alexander agreed.

Guy became the new angle in Deborah's presentation. She had been using a video of a young AIDS victim that was so sad that the employees were going back out on the floor in tears—effective, she told Guy, but a bit disruptive. So Guy became her "live" AIDS patient. He was attractive, he was earnest, he answered any question with ease, and he always included a few words of praise for Nordstrom's involvement in AIDS education.

Deborah and Guy gave their seminar thirty times to Nordstrom employees all over the area. "You're a hit, Guy" she told him after the last seminar. "I'm beginning to think you don't really need me."

Poor Deborah was way behind. By the end of that day, her charts and materials had been charmed into the trunk of Guy's car.

"I can do this on my own," he told his father.

Hope, rare and wondrous, befriended Alexander and stayed with him for days.

Going Public

In 1988, I mentioned to Glen and Guy that they ought to track their experience with this disease, write it down in a journal and share it with others. Glen, Guy, and Jane thought I was crazy at the time. In 1992, when Guy decided to go public, he didn't remember that I said that. I recall thinking, if only they could get up and tell their stories, maybe we could save somebody. It might make some sense out of losing them.

Guy assembled his props and planned his presentation. He couldn't wait to be invited somewhere, but knew he would have to make the first move. He called Eli Whitney High School, his alma mater.

To whomever answered the phone, Guy decided the direct approach was best. "Hello, my name is Guy Nakatani. I graduated from Whitney in 1986. I have AIDS, and I need to talk to your entire student body about it."

Guy was told he would have to speak to a counselor. Days went by and Guy called back repeatedly, but the counselor never seemed to be in.

"What's wrong with these people?" Jane asked Alexander, fire in her eyes. Her husband just smiled.

Jane also took the direct route. She called the principal at Whitney, an acquaintance, and explained that her son was giving HIV seminars and couldn't seem to get anybody down there to pay attention.

"I'm of a mind to give my friend Alice a call about this," she declared.

"Alice?"

"Alice Barnard, head of the school board."

The principal called Guy later that day. Guy spent an entire week at Whitney. He had learned from his experience at Nordstrom that small groups were best. "If I talk to an auditorium, I'll lose them," he explained to the principal. So he visited classroom after classroom. By the end of the week, he had given his seminar twenty times.

Word spread quickly, and Guy began to receive requests from other schools. He bought a personal organizer. He assessed the look he had seen at Whitney and went shopping. He learned quickly what to say and how to say it.

"He gets into their hearts," Al told Jane, "and then he lets 'em have it."

His first priority was to be effective. "You've been told this stuff before," he concurred with a group of high-school juniors. "I know you have. Some science teacher explained the whole thing to you, right? How boring was that?"

They shared a moment of appreciation before Guy turned on them.

"Hel-lo-o. Do you want to die?"

Guy crashed through the barriers to the place where they lived. "You think, this can't happen to me. I'm not gay. I'm not a drug user. I'm not uneducated. I run around with a safe crowd. That's what you're thinking, isn't it, deep down inside? Well, you may not be any of those things, but you are crazy."

Guy continued his rapid-fire, omniscient recitation of teenage life. "There's a party, a rager, and you wake up in someone's arms, and you don't really remember how it happened. Don't look at me like that! I've been there. I know everything about you.

"Or how about that one moment, and he really wants you to, and you know she hasn't been with anybody else, or at least anybody like that, so you take a chance in order to be loved and accepted?"

Guy paused, just long enough. "'I love you. Trust me.' Those words don't save lives," he said softly. "They didn't help me." His eyes bore into theirs, at close range, too close for them to turn away, and his voice began to rise.

"If anyone in this room can relate to anything I've just said, you need to get tested for HIV." He picked up a stack of papers in front of him. "Who wants a flyer?"

He knew it was working. Kids stopped him in the hallways to thank him personally, often with tears in their eyes. Periodically, he was challenged; once he was verbally attacked by a child whose parents also called the school, threatening a lawsuit if Guy was allowed to continue supporting promiscuity in the classroom.

"What are they talking about?" Guy ranted that evening. "I tell them abstinence is the best prevention." But Guy knew that abstinence, for the most part, wasn't real. "How many of you sitting here are never going to have sex? Because you guys could probably leave." Guy waited for the lifetime celibates to show themselves.

"Okay," he said, leaning forward and extending a finger, "for the rest, I'm talking to you."

"But what if I wait until I'm married?" someone would inevitably ask.

"Has your spouse also waited?" Guy responded.

A nervous smile. "Yeah. It could happen."

Most of the class rolled their eyes. Good, Guy thought. I've got them.

For younger students, he would then reinforce his point by asking them to participate in an exercise designed to show how easily AIDS spread.

He asked one girl to stand up. "What's your name?"

"Jennifer."

"Okay, Jennifer. Now I know you're going to be mature about this. Would you please shake hands with any four people around you."

Jennifer shook four hands. Guy turned to the class. "Jennifer is HIV-positive." Guy waited a moment to get through the self-conscious giggling. "Jennifer is HIV-positive, and she had unprotected sex with the four people she shook hands with, and they are now infected. Would anyone who shook hands with Jennifer please stand up?"

Invariably, the giggling ceased.

"Now would everyone who just stood up please shake hands with four more people? And now, would all of you please stand up?"

In less than a minute, everyone was standing. Guy stood in front of them, his eyes sweeping the room, urging them to look around with him, considering one another.

"This," he thundered, "is how it spreads! You've got to focus on not getting this disease."

One day, before the morning bell at Cedar Street Middle School, Guy waited among an unusually large group of seventh graders, dressed in a sloppy sweatshirt, shorts hanging down off his hips and below his knees, with a Nike hat turned backward. It took a while for the kids to figure out this was the guest speaker.

He was high energy, firing questions and facts at them quickly and confidently, engaging them easily. He charmed them out of their inhibitions until they were speaking freely, about subjects they would never broach with anyone out of their age range.

"Don't hold back," he reminded them. "Don't hold back with me now or for the rest of your lives." He was able to convince a fourteen year old that parents were not the enemy. "Talk to them," he said passionately. "Someday, they may be the only ones left you can count on."

When he popped a question and someone raised their hand, he turned to them and said, "Okay, go for it. Yeah, go for it," encouraging them, affirming them, no matter what their response.

With the younger ones, he always started with a little anatomy review. "Be mature, now" he grinned at them.

When no girl would say the name of the bodily fluid that comes from her vagina, he gently scolded them, teasing that he might have to ask the boys.

"There always seems to be some boy with all the answers," he told his mother.

"That was you, Guy," she reminded him.

Cedar Street was in my district. When Guy was invited to speak there, I composed an open letter for the parents at my own school, Robert F. Kennedy. I wrote that my son was HIV-positive and he was out speaking to kids and parents, and if any of them wanted to come, I would like to invite them.

My principal thought it was a wonderful letter, but she said she would have to run it by Mr. Harris, the superintendent. I remember groaning out loud, because he had been avoiding me like the plague. Literally. And sure enough, he said he didn't know how the community at our school would react, and there was no way that letter was going out.

By that time, Guy was already deeply involved in Saratoga High School, which was nearby. I said, look at Saratoga, they've practically adopted Guy, and he won't even send out a letter. When Guy spoke at Cedar Street, the superintendent put a little notice in the district newsletter, saying that Guy's seminars were not part of our curriculum.

I kept my letter as proof that I was going to send it out. Alexander said I was becoming an activist. I didn't know what he meant by that, but Guy had such an important message, I didn't want any of our parents to miss it. It scared me to think of how ignorant everyone was. I mean, look what happened to us.

· · · ·

James watched from the sidelines while Guy's role as an AIDS educator consumed him—and eclipsed their relationship. When Guy had come home from the hospital in January 1992 with a catheter protruding from his heart, he instructed James to stay away. As he recuperated from his second major bout with the affects of full-blown AIDS, James waited patiently, continuing the playfulness that had so endeared them during the months before he got sick. But the more he teased, the more he touched Guy in those secret places that had once delighted him, the more Guy backed away.

The knowledge that I was hurting James was in the back of my mind somewhere, behind my preoccupation with my withering body. I hated what I saw in the mirror.

The change came over me rather quickly. Within a week of getting my catheter, I was sure I had made love for the last time. I didn't even want to be touched, though eventually I found pleasure again in that feeling of skin meeting skin, so long as it wasn't sexual.

For months, James did little things to try to turn me on. But as hard as I tried to want him, I never got the feeling back. It was more than the fact that I didn't think I was attractive anymore—I might have learned to accept that. But I was teaching kids to stay alive by staying safe. If anything had happened to James, I don't know what I would have done. We had been lucky, but luck wasn't my strong suit.

Saving Lives

Later, James wished he had savored their last time.

"If I had known when you went into the hospital that we would never make love again, I would have kidnapped you," he told Guy.

It was as if we woke up one morning and he didn't want to be near me ever again. No kissing, no cuddling. It got so I waited until he fell asleep, just so I could touch him, carefully, without waking him.

He suggested I masturbate while he lay next to me. I thought this was a temporary solution, until he sent me to do it by myself in the shower.

Finally, I confronted him, and he recited his reasons. I cried and cried. I didn't care that he was skinny. And I didn't care that some parent might not think he was credible. What we were doing was totally safe. Anyway, I said, how would anyone know?

Guy had brought me to my sexual peak and left me hanging.

Alexander felt that the most significant outcome of Guy's work was the requests he was getting from parents. It was Jane's friend Pam who arranged an evening seminar at Saratoga High School that was attended by several hundred adults, many of whom were brought there by their children. Pam suggested that Al introduce Guy and say a few words about being his father. Guy agreed.

It was as if Alexander had been waiting his whole life for this moment. He stood at the microphone and thanked the people for coming. He said that they would be hearing a workshop on HIV and AIDS, and he hoped they would listen carefully to each word. He emphasized how urgent the message would be. Finally, it was time.

Alexander gripped the sides of the podium. "This is my son, Guy Nakatani," he said, swallowing hard. "He's here to save your children's lives."

The assembly rose to their feet, partly to greet Guy, but to pay tribute, too, to the courage of his father. Guy had to compose himself before he began. From that moment on, Alexander and Guy became a team.

When Guy started going out on his own, Alexander was just dying to go along. He had been thinking about retiring for a while, and when it appeared that Guy would welcome him as his agent and manager—more like an assistant, really, because Guy ran the show—he let go of his career quickly and painlessly. He wanted to be with our son and to feel like he was doing something about what had happened to us and to so many others.

I didn't have that sense of purpose, but there was something sustaining me. When Greg died, I thought that nothing more could happen. But boy, it kept happening. Glen, then Guy. It never stopped.

Maybe that's what keeps me going—the sheer wonder of surviving at all. I have to see if I end up crazy.

Alexander took phone calls, booked seminars, made the arrangements, confirmed the dates. When Guy spent the week at a school, Al brought him his lunch every day. His son was slowly getting weaker, and Al picked up the slack. Guy just kept going at the same frantic pace, and his father took it upon himself to make that possible.

By the spring of 1993, Guy and Al Nakatani had been to hundreds of schools and businesses. They were invited to Apple, Hewlett-Packard, and Lotus Corporation, community centers and libraries,

Rotary and Lions Clubs, churches, and even one art gallery. They had been all over California. They spoke in front of the National Asian Pacific American Families Against Substance Abuse in Washington, D.C. And of course they had taken their act to Hawaii.

Alexander began a scrapbook for the rising pile of newspaper articles about their work. He intended to add Guy's correspondence from schools and students, but the scrapbook was quickly replaced by a filing system, augmented by a dozen shoe boxes.

He no longer simply introduced his son. As Guy's warm-up act, he challenged parents—provoked them when he had to. His message was clear: Communicate with your children about the things you don't want to talk about, or risk losing them. There was hardly a parent who could resist him; he was living proof of the price of silence and separation between parent and child in the age of AIDS.

Alexander worried about a great many things, including the future of the program, in a low hum of brooding that followed him everywhere. He spoke often of Guy's "message." It was unique, he felt, among AIDS activists, but he was afraid that what made it special was the messenger. Other HIV-positive young people could be trained to say Guy's words, but no one could say them like Guy. A local filmmaker offered to donate part of his services to make a video telling Guy's story. Alexander, aided by Pam and Bob Dunnett, set up the Guy Nakatani Life Management Program, with the idea of continuing Guy's work after he was gone, and launched a fundraising drive to finance the first video, and then a second, and a third. Each one was a small, comforting victory for Alexander, who was battling many demons.

Of course, the gnawing center of his worry was Guy himself. Guy had created a new presentation for those schools who begged him to come back a second time. To the teachers and students who had come to know him the year before, the change in his physical appearance was startling. He was much thinner, his once muscular frame now slight. His face, still handsome and expressive, had aged; the lines that once framed his smile now etched a look of melancholy and detachment.

When he was not on stage, however, Guy's feelings were close to the surface. Frustration and anger, once emotions he stubbornly denied, weaved their way into his daily life.

The other day I was so pissed. The ignorance. I had driven to Dino's Deli. I wasn't feeling very good and I wanted a sandwich. I pulled up into the handicapped space and a lady came out, looked at me, looked at my nice black Acura, and shook her head, as if I was abusing handicapped parking. It enraged me that she would do that to my face, so I honked my horn and held my placard up for her to see. She still just glared at me, disapproving. I was furious, ready to get out of my car, show her my Hickman heart catheter, show her my body, tell her the names of my five t-cells. She was really fat, so I was going to say, I'm one-twentieth of your body weight and too weak to walk the extra fifty friggin' feet.

She was so ignorant not to know that disabilities come in different shapes and forms, and to pass judgment on somebody who goes through what we go through is totally unfair. I was angry at her, but I was angrier that she took up my time. I don't want to give any of those things— anger, frustration, this disease—the satisfaction of stealing the most precious thing I have left.

To his parents, the slow deterioration of his condition, the unsettling change in his physical appearance, and his total exhaustion were uninvited guests, insistent, troubling reminders of his mortality, which until so recently had seemed like only a dim possibility. When Alexander suggested that he accept no speaking engagements for the summer and spend at least a month recuperating, Guy didn't put up much resistance. A month in Hawaii was just what he needed.

• • • •

Even more than his health, Alexander worried about his son's character. As publicity mounted, so did the tension in the household about all the things Guy and, by necessity, Alexander were not saying to the world.

Guy, however, was adamant about not including the issue of sexuality in the talks. "If they know I'm gay, they'll dismiss my message as not having anything to do with them" was his argument, which

Alexander appreciated. After all, the Reagan administration had led an entire nation in thinking the same thing.

Still, he brooded about the consequences of such a tactic. He couldn't get away from the feeling that denial, flagrant and invasive, was dogging their tracks. He was increasingly threatened by this possibility, as if their omission was as virulent as the disease and would someday do them in.

James had little to say during the dinnertime debates over this topic. It hadn't taken long for him to understand: In order for Guy to be believed, no one must know he existed.

One night in early May, Guy asked James to accompany them to a parents' night at a large Catholic high school in San Jose. It was the third time Guy had invited him along, and, as he had been on each of those occasions, James was surprised that Guy would want to take the chance of exposing their connection. They had never discussed it between them, and each time James had an excuse to keep him home.

"Oh, thanks for asking," James tried to sound casual. "I'll stay home and keep Jane company."

"Mom's coming tonight. She has a teachers' meeting, so she's coming straight from school."

"I'm too tired. I sold two thousand today," James winced. Guy would know that was a lie; nobody sold two thousand in the middle of May.

But, instead, Guy was impressed. "Wow, I didn't think anybody could do that, Jamesy," he gave him a sly look, "except me."

James stayed home. Jane sat in the front row between Alexander and the school principal. It was one of the largest evening gatherings they had ever addressed; more than four hundred people were waiting for the father and son. As they had come to expect, many of the parents were accompanied by their children.

Guy was brilliant, capturing them quickly with his sobering list of facts and figures. He stopped to take a breath. "Any questions so far?"

A hesitant hand arose from the third row.

"Yeah, go for it."

A woman stood up. "These things speak for themselves, Guy, and

166

you present them in a very compelling way. But exactly what is your message to them? I mean, my child came home and told me that Guy Nakatani saved his life today. What did you say to him?"

Guy smiled. "Don't you mean, what did he say to me?" She looked confused, but from their places in the first row, Al and Jane nodded knowingly.

"You want to know if your child is having sex. Well, the answer, for the vast majority of you, is yes."

Guy's presence seemed to saturate the auditorium and command every molecule of air. He let them in on the secret, holding them spellbound as he relayed to them exactly what he had told their children, in exactly the way he told them. The transformation was evident, as the adults became their children, and the teenagers in the audience became Guy, already owning his words, perceiving the meaning of his questions far sooner than their parents.

Alexander ended the evening.

"You know," he said, taking the microphone from his son, "I never gave much thought to parenting. In fact, as I look back, I went through life thinking I had it easy. I never fully realized the awesome responsibility of being a parent, and in that respect probably never lived up to what I could have been as a parent.

"I missed the point. I needed to be at my kids' sides, every step of the way, believing in them and helping them. I needed to say out loud how I felt, especially when I was worried and fearful for them.

"Now, for Jane and me, our chance to be parents is just about over. We're going to have to build a future together, without our children. It's important for us to know that we've alerted you to the chance you have. If we were to remain silent about what we have learned, and the price we have paid, we would be betraying not only you, but our three sons. Our redemption is you, going home to your children, and doing whatever it takes to get lovingly involved in their lives. Thank you very much."

The ovation for Guy and Al Nakatani went on for five minutes. Afterward, the school principal passed the hat, and sixteen hundred dollars was collected for the Guy Nakatani Life Management Program.

Since Jane had driven her own car to the presentation, she went on ahead of them. Alexander and Guy rode together in a weary, yet satisfied, silence. Finally, father turned to son and spoke.

"You really got to them, Guy. You were on tonight."

"I hope so," Guy murmured, his fall from animated intensity painfully apparent. He didn't want to chat. He leaned back against the seat and tried to close his father out.

Alexander loved all of it. He loved watching Guy seize an audience. He loved being Guy's assistant, his spokesperson, his companion. Indeed, this was what he treasured most, spending time with his son, filling up those moments so completely that memories of moments lost, and those that had been recklessly discarded, were crowded out. He often used their drives to and from presentations as a private time for them to talk. Now was such an occasion. He had something on his mind.

"Guy," he began.

"Hmm?"

At this point, I knew that any attempt to discuss the issues of his sexuality and his public life would anger Guy. Jane would say I was badgering him, which I didn't understand. Guy was getting weaker. How could she want him to die with this unsettled? She just goes along, I thought, allowing Guy to make all the rules because he's dying. I suppose that's a mother's job. A father's job is to hope that his child lives well, even as he's dying. Who would begrudge me that?

"Remember tonight when the guild president told the story about her son saying you had saved his life?"

Except for the hum of the engine, silence filled the car.

"Well, have you ever thought about this? I think about it all the time. If that boy is right, and someday he has occasion to remember Guy Nakatani at a moment when he could be putting himself at risk, then he will have been saved by a gay man."

Guy's eyes flew open. "Maybe he's gay, too, Dad. Then one gay man will have saved another."

"Let's say he's straight," Alexander said evenly. "It's quite possible that a gay man is saving the lives of many straight people. I find that amazing and ironic, don't you?"

Guy was dreading where his father might be going with this.

"I'm just wondering," Al continued, "if the time has come for you to acknowledge your sexuality publicly."

"We agreed that it wouldn't be good for the program," Guy retorted quickly and firmly. "People will discredit me, and therefore everything I have to say about AIDS."

"I say those who are going to discredit you are going to discredit you. Those who will embrace what you say are going to be moved regardless of who you are. In the end, when you have a public profile and become influential, you have to be honest. Once people pick up the fact that you are running from something, that is what destroys the effort, destroys your credibility, destroys you."

Ignoring his father's argument, Guy defended himself. "I don't think it would be good to change now, Dad. If I announce to everyone I'm gay, don't you think they'll wonder why I haven't announced it before now? Let me tell you, Dad, I've never denied it. I've just avoided making it an issue."

"And unfortunately, that's worked for you. You're comfortable with the way things are going. But are you comfortable with yourself? No matter how many reasons we come up with to do it this way, don't you feel it's something of a deception?"

"Who am I deceiving?"

"Yourself. You're not saying who you are. You're not claiming your right to be who you are."

"I don't need to claim that right publicly. I've done it privately, and that's enough."

They rode quietly for several minutes while Alexander calculated what he was going to say next.

"I don't know, son. If you can't say publicly that you're a gay man, then you're still in the closet."

"I'm not in the closet!" Guy exploded. "I'm sick and tired of you not understanding this. My work doesn't have anything to do with my sexuality. It has to do with people dying and what I can do to stop it!"

Guy's voice lowered to a passionate whisper. "I just want to stop the dying."

His father, too, lowered his voice and said as gently as he could, "I know that, Guy, and I believe you are doing that. But HIV is not the beginning and the end of what you're about."

"You're wrong, Dad. I won't do anything to risk losing my effectiveness. I thought we had decided that."

"Who you are should not be a source of shame for you. God, it just eats away at me sometimes."

"Well get it together, Dad, because I'm not ashamed. I'm fine."

Alexander turned into the garage, and, before he had shut off the engine, Guy had begun the painful task of getting out of the car, moving into the house, and shuffling up the steps to his room.

"When Annie gets here, send her up. I need a massage," he called down to his mother. She and James had been waiting for them in the kitchen.

"What's wrong with Guy?" she asked, as Alexander sat down wearily at the table. James got up and went to the refrigerator, opened a can of soda, and stood in the shadow of the dining room doorway.

"I brought up the idea again that Guy might want to acknowledge that he's gay. And he just staunchly defends how he's going to deal with the issue, afraid of being discredited, guarding his respectability at the cost of his soul."

"Oh, Al, no. His soul is just fine. I agree with him. No one would listen."

"I don't believe that Jane—I never have. I watched those people tonight. It was like he had them under a magic spell. Do you really think the spell would be broken if they knew the magician was gay?"

Jane stifled a grin. "He was really good tonight. But I think it's his decision to make. He's just not comfortable with going public."

Alexander gazed at his wife. "You're not comfortable with him going public."

"You're right. I'm not. I mean, AIDS is one thing, gay is another."

"I can't believe it. My wife and my son feed off each other. You say you're still not comfortable discussing the fact that you have two gay sons, and he says he's not comfortable acknowledging who he is, because his mother still feels funny about 'the whole gay thing.' I say you're both pretty comfortable with denial."

"That's not true, Al. Guy's okay with being gay. He's just protecting me."

"If Guy's okay with who he is, then why isn't he being honest?"

"He's not being dishonest. He's just not saying anything."

Alexander sat brooding for a moment, staring down at the well-worn tiles of the kitchen floor. "Silence is betrayal," he murmured, his voice heavy with resignation.

And silence settled over the kitchen. Al stood up to go to bed. Jane turned toward the dining room, but James was gone. She followed her husband up the stairs.

"He's protecting me, Al. I think that's what it is."

Alexander turned to face his diminutive wife, all five feet, one inch, one hundred and five pounds of her.

"If there was ever a lady who didn't need protecting, it's you." He smiled. "At least not anymore."

JUST BE YOURSELF

I was one of the four hundred in the audience that evening. Three weeks later, my place had been established in the Nakatani household. Guy and I spent hours together: he on his couch, hooked up to the noisy medicine machine, and me on the floor, nestled in the pillows, tape recorder and notebook in hand.

The phone rang often, and it was almost always a request for Guy to speak. "I'm booking for the fall," he would say, "and you'd better get me now, because I don't know how long I'm going to be up to this." Guy liked a little gallows humor. "I'll be there," he would end a conversation. "Unless, of course, I'm dead."

The rest of the "family" came and went; James to Nordstrom, Anne to her physical therapy clinic, where she worked as an aide, and Jane to the safety of her third grade. Alexander was most visible during the day, answering the phone when Guy was in the bathroom or too tired to get up, consulting with his son over the week's speaking schedule, darting purposefully around.

I judged Alexander to be a good guardian, quietly mindful of his son's needs and sensitive to Guy's struggle to maintain autonomy despite his increasing dependence. He patiently accompanied Guy on his daily emotional ride, a seesaw pendulating steadily up and down, rarely a drastic change of mood, but enough to keep everyone off balance. The roller coaster came later, nearer the end, when he became like a weary child, who, at the end of the day, still has energy for one last ride.

On this particular day, Guy was to be immortalized in another of the videos being made about his life and educational program. This film would include the personal reflections of his family and friends, and the crew was already busy setting up. Soon, Jane, James, and Anne would arrive, having excused themselves from their jobs.

Catherine, now completing a master's degree in the Japanese language and already teaching in Japan, had flown in the previous evening for a visit and been recruited immediately by Guy for the video. I had been looking forward to meeting her, because Guy remarked so often that it was Cat who could fill in the blank pages of Guy's "wild" past.

At the moment, the Wild One was upstairs primping for his film debut, Alexander was offering his vision of the video to the director, and Cat and I were chatting over coffee.

Gazing at the young woman seated across from me, I realized that I had expected her to be shallow. The mention of her name always seemed to bring a smile to everyone's face; she represented a happier time, memories Guy cited reverently, and she received their affection accordingly. But there was never any further explanation of her life or her character, as if Guy's designation of Cat as his favorite "party girl" concluded all evaluation.

Indeed, I would wrestle often with Guy's influence over every particle of air that floated within the house. His heavy lever of control had by this time become for me a considerable distraction. To some extent, his loved ones simply allowed him to believe that his version of the nearby universe was commonly held. The disease, I was reminded, was uncontrollable, and Guy was fighting back hard in the only way he knew how. Some latitude was thereby granted to him; he could be right most of the time.

But Guy's authority seemed much more well seasoned. It was obvious that members of the circle were used to giving him permission to reign. Alexander and Jane, most often lovingly, sometimes with difficulty, arranged themselves around his need to be in charge. James, who looked to Guy to decide which socks to wear each morning, and Anne, whose obsession with Guy's nightly back rubs left her dizzy with exhaustion, also gave way to Guy's direction with some amount of intent. He had possession of the control pad, but everyone understood, perhaps better than he, what was going on in the game.

As an outsider who had been invited inside, I still needed my own control pad. So I considered Cat eagerly, breezing past the stories of social excess, looking for depth.

Blunt-cut black hair framed her pretty round face as she spoke, softly, wistfully, of her life with Guy. "I met him in 1988. He tried to convince me that he was the father of twins, Bobbie and Betsy. His story was so well composed, I just had to believe him.

"Naturally, the next time I saw him I asked how the kids were. When he couldn't remember their names, I told him that was pretty pathetic.

"Since he lived in San Jose and I in Los Angeles, we got together every three weeks with airline reservations he bought twenty-one days in advance. Guy was always a step ahead. Our every-third-week get-togethers involved shopping and spending money, bar-hopping and recovering from bar-hopping. On Sundays, we'd go to the beach for some pretty intense betting on skee-ball and air hockey.

"We were always drinking, dancing through the night at the clubs that Guy knew so well. More than once we pulled each other out of bathrooms and bushes, the one who had finished vomiting in charge of getting us home.

"It went pretty much downhill from there. My weeks at school became shorter and my weekends longer. I always planned to go home early Monday morning so that Sundays wouldn't be ruined by having to leave. But not being a morning person, I'd often miss my flight. Under Guy's direction, I would fax my papers to my professors and then follow up with a telephone call, carefully timed for when they would be teaching, leaving messages that my relatives were dying and I couldn't make it to class. By the time I graduated, half my family had been wiped out."

By this time, I was laughing out loud, wondering how the young woman before me, obviously intelligent, quietly poised, could ever have vomited into a bush. She continued, her voice tinged with melancholy.

"In 1991, when Guy got sick the second time, both of us knew the party was ending. He started giving his talks, and I left for Japan. I'm discovering my cultural identity there, I'm understanding more about my family. I wish Guy could be there."

Cat regarded me solemnly. "You know, despite everything he says about being Japanese, I think he would love what I'm doing. We started out like a pair of Peter Pans, Guy and I, doing a lot of flying around, not wanting to grow up. Maybe because everything that happened was so terrible, we both came tumbling down to earth. Maybe his new seriousness rubbed off on me. It could have been that way, because I let Guy be the leader. Anyway, we both chose to face our destinies.

"Of course," she stared at me intently, "he was the braver one."

Cat got up abruptly from the table and walked to the sink, placing her empty coffee cup next to the others that had accumulated on the counter. I watched her, waiting for what would come next, but she didn't look back at me.

The front door slammed. James arrived in a panic, bounding up the stairs, wailing about what to wear and how to fix his "Aqua Net hair." Anne and Jane also came in, each of them offering Cat and me a warm embrace, each asking about Guy's whereabouts.

"I don't know what he expects," Jane confided, as I poured more coffee and she joined me at the table.

"He expects it to be very professional," Anne remarked.

Jane laughed. "With all of us in it? Good luck."

Guy descended into the kitchen with as much energy as a healthy teenager. "James is so nervous. He's up there whining about his hair. He should be down here rehearsing."

Alexander had followed his son into the room. "This is his big break, Guy. He's never been a movie star before. None of us have."

The father grinned, obviously enjoying the preparations and the attentiveness of the crew. The telling of his son's story was what drove him and gave him comfort, what delighted and satisfied him.

"I've been wondering who will play me," he continued, eyes twinkling, "when this hits the big screen."

Jane gave her husband a suspicious look. "Who do you have in mind?"

"Robert Redford."

"He's not Japanese."

"He's handsome." Chuckling to himself, Alexander moved out onto the deck where the crew was setting up.

• • • •

"Just be yourself, James." Guy stood next to the camera person, hands on hips, scowling at his friends. James, Anne, and Cat had just been instructed by Guy to share their feelings about what it would be like after he died.

"If I need to, I can get Annie to cry in a minute," Guy had confided to me as the filming began. So far, not a tear had been shed. For almost an hour, the director asked a variety of questions that might stir their emotions and their ability to communicate them. They couldn't muster even a mild emotion, and Guy complained that it sounded like his death would be no big deal.

Guy was close to coming unglued. "This is so lame," he groaned, when finally James sat silently, head down, unable to do anything but nod in response to the director's gentle prodding.

"No, this is hard, Guy," Anne complained. "It's easy enough when we're all sitting around talking together. Then I can say what I feel or cry or whatever. I don't know how to do that on cue."

"Pretend the camera isn't there."

"But it is there," said Cat. "Maybe they could go hide in the bushes."

This brought a laugh from everyone as we imagined the camera person in camouflage, branches stuck to his head. James remained silent. From my spot near the kitchen door, I began to feel sorry for him. He looked like he would be glad to be hiding in the bushes.

Guy moved over to James and knelt down in front of him, obviously going for a more gentle approach. "James," he implored, "I don't understand why you can't talk about how you feel about what's going to happen to me. It's okay. Just let your feelings out."

The director said they were ready to try again. Anne rolled her eyes. James watched miserably as Guy moved back to his command post between the camera and the director.

"This isn't going to work," I murmured to no one in particular and was surprised when Alexander and Jane turned to me and nodded. We huddled by the door.

"James can't emote on command," Al whispered.

Jane agreed. "You watch. Guy's going to lose it."

Anne was beginning again. "It's going to be really weird when Guy isn't here anymore. I can't believe now that it is actually going to happen. I mean, he's pretty healthy and everything." She stopped, glancing quickly at Guy, and then at Cat, who turned helplessly toward James.

"Yeah," James said, pulling himself up in his chair, as if he could summon his emotions by sitting up straighter. "It will be weird."

Guy exploded. "Weird? Weird? You guys are talking about when I'm dead, and all you can say is that it's going to be weird!" He picked up a the little table next to James and set it down hard in front of them. Legs apart, bracing himself with his hands on his knees, he sat down and leaned forward into their faces. In unison, they shrank back into their chairs.

"I can't believe I have to coach you about what to say. After everything we've shared together, all we've been through, you'd think you'd at least be able to say you'll miss me when I'm gone!"

That was enough for both young women to begin weeping, and the director announced a break. The crew shuffled off the deck and back inside. Alexander and Jane didn't move. I considered joining the retreat into the house but decided to wait to be ejected. Meanwhile, our attention was on James.

Guy continued to rant. "You know this is important to me. I thought you cared about me more than this." James was glaring at him now, and I wondered what it would take to release whatever was gathering behind those eyes.

"James, you're the person who's supposed to be closest to me. You should be the one with the most to say."

That, apparently, was James' breaking point. "For months, Guy, no, for years, I haven't been allowed to talk about you at all. I can't tell anyone who I am. You don't tell anyone who I am. In fact, I don't really exist!" His expression stiffened and he sat back, staring at Guy with half-open eyes. "How do you expect me to suddenly tell everyone in the world how I feel about you when I don't exist?"

I've always been honest with James, from the very beginning. I had hardly kissed him before I had to tell him I was HIV-positive. He had a right to know. One time I told someone that I couldn't spend the night because I didn't have my toothbrush. Of course, he said use mine. And I was obligated to say, you know, I'm positive. If two people are honest about the kind of sex they're going to have, then I think it's okay. Of course, protection is the key.

After I fell in love with James, I eventually told him that no sex was the best sex. That still isn't settled between us, but at least he knows where I stand.

And I thought he understood about the talks. I had been straight with him: We would have to keep our relationship private. Not hidden. Just . . . quiet.

From the patio door, Alexander, Jane, and I held our collective breaths. James' words were harsh, yet so clear. I couldn't imagine what Guy could possibly say in response.

Guy, on the other hand, hardly missed a beat. "Well, James, now's your time to talk. You know we decided to keep my sexuality private, for the good of the program."

"I didn't decide."

"Yes, you did, James. You remember that time we were in the kitchen talking about it, and we decided people might not listen to me if they were thinking about how I got AIDS."

"I didn't decide that."

"Yes, you did. You were there."

"I was there, yes, but I didn't decide. I wasn't consulted."

Guy was momentarily derailed. "James," he began, his approach decidedly softer, "if you were uncomfortable with the decision, why didn't you say anything?"

At this point, James glanced nervously in our direction. I took one step backward into the house, believing instantly that my presence was the problem. I wasn't the problem.

"Because your mom and dad agreed to it, and I didn't feel I had a right to say anything."

"James, if the decision affected you, then you had a right to say anything you want."

"That sounds good, Guy. But that's not the way things work around here. I'm nobody."

The director came back out of the house.

"Guy," he said quietly, "maybe I could film the four of you talking together. That might get things started."

Guy perked up immediately, sensing a plan for damage control. He walked back toward us, nodding at his father. "Yeah. Then I can ask them questions. All they have to do is answer." He disappeared into the house, his voice trailing after him. "I have to pee."

At the patio table, Anne gathered up the pile of tissues she had accumulated and hid them under her chair. When one of the crew members tried to take away the tissue box, she grabbed it from him.

"Better leave that here," said Cat. Beside them, James pouted. A chair was moved in for Guy.

It took only one more try to film the scene, because Guy took over. Deftly, he got them to talk about what it would be like to be at his funeral, having children, even going shopping, after he was gone. Gradually, the emotions came. What sounded in the beginning like children reciting their lessons for a strict schoolmaster ended in a heart-tugging display of love among friends.

"He practically had to put the words in their mouths," Alexander lamented from our corner.

But Anne and Cat managed to find some words of their own. "We took so much for granted," Cat told Guy, as the camera rested on her tear-stained face. "I just want to play again, like we used to."

"I'm terrified," Anne wept, "to be alone. Of the pain you'll have to go through, and the pain we'll have to go through, too."

Satisfied, Guy thanked his friends. James had not uttered a word.

GAYDAR

In my opinion, a round table is best, a symbol of equality among the people who gather around it. The hope is that anyone can say anything while everyone else more or less listens.

With this is mind, I took my place at the Nakatani's kitchen table after the filming of *From the Heart*, the name that had been given to the new video. The table was round, and the chairs had wheels on them. The kitchen floor had a funny little slope to it, so that on one side of the table you tended to collide with the edge, and on the other side, if you didn't keep one arm propped up on the tabletop, you might find yourself rolling away.

I marveled at this particular table, where despite the seemingly limitless tragedy that stalked the house, coffee and conversation flowed easily. There didn't seem to be anything that was off limits; once, we had an extraordinary, laughter-ridden discussion, ranging from suicide to our least favorite vegetables. At another, graphic descriptions of gay sex accompanied baked salmon and wild rice.

On this evening, Jane nursed a cup of coffee while Anne, Cat, and I enjoyed a beer. I was on the side of the table that required holding on. While we talked, I was always moving a little, pulling myself back with one hand while I handled my beer with the other. It was a good distraction, because it kept me too busy to say much.

Anne was talking about spaghetti. "When Guy and I first became friends, we made a pact never to lie to each other. One morning, Guy asked me what I had for breakfast."

I must have raised an eyebrow, because Anne paused to explain to me that this was a typical Guy inquiry.

"Anyway, I was too embarrassed to tell him I had spaghetti. I love spaghetti. I told him I had french toast or something, I don't remember. Just recently, I confessed to him that I lied about it. I felt guilty for years."

Jane nodded. "He told me about that. He said you were really distraught. Over spaghetti."

We all started to laugh, but Anne silenced us by raising her beer bottle into the air. "You don't lie to Guy," she said dramatically.

Jane considered this for a moment. "But you know, he has not always been truthful," she said carefully. "Look at all those years he lied about being gay."

Cat spoke up. "That's a lie he had to tell. And it wasn't a lie, really, it was as if that whole part of him didn't exist."

"I think you're right," I said. "Avoiding a painful truth is not like Anne not wanting to admit she eats spaghetti for breakfast."

"Anne," Jane said, leaning forward on her elbows. She was on my side, so with the added weight, I had to cling to the table or risk rolling into the water cooler behind me. "When did Guy tell you he was gay? How did you feel?" Jane's earnestness surprised me. I wondered about the agenda behind her question.

Anne settled back in her chair (she was on the uphill side) and began her story. She liked the fact that she knew Guy well enough to be a storyteller and therefore an important resource.

"Life with Guy was fun," she began, and although Jane knew we were about to get more information than she had asked for, she smiled encouragement. "He drew me out of myself and made me brave, and I did things with him that I never imagined. Guy was important, and being his best friend made me important.

"It was Guy who gave me my first beer, after we jumped the fence at the drive-in movie. We were sitting in his truck, and Guy said, 'Okay,

Annie, here's a beer.' And then Jason broke the bottle, and the police came, and we had to check receipts and pay more money, and I kissed Timothy Dickson."

"Who's Timothy Dickson?" Cat wanted to know.

"Who's Jason?" I added, laughing.

"He turned out to be a slime."

I was about to ask whether it was Jason or Timothy who turned out to be a slime when Jane got us back on track.

"Well, what about finding out Guy was gay?"

"I didn't know that there was anything important left to know about Guy. Then one day we were sitting on the floor of my room, just talking about whatever we talked about, and we started laughing, and then we were wrestling and rolling over and over, and Guy ended up on top of me, pinning my hands to the ground.

"He started to lean down toward me, and I thought, oh, my God, he's going to kiss me. But instead, he got really serious and just stared into my eyes.

"'Annie,' he said, 'I have something to tell you.' He was scaring me. I asked him, 'Are you sick?' I thought maybe he had leukemia or something. And then he just said it. 'No,' he told me, 'I'm not sick. I'm gay.'"

December 30, 1985

Dear God,

I'm addressing this letter to God, because Guy warned me I can't tell anybody. Please give me the courage, strength, and understanding to conquer all my problems. Help! Guy is gay. He told me last night and today, whenever I think about it, it makes me sick. Is it natural?
How many gays are there? More than anyone knows?

When will I stop being so confused? I hate everyone right now. I'm so angry that Guy is gay. Why, why, why?

From, Anne T., who needs help

"I was astounded and hurt. I still don't know why I got so angry at Guy. I told him to leave my bedroom, that I had to be alone for a while.

We weren't really friends for a long time, six months maybe. But then one day we just started back up, and it was all right."

Jane had followed every word of Anne's story with rapt intensity. I had been watching her peer across the table, her face unmoving, as if there was something she was waiting to hear. Now she shook her head in firm agreement.

"That was the way I felt, too, astounded and angry. I yelled at him and he left." She paused, remembering. "He went down the street. It was his friend's mother who comforted him."

We all turned to look at Jane.

"I don't blame him for going there," she said, beginning to weep. "I rejected him, just like he imagined I would."

Her honesty so disarmed us that we could do nothing but sit and watch her cry.

I couldn't help but think of my own family. I wanted to believe I was totally enlightened, and indeed the searing prejudices thrust upon Jane in her youth had apparently alluded me. I was much more comfortable with Guy's sexuality than Jane was, but then I was not his mother. Whenever I considered the possibility that one of my children might be gay, I figured it would be fine with me. But my stance remained untested.

I reached for her hand, but Jane had drifted far away. Her voice quavered as she whispered words that were surely familiar, a litany of regret that must follow her everywhere, preying relentlessly on her guilt.

"If only I had known, perhaps I would have reacted differently. I didn't know. It was the way I was brought up."

We were all crying, feeling her pain and her frustration. No one spoke, though I know I wanted to. I wanted very much to help her search her past for an explanation, but this was not her way. Whereas Alexander, I was learning, struggled with his demons, Jane let them be.

After a minute, Jane reached across me for the box of tissues perched on the counter. She pulled out a handful for herself and threw the box down on the table. We all began blowing our noses at once.

Predictably, Jane started to laugh. A moment of emotional breakdown was fine but wallowing was definitely out.

"Look at you," she admonished us. "You're so easily influenced."

"Like sheep," Cat giggled.

"Lemmings," I corrected her, draining my beer.

Jane stood up and cleared the table of our empty bottles and her coffee cup. "It's a good thing Guy isn't here," she remarked. "Whenever I cry, he laughs at me and starts running around looking for Kleenex. 'There she goes,' he says."

I had been meaning to say something about that. In my mind, Guy, James, and Alexander had teased her one too many times about the Kleenex. I was about to jump into a speech about men and emotional accessibility when the water cooler gurgled.

"Greg," Anne announced solemnly.

"What?" I didn't understand.

Jane smiled sweetly at me. "My son Greg. He's getting a drink of water."

Everyone must have enjoyed the look on my face.

· · · ·

Gaydar.

That was the answer Guy gave to our eleven-year-old daughter when she asked him how you could tell if someone is gay.

"Gaydar," he said, "is how I can tell." We were sitting at an outdoor cafe, eating ice cream, Al, Jane, Guy, James, and Anne, my husband Chuck and I, and all six of our children.

"Come here," he beckoned her, making room for Kristen on his chair, in which they both fit nicely. She snuggled up and looked into his eyes, a big smile on her face.

"You're in the fifth grade. Hmm. Do you like boys?"

At this point, Alexander leaned over and nudged me. "Notice he didn't say, 'Do you like boys yet?'" I looked at him. He nodded and went back to his ice cream. Kristen was giggling and trying to hide under Guy's arm.

"I guess you do," he laughed, rolling his eyes at Chuck and me. "So, do you know when there's some boy in your class who's interested in you? I mean, can you feel him liking you a little bit?"

Kristen became quite serious. "I think so," she said.

"How can you tell?"

"Well, usually they start acting really weird around me."

Peals of laughter rippled across the sidewalk, and passersby glanced at us and smiled.

"So you get a signal, then, that something's going on. Kind of like radar."

"Yeah, I guess."

"And would you be looking for a girl to act like that toward you?"

"No."

"Well, someday, a girl might do that."

"That would be funny."

"If that ever happens, do you think you could tell her nicely that you aren't interested in her that way, but that maybe you could be friends?"

"Yes, I could do that."

"Good, because you wouldn't want to hurt her feelings."

My daughter shook her head up and down knowingly.

"Well, Kristen, I know when somebody is interested in me, too. It's hard to explain. I get a signal, just like you. Only I'm not looking for that signal from a girl. I get that feeling from another man."

He stopped and shrugged. "That's gaydar."

We all watched silently as Kristen and Guy stared at each other.

Finally, she asked, "Did you use your gaydar on James?"

"Sure."

Across the table, James swirled his tongue around his cone and nodded. "Yeah. Otherwise, he would have missed me."

· · · ·

One morning, Guy called at 6:45. I was still in bed.

"Are you coming over today?"

186

"Why?" I said, rolling over to peer at the clock. "Do you have a story to tell me?"

"I'll think of something." He pressed on. "When do you want to come? Come early. Come now. We can talk, and then we can go out to lunch. I feel like pizza."

"Guy . . ."

"Okay, get up, get dressed, do whatever. Eat breakfast. Take care of the kids. Whatever. Then come."

"If I do all those things, especially the 'whatever,' you'll never see me," I laughed into the phone.

"See ya." A loud click in my ear.

When I arrived a few hours later, Guy was still energized. Now hooked up to his machine, he had spent the morning going through his closet, pulling out piles of things he no longer wanted or needed.

"I've lost so much weight. I'm down to a size small."

"Oh, Guy," I stammered. He was shriveling up, and the worst was yet to come.

But across his face came a look of glee. "It's no big deal," he said excitedly. "I don't usually have such a good reason to go shopping. Now it's legit."

"Well, anyway, God bless you, ten times." I have a friend who always says that, and I figured in Guy's case, once was definitely not enough. "You're in a good mood," I observed.

"Yeah, I am. Sit. Ask me anything."

I was silent for a moment. Questions, not completely formed, were beginning to come to me, blank spaces in the life story he was relating, questions that I worried were unfair or crossed some unspoken line of defense.

"Guy," I began, "when Glen was so sick, did you ever think that you would someday be going through the same thing?"

"Molly," he said, narrowing his eyes and answering immediately, "when Glen was sick, I was well. I was so well that it was easy to stay separated from Glen. Whatever was happening to him wasn't going to happen to me."

"Because you were in denial?"

"Maybe." He gave me a crooked grin. "Being in denial always helps." Guy shifted on the couch, rearranging his blanket, smoothing down his slightly rumpled T-shirt. "But remember, we hadn't been close for years. It was as if I didn't have a brother."

"So," I tried again, "when you looked at him, you didn't see yourself?"

"No. We're totally different." Guy waited expectantly for my next question.

I was still trying to get him to answer the first one. "Perhaps the two of you were different, but the experience of this disease . . . "

"Glen was a weird kid," Guy interrupted. "Very introverted at a young age. If you were trying to imagine the opposite of me, you'd think of Glen. He was so into himself."

I didn't know what to think. Guy kept going.

"Macramé. All on his own. Stitching. A lot of time in his room. Very sneaky. Glen stole some silver dollars from Greg and set it up like I did it. I got busted, and my parents didn't believe me.

"I remember when Glen was eleven or twelve and some kids were coming down the street to beat up on everyone. Glen was the only one who said, 'No, they're not going to do it.' I don't know what he was thinking. Everyone was running but Glen. And Glen got the shit beat out of him.

"He hid his life from us. He was the king of the manipulators. I couldn't believe what he got away with." Guy paused. "So you see, Molly, I couldn't really get into what Glen was going through."

Often when I talked to Guy, I had the sense that we were sailing. The wind would pick up and move us along until we were going at a really good clip. We could have tacked, and I almost always wanted to turn and go back the other way, to get to know this space of sea by traversing it again and again. If we could only let down our sails and drift a bit, I could lean over the side and gaze into the depths. But somehow, we'd just glide across the surface in one direction, until we were home again, and I wasn't sure how we'd gotten there.

Once more, I returned to the obvious. "I guess I just can't get away from the fact that you both have the same disease."

Those fathomless brown eyes stretched open, taking me in. "You know," he said, running his slender fingers through his hair and nodding slightly, "there is physical evidence of his success at Jack in the Box. He was proud of his work. He would criticize the tables that hadn't been set up within his guidelines. I can understand that. At Nordstrom, I was very hard on the people who worked under me. Everything had to be just so."

"So," I tried to rope him in, "you had a similar work ethic?"

"Not really. I had a flourishing career as a manager at Nordstrom. I would have gone far if I hadn't had to quit. Glen worked a little and tried to go to school, but he dropped out often. His social life, whatever he was doing out there, always seemed to overtake everything else. I'm just saying that he took some pride in his work, even then."

Guy moved my little tape recorder nearer to him on the couch. He was telling me everything he thought I needed to know.

"I think he finally found his identity. He was content. But he was still different from what society calls normal. I couldn't relate to him for a long time."

A dark form hovered just below the water. We passed it by.

"And now that he's dead?" I asked.

Guy sighed and leaned back on his pillow. He stared at the ceiling as he spoke. "Glen's death was very hard on my parents. You'll have to ask them about it. It was two days after Thanksgiving. Glen was really scared. It wasn't a good death. You know, I'll never forget that Thanksgiving—that's when I stopped being separated from him."

I sat forward, eager to hear what might come next.

"Glen had been in the hospital, practically on his death bed. The doctor let him come home for Thanksgiving. He was down here on this couch while everything was being prepared upstairs.

"When it was time to eat, he said, 'I'll come up.' He was in no shape to come up. None at all. I remember him struggling to stand, and how gaunt and sick he was. My dad finally had to help him a little.

"For the first few minutes, he just sat at the table, totally winded. But the fact that he was part of the family again, sitting at the table at Thanksgiving—it meant something.

"But he couldn't really eat. It was pathetic. Everyone had their plate filled, and Glen had this little piece of turkey and this tiny clump of potatoes. He didn't last five minutes; he had to go back down."

Guy's voice softened and his eyes misted a little. "But you saw where the value was. He had come home."

I was sniffling too, and I reached for a tissue and plunged my hand into a box of rubber gloves instead. Just then the phone rang, and Guy hunted for it in the folds of his blanket.

"Hello?" said Guy, smiling and mouthing *James* to me. "Well, I missed you too. What?" He started to chuckle. "Oh, here it comes." He looked at me and rolled his eyes. "What kind of investment?"

I watched Guy talk to his lover, eyes twinkling, his voice gentle and teasing. After only a moment, he said, "Okay, Jamesy, gotta go. Molly's here." He paused. "I'm telling her everything."

"That ought to inspire trust," I commented as he hung up.

"Oh, he doesn't really care what I say. He's too busy becoming a mogul. Some big deal with a guy at work. Wants to invest all his money." Guy reflected for a moment. "He doesn't have any money. Do you think he's going to ask me for a loan?"

"You've got money?"

"Sure. Now, where were we?"

"Glen."

"Oh yeah. The first time I saw Glen as a human being and not as my brother who ran away and ruined everything was when I went to visit him at Letterman Hospital the first time he was sick. Let me tell you, Molly, it was enough for me to get my butt in the car and go all the way up to San Francisco just to see him. I still didn't feel strong feelings for Glen. Nothing positive.

"I walked into his room, and all I could see was the foot of the bed. He was so skinny—until I saw his head, I didn't think he was in the room. I was shocked. I thought, wow, this is real. And while that was hitting me, he sat up to eat his lunch, and from beneath his tray you could see his little legs sticking out of his gown. It was like when the house falls on the witch in *The Wizard of Oz* and her legs shrivel up and disappear. In another minute, there was going to be nothing there.

"But I thought, this is a human being going through something that no one should have to go through. And my brother had never said a word to me. Never a complaint. He had this smile when I walked into the room. He didn't make me go through it with him—you know what I mean?"

"So your feelings for your brother did start changing, even before Thanksgiving?"

"Hmm. I guess so."

"Did you forgive him?"

"To a degree. It was weird to have anything at all going on with him. For the longest time after that, my feelings for Glen had changed, but still, he would come home and we wouldn't say hello to each other. He'd go downstairs, do his thing. Other times he drove me crazy. He would talk and talk about nothing. I remember him telling me one time about his Air Force locker and how everything had to be in a certain order, and he went into total detail about it. You see, when we talked it was about nothing. And even that was rare."

Guy brightened. "I thought of a similarity."

"What's that?" I was finally sure of what he was going to say.

"We both have inner strength."

"Whoa," I murmured, still picturing the inside of Glen's locker.

Guy's machine began to beep, and he turned it off and unhooked himself. "Gotta pee." As he moved slowly up the stairs, he called down an order to me.

"Lunch."

"Okay," I called back. "Where do you want to go?"

"Anywhere you want, Molly, anywhere at all."

· · · ·

191

I certainly wanted to go to Hawaii. The Nakatani family would begin their stay on the island of Maui in late July. I was invited for a week in August.

I was delighted to be included and saw it as a chance to be with various members of the circle in a relaxed, comfortable atmosphere. Initially, everyone looked forward to it. Guy would breathe the Maui air and start feeling better. Jane would take walks and cook wholesome food for her son. Alexander would play golf. James would work on his tan. Anne would work on her body. I would bring my tape recorder to the beach.

In the weeks that preceded the trip, however, complications arose. In bits and pieces, I came to understand that Alexander was less than thrilled with the fact that his family vacation had swelled to seven, including James and Anne and me—still somewhat of a stranger—and Cat, whom Guy invited at the last minute. On top of that, I discovered that James had pouted for days when I was included on the roster.

"Guy has a new friend," he told Anne. "Just one more person for me to share Guy with."

Later, Anne confided that she, too, had been threatened by my presence. "It's the way he does things: This is Molly. She's writing about me. She's coming to Hawaii. Move over."

Over Guy's objections, I demanded a short family meeting to ask permission to join the vacation. Alexander said he would probably be gone by the time I came. Jane said she'd be glad to have another "grown up," which produced a chorus of boos from Guy, James, and Anne. Personally, I was glad to be put in my proper place with the older generation. In any case, I rearranged my week so I wouldn't step on James' time with Guy.

Eventually, it was decided that Alexander would be there with Jane, Guy, and James. Anne would arrive, and Al would leave. Cat and I would arrive, and James would leave. James complained that he was going to miss all the fun.

A much more serious problem was Guy's health. The cyto-megalovirus that had claimed his right eye was threatening more of what was left of his sight. Usually kept in check by the human immune system, CMV is a primary cause of not only blindness, but dementia and death in AIDS patients. As it had since I met him, Guy's ever-increasing daily dosage of gancyclovir was exacerbating his nausea and diarrhea and no longer protecting his left eye. In addition, the hours spent on the couch, feeding the medicine into his body, had stretched into a majority of his "good" time, as he put it.

"I've been thinking," Guy said to Jane and me one day while we were eating lunch at their house, "that I should let my eye go. I'd have better quality of life, at least for a while. No diapers would be nice."

I cringed. Diapers had become a necessary part of his ability to perform in front of a room full of kids. He even shared his problem with "the runs," painting for them a graphic picture of the indignities of living with HIV and AIDS.

"What will really kill me," he said wistfully, "is not being able to shop."

Jane had a plan for that. "We'll just have to be there to describe everything for you."

Guy scowled playfully. "In detail, Mom. Yellow isn't just yellow, blue isn't blue. It's canary yellow, or periwinkle blue. And silky isn't the same as satiny. I've heard you intermix them.

"And Molly will be of no help," he gave me a look of mock distain, "her belt and shoes are a mishmash."

"What," I protested, "is he talking about?"

Jane gave a practiced reply. "Belt and shoes must match. Black with black, brown with brown. Leather with leather. No plastic."

I looked down at the empty belt loops on my shorts.

"What about no belt?"

Guy made the sound of a buzzer. "Not a match. You lose."

I groaned.

"That's okay, Molly. I'm getting used to you. The eclectic look."

Granted, I based my wardrobe mainly on what was out of the wash, but I felt that most of the time I looked somewhat together.

"I'm not that bad." I tried the high road of defense. "Anyway, I didn't know my apparel was being evaluated. What about who I am, as a person?"

"That doesn't matter." A grin spread across Guy's face. "It's not who you are, it's how you look."

"A philosophy for life," I laughed.

"You betcha. And if I'm blind, how am I going to be sure how I look? And then," he continued with a flourish, "how will I know who I am?"

"Somehow, I don't think that will be a problem," Jane snorted.

Despite his tenacious good humor, the devastating choice facing Guy shrouded the household in gloom for weeks. Then just one week before the first group was scheduled to leave for Hawaii, an amazing development in Guy's CMV treatment provided a new option—twice a week, an eye specialist in San Francisco would inject the gancyclovir directly into Guy's good eye.

"If I can stand it, it's a good solution," he explained to me. "The medicine will hit the problem area and not wander around the rest of my body making me sick. And I won't spend every waking minute chained to the couch."

The thought of a needle being stuck directly into my eye was enough to make me sick, but Guy seemed to take it in stride. After his first injection, it was reported that he had survived and survived well. On the next appointment, Alexander took the video camera and taped the entire procedure. Reluctantly, I joined the family that night to view the video. I survived fairly well, too.

Alexander was excited. "We're going to show this video to the kids in his next seminar." His eyes were gleaming. "It'll scare the hell out of them."

"Oh, Al," said Jane. "They'll be swooning in the aisles. You'd better warn them. We're going to get calls from irate parents."

"Good," he declared. "I'll take the opportunity to explain to them what they *really* ought to be worried about."

Guy's doctor found an eye specialist who could perform the same procedure in Honolulu. During his vacation, once a week, Guy would fly to the clinic on Oahu. Quietly, Alexander calculated the extra expense of the shots and one round-trip flight between the islands every week for four weeks. Even with insurance, the treatment would cost nearly two thousand dollars.

"Holy cow," he said, once the figure was before him. "But look what it's buying him," he remarked to me. "Sight, quality of life, maybe even some time. Since these injections are closer to his brain, they'll protect him longer from dementia."

Two weeks into the trip, a specialist was located who practiced on Maui; the flights ceased, and Guy became even more accepting of the routine. Over the phone, Jane reported that all was well, except that if the doctor broke a little vein in his eye, which seemed to happen every other session, Guy had blurred vision for at least twenty-four hours.

The hardship, it seemed to me, was unimaginable. It made me think of something Guy said to the students and their parents during his talks. He would list all his medicines, how much they cost, and how sick they made him feel.

"And for what?" he would ask them, his voice strong and clear in the stone silence that blanketed his audience. "This isn't the flu. I'm never going to get better. It's just going to get worse and worse. And then I'm going to die."

There was never a cough or a shift in a seat. "Please," he was pleading now. "I don't want you to have to go through what I'm going through. The next time you're faced with a choice that could give you this disease, think of Guy."

"Please," he implored them again, punching each word through the tension he had created, "remember me."

I've often wondered how many lives he saved. There could be many. Surely there have been a few. Just one would be a magnificent victory.

THE CHANGING SEASON

I arrived at the airport in Kahului, Maui, on the evening of August 5, 1993, and walked slowly down the long covered walkway between the gate and the terminal, allowing happy vacationers to pass me by. I wasn't a tourist this time, but I also wasn't quite sure in what capacity I had arrived on this island.

Since May, I had gone from an observer and supporter of the Nakatani cause, to a recorder of their lives, even a confidante. With this trip, the lines were blurring even more; I was here to be with a dying friend and with those who loved him, but still I felt the laptop computer I was lugging along was my ticket to their private party.

"I don't want to lose any time," Guy had said when he extended my invitation. He had things to tell me.

Jane and Guy picked me up and drove me to the condominium they had rented in Wailea. On the way, I drank in the sights—the ocean, always breathtakingly beautiful, the welcoming palms, the roadside stands overflowing with the bounty of the islands. I felt my body slowing down.

"Our place is so great," Guy exclaimed as he opened the door of the white stucco condo. "No stairs!" It also had a patio, where we could enjoy breakfast while looking out on luscious green lawns that stretched down in the direction of the sea until they blended into a horizon of colorful flowers. Its cozy living room had enough couch space for everyone to nap at once.

That night, after the dishes, Jane curled up with her book, and Guy disappeared into the bedroom to wait for James to call. When he did, we could hear Guy giggling down the hallway.

"All better," Jane commented. There had been tension between the two, to say the least, just before the trip. The video fiasco. Guy's complaints about James' pettiness and jealousy; James didn't understand his needs and was forgetting how sick he was. In turn, James whined about gaining weight and his grueling job and Guy's trying to control him. Guy said James couldn't make a decision without him. James said he was so used to Guy making all the decisions, he didn't know how anymore. Guy said James had to learn to be more independent. James, on his own, bought some new pants, which Guy said made him look fat. He took them back.

Apparently, the magic of Maui had rekindled their love. Twice during dinner, Guy declared that he was miserable without James, a considerable change from not wanting to be in the same room with him just three weeks before.

Undoubtedly, Guy was feeling better. The untainted air, the chaste blue waters, the cloud-capped mountains—something cleansed him, renewed his hope. Watching a Guy who was nearer to what he had once been, a young man I would never know, I noticed his weight had risen slightly. His step was not yet lively, but the shuffle was gone. This plague created a drum-tight world, a maze without a door or window or even a tiny crack in the iron-ribbed walls. But here, the island breeze flowed through that maze, and the illusion of hope came with it.

"I might move here."

Guy and I were swinging, timidly, our feet never leaving the ground. On our patio outside the condominium, we watched geckos scurrying through the vines of flowering bougainvillea from our little swing with plush cushions and a canvas cover to protect us from the overly friendly Maui sun.

"I get well on the island. When I go home, it will take a while, but

I'll start feeling really lousy again. Moving would be hard on my mom. If I could hold out two years, it would be ideal, because she could retire and get benefits. If she quits now, she takes a pay cut."

I pondered his words. Two years, I thought sadly, might be a bit of a stretch. But beyond that, I was surprised at how threatened I felt. I couldn't imagine the story continuing without me.

I said softly, "I'd miss this mess." He raised an eyebrow.

"Is that what we are to you? A mess?"

"Not at all. It's a term of endearment."

We swayed silently for a while. "You know," Guy began again, "if I could, I'd never go back. I'm changing, physically and emotionally. I just can't give that much anymore. I'm glad I don't have any more seminars until the fall." He brought his hands to his chest. "I don't know where it would come from."

I watched his fingers spread wide and run down the length of his shirt, prodding here and there, as if he was mining for energy beneath the cloth and skin that covered his flagging spirit.

"If you quit right now, Guy, it would be enough. You've reached so many young people—and not-so-young people, too, like me." I leaned on him affectionately.

"Thirty-seven thousand." He stopped the swing. "Thirty-seven thousand people, so far." He started us up again. From our comfortable seat, Guy looked toward the ocean, the wind coming up and ruffling his hair which, despite the slow thinning, still begged to be touched.

"I know I have it rough physically now, but I'm not going to feel this way forever."

"Hawaii is doing wonders for you, Guy."

"No, that's not what I mean. From what I've been told, it may be an even better situation once you move on to another life."

Our swinging stopped again. Guy continued to speak, his eyes still reaching for the slender blue line of the sea. "When Greg died, I realized how infinite death is. I always thought my brother was going to be there. I thought we would share family gatherings like Christmas and Thanksgiving. It was hard to cope with it, the physical nothingness, his not being there anymore, ever. But then I began to feel Greg still around me. I became spiritual, without my even knowing it. And I accepted death, because I could still feel Greg—he was still somewhere."

Guy turned back toward me slightly. "You'd think after Glen, I'd be scared shitless. But I'm not. Instead, I think about seeing my brothers again. That helps a lot.

"You know what my mom wants me to do? She wants me to tell Greg and Glen how stupid they were to get themselves dead. And then I'm supposed to give her a sign that I've talked to them."

"I want a sign, too, Guy," I said. "Can I have my own sign?"

"I'm going to be busy."

The bougainvillea stirred, and a warm breeze wrapped around us comfortably. Guy leaned back and sighed. "I want to be buried here, next to Greg. In a sense, I'll just be coming home. I'm doing a lot of that these days, you know, wearing my whale's tail, getting into all the symbols of the islands."

Guy had been wearing a gold whale's tail around his neck for as long as I had known him. His mother and father, as well as Anne and James, wore them. I took it to be the sign of the circle.

"And to think of all that time and money I spent trying not to look Japanese. My curly hair and my blue eyes. Now I'm proud of being Japanese-from-Hawaii." He smiled and shook his head. "I was a little crazy."

I drew a quick breath when a daring gecko slithered over my foot and into the bushes behind our swing.

"Ooh, brave," Guy commented.

"That lizard?" I asked, eyeing the shrubbery.

"No, you. James is scared to death of those things." We watched the gecko venture out from under the bush and disappear into the grass.

"What I'm afraid of is just before I die. I'm afraid of dementia. But I keep telling myself I'll be going to a better place. Not that this place isn't wonderful, and I'd rather stay longer. It's just that the process of life doesn't stop at death."

Reaching for his hand, I asked, "Did you figure all of this out yourself?"

"I've been processing," he agreed. "Some people don't have a clue what I'm trying to say here. Death is just another step in life. I don't know what to expect when I'm dead. It could be a million different things. It could be heaven, where it's beautiful, you know, cloudy, kind of hazy, but with sun and hope. Maybe I'm going to be in people's thoughts, helping them. I'd like it to be that way."

I smiled. Leave it to Guy to give advice from the grave.

Jane came out onto the patio. "Are you ready to go?"

Guy straightened up. "We're going to my grandpa's house today. And on the way back we'll visit Greg and Glen." He glanced at me. "Will you come?"

"Of course."

Jane offered her son a bag of potato chips. He took one and settled back on the cushion, munching thoughtfully.

"It's been hard for me to visit Greg. I was going to go by myself, but James was here and I kept avoiding it. So now we're going together, and I'll just shut myself off. I figure I'll go alone next time." He gazed at his mother and reached for another chip. "So what do you think of that?"

"Why do you need to go alone, Guy?" Jane asked. "Are you saying it's not resolved? That you never said good-bye? Or that you had problems with him?"

"Yes, yes, and no. I didn't really have problems with Greg." Guy considered his next chip, slipped it in his mouth, and continued crunching. "I didn't deal with it when he died. At least now I talk about it."

We slid over so Jane could join us on the swing, and the chips could be passed back and forth. "You were so closed off," she said. "You kept going on the outside, like nothing had changed. That worried me." She paused. "But of course, none of this is ordinary. Our falling apart has been nothing compared to what I would expect.

"My therapy has been talking to Al. I don't know what I would have done without that. The worst is in the middle of the night. Sometimes I'm lying silently beside him, and I'm crying or deep in thought. He always seems to know, and we start talking. Or in the morning when I wake up. That's why I get up so quickly."

I had noticed that Jane could be sound asleep one moment and cooking breakfast the next.

"I guess I'm fighting," she concluded.

"Fighting what?" Guy asked.

"Thinking," she replied ruefully.

Jane and Guy started to swing us with enthusiasm. Soon we were laughing uncontrollably.

"Wait," I yelled. "I'm going to throw up!"

"No, Molly," said Guy as we came to an abrupt stop. "That's my department."

• • • •

On the way to Grandpa's house on the mountain, Jane, Guy, and I drove through the towns of Kahului and Wailuku, where the atmosphere was still richly old Hawaiian. Only moments later, we were high above city streets, turning off Kea Road, inching down a steep driveway. From the front, it was not an extraordinary house. It had a garden, not particularly well kept by the caretaker Jane and Alexander had hired, and a front porch, which was empty except for an old table with a sheet over it and a couple of packing boxes.

We entered the sliding doors and took off our shoes. The same warm, easy breeze that seemed to make the whole island gently sway moved through this house as well. In Hawaii, inside and outside are the same.

I crossed the room and stood before an enormous wall of windows. The view was astonishing, a sweeping panorama of beauty. To the left, Kahului Bay, and in the distance, the Haleakala Mountains and the volcano beyond. Below us, sugar and pineapple plantations, and to the right, Maalaea, the meeting place of the two sides of the island. I knew we were on a tiny island, but what lay before me seemed as vast as it was exquisite.

"C'mon," said Guy, leading me away. "Let me show you how to do the Grandpa thing."

Jane's father had died in June after a long illness. She explained that his spirit was still new, but since the forty-ninth day after his death had passed, he was, thankfully, no longer trapped in his house.

A long coffee table was set up in front of the windows. "Do what I do," Guy instructed. He knelt down, sitting on his heels in front of the *hotokesan*, the shrine, for Grandpa. Taking up most of the altar was a detailed model of a Japanese house, painted black with sloping roofs and large doors that opened up to reveal steps inside. On the center step was a statue of Buddha, and to the left what I later learned to be Grandpa's spirit name carved into the wood. His picture peered out at us, an austere-looking man in a starched white shirt and tweed sports coat, the kind that might have suede patches on the elbows.

I knelt down beside Guy. He took a long incense stick out of a cardboard box and lit it, motioning for me to do the same.

"*Senko*," he murmured. Incense. We put the *senko* in a small brass bowl filled with sand, and the sweet smoke rode the breeze through the room.

Next, Guy picked up a wooden stick and, with some degree of ceremonial flare, struck a gold chime that rested next to the incense. Bringing his hands together in the traditional prayer position, he bowed his head. I did everything Guy did, until the two of us were left with hands clasped and our heads bowed.

"Isn't that neat?" Guy perked up. "You can do that anytime you want to now. You won't need me."

· · · ·

Our stop at the Maui Memorial Park was brief. Guy took me to see the graves: Jane's mother, father, and brother, and Glen and Greg. Next to Greg's name there was a blank space.

"For me," said Guy easily.

Jane had brought flowers and greens from the house. She filled a bucket with water from the hose attached to the mausoleum and decorated each grave while Guy and I relaxed on the grass. In the distance, the ocean sparkled.

Around us, other visitors sat by the flat headstones, and I noticed that many of them seemed to be talking. One man was quite animated, waving his hands in the air.

"They come here all the time," said Guy, reading my mind. "They talk to their dead relatives, keep them up-to-date on the family gossip. Sometimes they even bring a little picnic."

"It's pretty here, isn't it?" Jane walked over to us. "Peaceful."

I smiled at her.

"You know, someday we'll move here, and we'll live in that house. From my kitchen window, I'll be able to see my three children."

I put my arms around her, and we shared a few tears. After a moment, I glanced up. "Oh, no," I said. "Look at your youngest."

Jane turned around. Guy was lying on the grass, having assumed the "laid out" position, complete with flowers poking out from his folded hands.

"Don't I look good dead?"

Jane shook her head. "You little shit."

We got back in the car. From the top of Kea Road, we could almost see across the island, where the sun would be at its most brilliant, a red-yellow fireball igniting a long taper of light across the ocean, soon to vanish into the azure abyss. But we drove away from the sunset, dropping into the valley, back to the condo in Wailea. Anne and Cat would be waiting impatiently for our return. We had big plans for the evening.

· · · ·

We set out for Mama's Fish House, to this point in my life my favorite place to eat, talk, and celebrate.

Jane was at the wheel with Guy next to her, and Cat, Anne, and I were in the back. We played a Kenny Loggins tape, and Guy reclined his seat so that Cat could massage his head. The music, the beauty of our surroundings, the feelings inside the car—I wondered if this was how astronauts felt, free-floating, safe inside their airtight capsule, glancing outside a porthole and suddenly perceiving the meaning of life.

Winding up the coast from Wailea through the town of Kuau, we found Mama's hidden from the road, at the end of a lane dense with trees and island flowers. We were early, so Anne, Cat, and I walked across the palm-studded lawn onto the beach. We took off our shoes, sat down, and dug in our feet. Cat started picking up handfuls of sand and letting them run through her fingers; soon Anne and I were doing the same. The sand felt smooth and even to the touch. It was perfect sand.

We sat silently and watched night slowly descend, reaching down to touch the deep liquid blue, pouring wine-colored darkness into what had been an endless space of pastel sky. A yacht moved down the shoreline, its bright lights leaving a trail of glitter across the water. We could see people moving about the deck, and we knew what was happening there: the music, easy and mellow, the absentminded gaiety. The ocean separated us.

As though on cue, we jumped up and walked back to where Guy and Jane were waiting on the crowded patio in front of Mama's. Our table was ready. We were led through a massive door made of puzzle-piece sections of mahogany, oak, redwood, and walnut, and in the center a koa dolphin. Inside, bamboo-lined walls and rich mahogany beams and studs surrounded tables covered with blue-toned Polynesian prints. The atmosphere was loud and festive.

On Guy's command, we each ordered a different exotic drink. Jane and I stuck with daiquiris, but the younger group were much more adventurous. Anne and Guy decided on a Chi chi and a Coco-loco, respectively.

Cat went last. "I'll have an Orgasm."

"No problem," said our waiter.

When the drinks arrived, Anne raised her glass. "To friendship," she said, and then Jane and Cat toasted the noticeable improvement in Guy's health.

"To this holy place," I added, and we drank.

"Okay," said Guy. "Pass 'em around."

"Guy loves to do this," Anne told me, as my strawberry daiquiri was replaced by her Chi chi.

It was slowly dawning on me that Guy's drink was coming my way. I looked up to see Jane's eyes on me.

"I'll have some of Guy's," she said, reaching across for the tall glass that had been served with a plastic parrot perched on the side. She took a sip. "Umm. That's good." She handed it to me. "Want to try it?" She gave me a little nod. It's okay, her smile was saying.

I knew that, I said to myself. And Guy's Coco-loco, I decided, was not for the weak of heart.

Cat turned to me. "What did you mean, this holy place?"

"I know what she means," Guy said solemnly. "Hawaii was my escape from reality, coming here as a child, picking up and leaving everything behind. Up at the house, I would watch my mom picking papayas and think how beautiful she was, how she belonged here. And at night, when the little lamps across the yard were shining all in a row, I believed it was a bridge and that angels were on the other side."

Guy sipped his drink. "It's always been a holy place for me."

"Holier than Nordstrom?" said Anne quickly, as if to keep the light-hearted breeze that swirled around our table from dying down.

But Guy smiled broadly. "And Polo and Ralph Lauren. Friggin' divine."

· · · ·

Dinner was gastronomical heaven. We ordered five different kinds of fish and ate off each other's plates. It was an especially good arrangement for Guy, who could just about manage one bite of everything. Wine was added, and we created a bit of a commotion, our forks flying back and forth across the table, our conversation loud and, to any nearby diners who may have tuned in, interesting. Provocative. Raunchy.

"When Guy tells me what to do, he's both gentle and slick. It makes you want to do what he says." Anne's eyes were bright from the wine and freedom of speech—the law of our table.

"You make me sound like a manipulative jerk," Guy said pleasantly, reaching for a piece of my filet of sole.

"Why'd you want me for a friend, anyway? Did you need a slave?"

"Oh Annie, I was attracted to you because of you." It was a good beginning, but he went on to blow it. "Because in my opinion, you weren't pretty, you didn't know how to dress, you had no hairstyle. I went out with only the most popular people, the best dressed. I'm saying this now so you'll realize I had nothing to gain by being your friend." Anne stared at him.

"You know what I mean. I liked you."

Our intrepid waiter came by to inquire if we needed anything.

"Can you go pee for me?" Guy asked him.

"No can do," he replied without changing the expression on his face.

"I couldn't believe you called me," Anne continued, rushing by Guy's dismissal. "I was so scared of you."

"Why?" Jane was incredulous.

"This was Guy Nakatani. King Cool. He even knew how to smoke a joint. I didn't know anything. He had to explain to me why guys get soft after—you know."

I could feel my eyes widening.

"Why do you call it a 'boner' when there are no bones in it?" she responded to my look. "Guy had to explain all of that to me."

Guy was still picking at what was left of Jane's dinner. "She didn't know what a rectum was."

"Excuse me?" Typically, I couldn't quite keep up.

"Rectum." A few looks from adjoining tables.

"We were over at our friend Kim Johnson's house, and her dog had just had puppies. Mrs. Johnson said there was a problem, because one of them was born without a rectum. And Nastasia says, 'What's a rectum?' Everyone laughed, except Mrs. Johnson. She probably didn't want to be rude."

"She probably thought I was a nice girl," Anne commented.

"What's this about a joint?" Jane demanded. Through the years, she had heard all the Nastasia stories.

"Dad knows I tried pot."

"I didn't. You have confessions to make to me."

"Oh," said Anne soberly. "We never did anything more than pot, like coke or crack or IV anything. And it was just one hit."

Jane shook her head, thoroughly disgusted.

• • • •

Coffee and five magnificent desserts were ordered and, when they arrived, they began to make the rounds.

"Umm," said Cat, her mouth full of Jane's fudge brownie covered with macadamia nut ice cream. "This is to die for." She shot a look at her sick friend. "Sorry."

I had been waiting for just the right moment to ask Guy and Cat about their engagement on the night of Glen's death. Clearly, this was it.

"So, do you two want to tell me what you were thinking about? You really were going to get married? Exactly how was that going to work?"

Guy seemed surprised. "Who told you about that?" He surveyed the table.

"You're not the only one talking to me, Guy."

"Yeah, she's the group therapist," said Jane.

Cat sat quietly, her coffee cup poised in midair, a serene smile on her face. "Hmm," she said, as if she was just remembering the incident. "We were going to get married."

"It was going to be great," Guy pumped one hand up and down while the other waved his fork in Cat's direction. "After the wedding, which was going to be the party of the year, we were going to set up a business together."

Cat regarded him lovingly. "At first I thought he was joking. Then we started talking, and pretty soon it was like, this might be a good idea. We would live together and do all these fun and crazy things and not be so far away from each other. Eventually, I guess the idea just went away."

I cut to the quick. "What were you going to do about sex?"

Guy's mouth was full of raspberry torte. "No sex."

"Hmm," said Cat. Many of her sentences started that way. "We were going to have lovers."

"I'm picturing you and a whole lot of men."

"Yeah," she giggled.

"What were you going to do about kids?" Jane inquired.

"Hmm. I think we were going to have them with other people," Cat looked at Guy.

"You know what, I always planned on kids. I didn't understand what my parents were talking about after Greg died—you know, no chance for grandchildren, the end of the Nakatani name—because I fully intended to have children. Of course, I fully intended to stay alive too.

"In fact, I still think about it. The other day I asked my dad, 'Would I be a good father? Would I be too anal with my kid and make him grow up totally paranoid?' He said you're different when you have kids than you thought you were going to be. He said he thought I'd be a good father."

Beside me, I could feel Jane crumbling.

Guy regarded his mother. "When you raise a child, you feel like you've accomplished something, helped someone develop. Well, I feel like I've done that with other people. Not in the same way, maybe, but something like being a parent."

"Thirty-seven thousand, so far," I interjected.

"You would have been a great dad, Guy," Cat stated softly. "You're a charismatic person. You're passionate. Loving."

We all turned to stare at Catherine.

Guy smiled, pushed away the last of the *tiramisu,* and pronounced dinner over.

• • • •

The phone was ringing when we walked back into the condominium.

"It's probably James. Tell him I hadda' pee bad." Guy disappeared down the hall.

"Hello," Jane cooed into the phone. "Yes, he's here. I guess you can talk to him, but only if you say you love me."

Cat, Anne, and I were stuck to our places in the middle of the living room. After a pause, when we assumed James was complying with Jane's request, Jane laughed and put down the receiver.

"Gu-yyy!" she sang, "your lover's on the phone."

We weren't going to make it easy for him. The first pillow flew around the corner and hit Guy squarely on the head as he lay sprawled out on his bed, talking animatedly to James about Mama's Fish House. Still holding the phone, he rolled over, and with amazing force shot it back. Soon each of the four women were in a room, stockpiling pillows, and the battle then ensued.

In the end, we were all in the living room, pouncing on each other, launching our pillows from point-blank range. Guy had long since slammed his door shut, abandoning the fight. Sweaty and laughing, we called a truce.

We waited. We could hear a low murmur coming from Guy's room.

"Didn't they already talk, just before we left?" Cat asked. We were settling in for another round of chatter.

Anne replied sweetly, "That doesn't make any difference, Cat. They're in love—for a change."

"I'm glad," Jane stated firmly. "Guy's happier than I've seen him in a long time. And if he's happy, I'm happy."

After about ten minutes, Guy joined us, beaming. "Silly boy," he quipped, snuggling down into the couch, his head on Jane's lap.

"Ooh, Guy," said Anne, "you sounded so gay just now."

"I am gay."

The comment seemed to astound everyone.

"But what about when James starts to flame, and you tell him to stop acting like a fag?" Jane stroked Guy's forehead.

"One fag is allowed to say that to another." Grinning smugly, Guy closed his eyes, enjoying his mother's touch.

"You see, Molly, James and I would never kiss . . . "

Up went my eyebrows.

". . . in front of my mother. Now, if I still was into real kissing, you know, more than a peck, I would be gutsy. I still hold his hand while we're watching television. But it used to be that nothing ever happened around Jane.

"Massaging is different. James could touch me for four hours that way, but she couldn't take me kissing him. Not gross kissing anyway."

Jane just kept smiling down at her son. He opened his eyes.

"When she thinks of two gay people, she thinks of sex and not emotion." He had our attention. "Sex, to me, what made it pleasurable, was the emotional bonding that happens during the act of making love. What's hard for me is how people separate it all the time. Gay or straight, how can you make love one night and then never see them again?"

A shadow passed through Guy's expression. "No one said it's okay to love someone of the same sex. You feel so dirty and humiliated. I've felt that way, I really have!"

His eyes darted around the room, catching each of us in turn, demanding that we hear him. "Gay people desire the same emotional connection as anybody else. We just aren't allowed to look. And if we're ever lucky enough to find it, we're supposed to keep it to ourselves, because it makes them uncomfortable."

I didn't feel very happy at that moment, being one of "them." But Guy's words were profound. He was sounding like a healthy gay man.

Jane studied Guy's face on her lap. "It was the way I was raised," she said.

Guy groaned. "You're straight, Mom. And you grew up in a straight world."

"Like the rest of us," I offered.

She turned on me. "Then tell me why you don't have the feelings I do."

I took a breath. "I used to have a problem imagining gay behavior. I don't know how much of this is conditioning. The idea of two women didn't bother me very much. I had loving relationships with women, and affection was easy. I could see it. But two men—that was harder."

"And you've gotten over that now?" Jane asked.

"I've come to know and love gay men, so it's not hard to imagine them loving each other. I wish I could say I didn't have to work at it. But I also knew I had to change."

Jane looked discouraged. "I wish I felt that way."

Guy sat up, declaring, "I think it definitely is conditioning. As a gay man, it used to gross me out to think of two women doing it together. I couldn't fathom it. Now I'm at the point where I'm uncomfortable visualizing normal heterosexual sex."

"Normal?" we challenged him, almost in unison.

"See, I'm conditioned, too. The point I've been trying to make is that if you say, for example, Molly and Chuck together, the first thing people think of is not, how do you think they have sex? If you say, James and Guy together, the first thing people think of is two dicks touching each other. Molly and Chuck could have an abusive relationship, and James and I be the most loving, giving couple in the world, and they wouldn't care." His frown deepened.

"You make a good point," I conceded. "On behalf of the entire universe, please accept my apology."

Guy disallowed my sincerity. "Don't you see," his voice cracked and tears rushed to his eyes, "that's why I'm sick!"

Jane's cheeks dampened instantly as she moved next to Guy and embraced him.

"If only someone had said it," he whispered imploringly.

"Said what, Guy?" Her face was losing its color.

"That it's okay to be gay. That I could live my life and find love and be successful, even though I'm gay." He was sobbing now. "God, Mom, gay was the last thing I wanted to be."

I found myself shivering. The comforting island air had deserted us; a chill, not unlike the first sign of the changing season, swept through the room. We all felt it; Anne got up and closed the sliding glass door.

Jane was trembling, too, but I didn't think she was cold. She was terrified.

"When, Guy? When could we have said that?" It was a trial, and Jane was the accused, rising to receive the verdict.

"When you found me with Derek. If someone had said then, "It's okay," things might have turned out differently."

Guilty, I thought. We waited for the prisoner to break down, but she barely flinched. There really wasn't anything more anyone could do to her.

Still, I wanted to save her. I sat silently, making some mental calculations: When did you get sick, Guy? In June 1986, hadn't the behavior that infected you already occurred? But Jane accepted her fate with such graciousness, I stifled the obvious questions.

"It's like a marriage, Guy," she said evenly. "Each step you take, you learn. I can't say I'm sorry for that because I can't go back. I didn't know. Look at us. It's death, because of our ignorance. You say you wouldn't have been promiscuous if we had said it's okay to be gay. Maybe not. But I didn't know to say it. I didn't know anything."

The sound of our weeping, I believe, must have been a comfort to Jane and Guy. The room warmed a little.

"I always imagined Greg would be the one," Guy murmured. "He would have said it, if he had the chance."

Was he taking Jane off the hook? She was right. It was too late to make things come out differently. The tragedies of the Nakatani family were written in stone.

· · · ·

I thought the others were in bed. I was alone, curled up in one of the comfortable chairs that looked like a clam shell with cushions, my eyes reading without comprehending words on a page of a book in my lap. The day, which had been glorious for the most part, had ended harshly, or so it seemed. I was feeling in need of a little comfort.

Sleep, I directed myself. I wandered down the hall toward the room I was sharing with Jane, slipping in quietly so as not to wake her.

Her bed was empty. Back in the hall, I saw that the door to Guy's room was open. My first response was measured alarm; Guy had so easily bounded through the day, his illness thoroughly neglected. Perhaps the virus was reasserting itself, and Jane was nursing him. I took a few steps closer to the door and peered inside.

Guy was lying on his stomach, stretched diagonally across the queen-sized bed. He wore only a pair of shorts, folded down so that a narrow strip of his thin body was covered. Jane was kneeling next to him, spreading oil on his back with long, even strokes. Guy's body glistened.

From the doorway, I watched her hover over her son. It was a bold love I was witnessing, although through her fingertips, he felt only tenderness. It was as if each caress linked them eternally, indestructibly. A mother's passion for the child she would soon give up—it was simple, really, yet almost unexplainable.

Jane looked up and saw me. She smiled and whispered, "Come," moving over a little to make a place for me. I crossed the room and knelt next to her. Hesitantly, I put my hands on Guy's back.

She placed her practiced hands over mine and together we began to move, the oil smoothing our way. His skin was warm, wonderfully soft, as I remembered my babies' had been.

Eventually, she let go. Side by side, we worked to soothe him, and he sighed contentedly beneath us. But clearly, it was her power that guided my hands, that had disarmed me and now gave me comfort.

SECRETS

My last day on Maui. We went to breakfast at the Tasty Crust, a local coffee shop.

"It's been here since I was born," said Jane as we drove into the crowded parking lot. "And it's always been the Tasty Crust. The bathrooms are old, but Guy likes it."

Breakfast was a significant cultural experience for the one haole in the group. We shared our long Formica-topped table and our soy sauce with Japanese-from-Hawaii families who had brought all the generations together for their morning meal out. I ordered an entire plate of fried rice just for me.

"Last night I made a decision, Mom," Guy declared while he ate his *saimin*, noodles with broth, and rice. We enjoyed watching the return of his appetite, an act of trickery that thwarted the virus and fooled even death, sending it to choose from among the more weak and emaciated.

"I'm going to tell you the two secrets I thought I'd take to my grave."

"In front of all these people?"

Guy surveyed our corner of the table while Anne, Cat, and I tried to appear uninterested.

"Yeah, them too. Actually, Annie already knows."

Midbite, Anne gave us a blank look.

"Okay." Guy put his fork down and took a deep breath. "When I was eighteen, I had gonorrhea."

Jane didn't say anything, at least to Guy. She was trying to flag down our waitperson. "Can I have some decaf coffee?" she called over Guy's head as an intense-looking young busboy rushed by.

"Do they have decaf coffee here?" Anne wanted to know.

"Sure. But I don't think they have espresso." She leaned around Guy toward the kitchen area, searching, obviously, for the espresso machine. The rest of us leaned, too, except Guy, who had stopped eating and was glaring at his mother indignantly.

"Mom, I just told you I got an STD, and you're ordering coffee."

I peeked over at Cat.

"Sexually transmitted disease," she reminded me.

"Glen had gonorrhea," Jane commented.

"Yeah, and I remember you were really disgusted."

Jane sighed. "Guy, you've got AIDS. At this point, I can't get excited about gonorrhea."

The coffee arrived. Cat ordered orange juice. Jane sat back, cradling her mug. "So what's the other secret?"

"Okay. I can't believe I'm telling you this." Guy paused for dramatic effect. "Remember that Honda Prelude I had?"

"No."

I began to feel sorry for Guy. He was spilling his guts, and Jane wasn't catching them.

"The Honda Prelude! Your remember, the black one I had before I started driving Greg's truck?"

Jane looked like she was really trying to make a connection.

"Well, anyway, remember that I came home, and it was smashed? I told you that somebody hit me and ran off. Hit and run. Well, actually," he sat back, glancing at Anne, bringing his hands together confessional style, "it was me who hit and ran."

Jane's eyes widened.

"Yeah. I just wouldn't want to die without telling you I lied. Anne was with me."

"Hey, wait a minute," Anne yelled.

He said sternly, "Annie, I just think it's time to tell the truth. We sideswiped a car and were afraid of having to talk to the police, so I just got out of there as fast as I could."

"Guy, we didn't sideswipe a car. And it was parked. It wasn't like we crashed into somebody and left them bleeding on the street."

"Okay, okay. I just thought you might feel better, too, getting it out after all these years."

"I would have felt fine holding it in forever, Guy, just like you made me promise, cross my heart, hope to die, the whole thing."

Jane sent her son a loving look. "Guy, I can't believe you've harbored all this guilt all these years. To me, these things are insignificant."

"These are the things I needed to tell. I couldn't hide them anymore."

• • • •

After breakfast, we took Guy to the clinic for his eye shot.

"Would anyone like to come in with the patient?" An elderly Hawaiian nurse stood at attention next to Guy, her arm around his shoulder. He grinned back at us.

"They can't handle it," he explained, "and obviously none of them cares enough to overcome their fear of needles and come in with me."

"Fear of needles in the eye," Anne clarified.

The nurse made a clucking sound with her tongue that I hadn't heard since my grandmother scolded me for not cleaning my plate. "Come with me, dear," she said soothingly as she led Guy through the door of the clinic. The last thing we saw was his left hand trailing behind him.

Cat inquired sweetly, "Did he just make an obscene gesture?"

"He flipped us off, the little shit," Jane laughed.

An hour later, Guy emerged, considerably subdued. "I can't see," he complained. "Everything's blurry, and now I'm not going to be able to shop in Paia."

We drove up to the little coastal town anyway. During the sixties and seventies, Paia had been Maui's hippie colony, and remnants of that age, storefronts and fences still decorated with rainbows and daisies, could be seen in the colorful village. Unfortunately, Guy could barely make out the street, much less examine the merchandise, and when he made an attempt to be gracious, urging us to wander around while he stayed in the car, we started back up the coast to Wailea.

Once back in the condominium, Cat and Anne headed for the pool, and Jane retired to the couch with her book. Within minutes, she was dozing, her glasses askew, her book resting awkwardly on her chin.

"Isn't she cute," I commented to Guy.

He squinted her way. "Yeah," he grinned, "she is."

We sat facing each other in the clamshell chairs.

"Can you see me a little?" I asked hopefully.

"I can see your yellow shirt. It doesn't go with the blue shorts."

"Okay, that's it. No more sympathy." Across the room, Jane snored softly.

"I worry about my mom," said Guy in a low voice. "She looks to me for approval. If we say, should we go to the store, where should we eat lunch, she looks at me, instead of choosing herself. It's the kind of thing James and Anne do. I guess I attract people like that."

I found myself in the familiar position of deciding whether or not to comment.

"Like when we went shopping. She told Dad, well, I didn't buy the dress because Guy didn't like it. And I had simply said to her, I don't like it because it makes you look too boxy, and it fills your bottom half too much. But she said it was comfortable. So I said, my philosophy is if you can look good and still get something comfortable, it's better than going for comfort in something that doesn't do anything, you know? It was forty-eight dollars. I told her, that's half a Polo shirt. Think about it. But if you like it, go ahead."

"You intimidate her, Guy," I offered a futile protest.

"That's when she's going to feel the loss of me, at those moments." His face clouded. "I want her to be strong all over."

"She is strong, Guy. She's a great woman."

His brown eyes steeled into mine, as if everything was clear, the images and the ideas equally distinct.

"There's no other relationship like the one I have with my mom. It's what I've always wanted in a best friend. The other day, when we were shopping in Kihei, I wanted to tell her: You know, I'm really glad you're here with me."

"Did you?"

"I didn't want to make her cry. We were having so much fun, I didn't want to stop the moment. She's laughing all the time. It's been a while."

"I'm glad I'm here to see it."

"Yeah."

I marveled at Guy, patiently waiting for the blurring to recede, hoping to regain the use of his one good eye tomorrow, only to have two or three days of questionable vision until he can return for the doctor to pop another blood vessel.

"So," he straightened out his legs and grasped the sides of his chair. "What do you want to talk about? You've got an hour or so. Don't waste it."

I had been waiting for a window of opportunity. "Remember how you always say I can ask you anything?"

"Uh-oh," he laughed, gripping the chair even tighter.

"Is it still all right?"

"I wouldn't have said it otherwise."

Maybe not, I reflected. "Okay. This is a tough question, but it's been on my mind. Do you worry about the time between becoming infected and being diagnosed, that maybe you infected somebody else?"

Guy's response was quick. "I guess that's possible. I don't worry about it. There's nothing I can do about that."

"Did you go back to try to find anyone?"

"Sure. I told who I could. No, I'm not worried about that at all." He shifted in his chair. "I was just a big safe-sex advocate."

"From when, Guy?"

"From since I've known."

"Known . . ."

"Known that I was sick."

"But before that?

"Well, I was and I wasn't. I didn't follow it much before I got sick."

"Was there a moment when it hit you: Oh, my God, this AIDS thing, I'd better be careful?"

"Not really. It was never, I'm going to lose my life if I don't have safe sex."

"You never owned it, then."

"Never. Until James, of course."

"You and James never had unprotected sex?"

He paused, almost imperceptibly, and then he said, "I tried to be safe. He's negative, thank God."

I understood that he didn't want to talk about James, and I felt no need to pursue it. I sensed that things were changing between us. Now, when we talked, Guy no longer watched me, calculating our exchange, like a defense lawyer gauging his jury. I sensed his slow movement toward the witness box, where he would try hard to tell the whole truth.

"You were diagnosed in August 1988. That's pretty late in the AIDS crisis not to have noticed what was going on."

"It's not that I didn't notice. I just didn't think it would happen to me."

"That's just what you tell the kids."

"I wasn't into that. I was clean. I had goals. That's the mentality I had. And the people I slept with were handsome and clean. Healthy-looking."

"Did you ever pick someone up at a bar?"

"Yeah," Guy laughed dryly, "but he was still good-looking and clean. My problem was lack of education on the subject of HIV."

"That surprises me. Your life is so ordered—you're very deliberate about everything you do."

"But not when it came to my sexual identity." Guy's voice held a hint of disgust. He was becoming agitated, rocking back and forth, as if he was deciding whether to hold back or leap free of his chair.

Instead he continued, passionately. "It wasn't ordered. It wasn't organized, because I was in conflict. I was in such conflict. It was very humiliating for me. God, if there was one thing I could get rid of, you know, to not have, it was being gay. I felt it, the threat of this thing, this gay plague. I saw it there, but the stronger part of me said, you know, I'd just as soon die."

Guy struggled, his body twisting this way and that, his face taut with the strain of maintaining his composure. I glanced over at Jane for an instant; she had removed her glasses and put down the book; her body was turned away from us, snuggled into the fold of the couch.

"I didn't know what kind of death it was going to be, you know what I mean?"

I tried to send him a look of encouragement.

"There's an aching part of you that wants to give up having to fight and struggle and work it out, work it out. You think about suicide. But I would never have done that to my family, not after Glen. But God, it would have been so much easier."

Guy lifted his eyes toward the ceiling, as if he could keep the tears pooling in his eyes from running down his cheeks. "I never thought it would be better, just easier. There was an easy way out . . ."

I watched as some sort of self-induced intoxication overtook him; he was slurring his words, remembering, it seemed, how it sounded to be uninhibited.

"This whole AIDS thing. I've been trying to explain it to you. People know that the result of being promiscuous is death, but death doesn't seem so bad when you go through a lifetime of conflict. Don't you see? Sometimes, leaving seemed like my only option. Inside, I was at war, and outside too, with everybody else."

There it was. Now that the words were out, floating menacingly in the air between us, I wasn't sure what should happen next. We could stop, not make things any worse. Instead, I took a tiny step forward.

"You've never shared any of this before."

"I never thought I would. When we decided to write a book, I thought it would be more, you know, surface." He pushed away stubborn tears with the back of his hand.

"But I mean, inside, there's a part of me that's a very troubled little boy."

"Oh, Guy." I was struck with a sense of total inadequacy. "We did this to you," I began hesitantly.

"Yeah, society, and the way things have always been, killing whatever scares them, before they even know it might be something good, like a human being."

Guy's eyes connected with mine, entreating me to help him, as if what he was about to utter was the hardest thing he'd ever had to say.

"I still can hardly believe it."

"Believe what, Guy?"

"That some of this is not my fault. I still have to tell myself every day, Guy, you're okay. What you feel is normal, and what you think, and the things you've done, even all of that is okay, because you've taken responsibility. I'm still a good person."

"Of course you are."

Suddenly, his words weren't slurred anymore. "So, let me tell you, Molly, you're going to see a side of me I'd never thought I'd let you see. I thought I could get by without doing that. But it's different now—I'm making my confessions, I'm remembering my father saying that he is proud of me. Things have been left out. You see that, don't you?"

He took the tissues I handed him and blew his nose.

"I've known there were holes in your story, Guy, I just didn't know what they were."

"And now you do?"

"I don't know. Do I?"

We squared off for a moment, the two of us tucked in our clamshell chairs, wondering how much more to ask, how much more to say.

"All I ever wanted was a man to love. I was searching for love, and I couldn't get it from a woman. If only I'd been told, it's okay to look in that other place. It's okay to be gay, you'll still succeed. That's all I needed to hear. Then I tell you, I would not have gone searching for love through sex. I wouldn't have done that! I wouldn't have had a need to do that. Those words would have changed my life."

"They didn't know to say them, Guy."

"I know, I know, and I don't want them to feel guilty. My mother feels terrible after what I said last night. And my father says every day that he's so angry at himself that he didn't know. I understand. It's like not knowing that you left the pool gate open and your kid drowns. But in this case, you didn't know there was a pool gate, and worse than that you weren't even there. You want to go back and redo it so someone can point you to the gate and you can close it. But nobody says anything."

"You are, Guy."

Despite his agony and the passion of his argument, Guy smiled.

"Yeah, I know. I'm telling everybody to close the goddamned gate."

• • • •

The words that were spoken between Guy and me that afternoon would not leave me alone. Never, during the year I spent immersed in their lives, did I ever come away easily, untouched by their story or unchallenged as to my part in it. Whatever distance I could manage between my life with them and my real life became very important; when I was driving home, I knew I had only a few moments to change back into a wife and mother. Chuck suggested I stop on the way, to widen the space, give myself more time. It wasn't that he didn't want to share it with me—not at all. "Tell me everything," he would say. Rather, he understood that I would be compelled to share it with the people I loved, and sometimes the burdens I brought home would be too much for us and better left outside the door.

I left Maui, and on the plane that night the questions returned to me again and again, like a song you can't get out of your head. What did it mean that Guy was spending his last days using all of his seductive powers to scare young people away from unprotected sex, and therefore save themselves, and yet he couldn't tell them it was okay to be gay, which was all he said he needed to save himself? And in his conflict, what issues made their way to me?

Was there something I hadn't told my children, something that now seemed as logical as it was, admittedly, unusual? "It's okay to be gay"—as simple a sentence as "It's okay to be afraid of the dark" or "It's okay to have brown hair," spoken not because the need had arisen, but simply because it was true. When Chuck and I said "just be yourself," did they hear the words clearly, without the echo of unspoken conditions? Or had we unknowingly failed to offer that specific reassurance that Guy claims would have saved him?

I was glad to be on a plane, with a few hours left before I came face-to-face with the ones I loved. There would be shouts of greeting and long, hard hugs all around, and behind them the questions, waiting, demanding answers.

REVELATION

By the end of August, the Nakatanis were back in San Jose. For the second time in a week, I arrived at their home to talk to Guy, an appointment arranged by Guy, confirmed by Guy, and then abandoned in favor of an errand or excursion with James.

Alexander, Jane, and I were standing in the entryway.

"You don't mind, do you, Molly?" Guy was sitting on the step down into the living room, tying his shoes. "Stay here. Eat lunch. I'll be back."

James bounded down the stairs, slipped on his sandals, and opened the front door. "I'll back the car out of the garage. Come when I honk."

The door was almost closed when his head popped back in.

"Hey, Jane," said James slyly. "Guy and I are getting married, and we're going to invite all the people you work with to our ceremony."

"No smart-ass remarks," Jane retorted. The door slammed, and Guy stood up, an act that required a noticeable amount of effort.

"Guy," I decided to be direct. "Are you avoiding me?"

"Noooo. I can't wait to talk to you."

"I'll bet."

"Two o'clock. I promise."

The horn sounded, and they were gone, leaving the three of us lined up next to the shoes.

"Well, this is silly," I said. "I guess I'll be back at two."

"Oh, stay a while. I made your coffee." Jane went into the kitchen while Alexander ushered me into the living room, where we sat on the couch beneath the portraits of the three sons. Jane carried in our cups and settled into a chair across from us.

"I see you and Guy have become real friends," Alexander said with a smirk.

"Because he's trying to manipulate me? Is that the seal of approval?" We shared a laugh.

"Well, from what I've managed to pick up from Jane, and what little I've dragged out of Guy, he's allowing himself to creep down off the pedestal and see what humanity's all about."

I regarded Alexander curiously. "How did you figure that out, I mean, if Guy isn't really talking . . ."

"Oh, he's said a few things. And he told Jane that if we'd said it's okay to be gay, he wouldn't be sick. Molly, he doesn't think it's okay to be gay. He never has. I think he's finally trying to love himself.

"Next, he's avoiding you. Because to be okay with himself, he's got to admit who he is and everything he's done because of who he is. He's terrified of that and," a flicker of glee danced across Alexander's face, "of what might show up in print."

He settled his gaze on me. "So keep after him. It's all in your hands."

"Oh, great." I'm in way over my head, I thought. I had agreed to tell a tale, and I knew from experience that in the telling, there would be other possibilities—a heightened awareness, perhaps, and a degree of transformation. But it appeared that I had somehow become responsible for trapping the truth and forcing it to reveal itself. If so, I was not up to the task.

"I'm not a therapist. I'm not sure what to do with whatever he's been hiding all these years. Maybe he needs a professional."

Alexander was gentle. "Molly, he doesn't have time for therapy. He needs a short visit to his past, to dredge it up and be all right with it. He's capable of this kind of process. He's brilliant, emotionally, and he understands everything that's threatening him right now as feelings.

That's what he tells me, 'Dad, I can't believe the way I'm feeling.' Fear, anxiety, insecurity—these are new emotions for him, really. His confidence has abandoned him."

"I know how he feels."

"He doesn't want to be unsure of himself. He thinks it's a waste of his precious time. He'll do what it takes to get through this."

"And you think he needs to tell . . ."

"I believe he needs to tell you, the writer, his friend, who might not only help him bring it up and deal with it, but turn around and tell the world, so to speak. Don't you see? He wants to come out."

"I had thought he was out."

Alexander shook his head sadly. "You know that's not true. So does he."

I looked at Jane, expecting at least a mild objection. She had been sitting quietly, her eyes moving among the images on the wall behind us. She was staring intently now, hardly breathing, at the portrait of Glen.

"He needs to feel safe," she murmured, as if she was still off somewhere with her oldest son, trying to come back to us. Finally, she pulled her eyes away and directed them toward me.

"When he lets go, he's got to know who's going to hold him. Alexander and I, James and Anne, and now you, Molly—we are all part of the struggle he has inside. When he lets go, he has to know things won't change, like they did with Glen."

She stood up. "He trusts you. Please tell him that no matter what it is, it's okay."

As his wife started across the living room, Alexander was in clear distress. "He knows that, Jane."

"Then remind him."

Alexander persisted. "I don't think we're the problem. It's not us he's angry at. He's angry at himself."

She turned and faced us from the entryway. "I'm just telling you how I feel."

Jane moved away slowly, followed by five sets of eyes in a room thick with memories.

• • • •

226

Usually, whenever I arrived at the Nakatanis' front door, I simply walked in. That had been Guy's instruction so he wouldn't have to get up from the couch when he was hooked up. But when I returned later that day, I hesitated, my hand poised on the doorknob, conscious of strange vibrations within. Farther down the long porch, the curtains rustled, and from somewhere inside the house came a faint thump. I knocked lightly.

When nothing happened, I opened the door, cautiously, calling Guy's name. I moved inside. Suddenly, Guy was in front of me.

He screamed. I screamed. The door slammed behind me, and James jumped out, clad only in a towel. The two of them had to lean on each other, overcome with the hilarity of it all, while I nursed my racing heart.

"You little shits," I yelled at them, borrowing a phrase from Jane.

"You're so easy," Guy teased me. He turned to James, who was already on the first step, on his way to their bedroom. "Oooh, and so are you, sweetie."

James wiggled his rear end vigorously. "Oh, God," I groaned, shielding my eyes. The towel must have slipped, because Guy shrieked with laughter, and James made a great deal of noise leaping up the stairs.

Guy and I resumed our places downstairs in the den, he on the couch, under an enormous pale yellow afghan his mother had recently completed, and me on my pile of pillows. The tape recorder was in its usual spot, on a low table next to the couch. I rarely noticed it there whenever we talked, and I didn't think Guy did either, except for today, when it could have been a ten-foot wall topped with barbed wire, complete with sentry and machine gun. I didn't know how we would reach each other.

It was Guy who came up with a plan.

"Are you cold?" he asked. Often, we had our hottest weather in September, in time to finish off the lingering green of the hills and send children off to sweltering classrooms, further endearing them to education. Inside the Nakatani house, the air conditioner was on overdrive.

227

"Here, we can share it." Guy spread the afghan my way, until we were connected under its long yellow softness.

"Thank you," I said.

"You're welcome."

"So, what do you want to talk about?"

"I thought that was my line."

Guy poked his fingers through the weave of the afghan, separating the yarn loops, creating his own design in the wool.

"You were right about the holes."

I remained silent.

"I've been feeling these things. That's the way it's always been. I have to understand why I'm so agitated. With the disease and everything, I can't have this. Everything I am is what I feel."

"I'd like to understand what you feel."

"You can't. You've got to understand what's happening here. You're going to dig, and sometimes you're going to dig too hard, and then you'll leave me by myself. It's easy to be in your presence when I bring these things out, but then you'll go home, and I'll be left. So you want to be careful."

Don't give in, I struggled with myself. Stay where you are and wait. Suddenly, I remembered that I had something to offer Guy in exchange for any self-incriminating testimony.

"Your mom said to say that it's okay."

"It's okay?"

"Her exact words."

Guy considered this for a moment. "I've never really been afraid before. But go ahead. Ask."

"What happened, Guy?"

Glen happened. Everything always goes back to Glen.

"Up until Glen left, life had been pretty innocent. My two brothers and I went to school, they walked me home, or we went to Georgie's, the baby-sitter. I spent a lot of time with them.

228

"I played with the kids on the block. The twin girls down the street. We traded matchbox cars. Pretty normal. They had Barbies, and I had a G.I. Joe doll. He had chicken legs that made me cry.

"When school got out in June, we would eat out in the Summer Fun Play House, made out of wood and cardboard. We painted the sign with nail polish. We looked in the encyclopedia for dogs and chose which dog we wanted to be.

"I took a shower with my dad until I was nine years old. I used to have this little bucket to catch the water dripping off of him. It wasn't kinky; it was just so free. We took our last shower together the night before my brother left.

"Glen took the innocence with him. He was no longer a topic of conversation at dinner. When Glen did come up, everything was very, very tense. I had to be perfect from then on, me and Greg, to make up for what he'd done. That meant that I could never go to my parents with my problems. I would not be a worry to them. I would have to build up a group of friends who would take their place.

"The problem was, how to make friends. I saw myself alone in a town of white people. I felt different. I saw that the first people who were invited to parties were blue-eyed blondes. What made them popular was they looked good. The new Nike shoes. I realized, I'm not going to make it on looks alone, I have to outsmart people. I'm going to have to make sure my personality shows.

"Junior high school was hard. I felt so Asian. Instead of being smart, I would be the clown, the life of the party. I remember there was this girl named Bernice Wong. She was really an outcast—big thick glasses, buck teeth, funny clothes. No one wanted to be her friend or sit by her. She happened to be Chinese, but people clump all Asians together. I spent a lot of energy staying away from Bernice.

"The sexual urges I had been feeling for as long as I could remember were getting stronger. As a kid, I did all the things everybody does, except I had a secret: I wanted to do them with boys. The first time was with this kid named Mike. He was four. I was five. We explored each other, not really much of anything. Then there was Robert, who was several years older than me. We got together on more or less a regular basis for a lot of rubbing. It was mutual. I don't think I felt funny about it.

"That changed with Aaron. He was a lot older than me, fifteen maybe, and I was ten. He got me in his house, and at first I was so nervous; it was a touchy-feely type of thing, and then he took my head and bent me down and made me take his penis in my mouth.

"I felt really disgusted and scared after that. I stayed away from anybody else's body parts for a long time. I remember thinking, I don't like doing that with men. Maybe I'm not gay after all."

I sat very quietly, giving Guy my full attention. In the beginning, he was very calm, unnatural almost, as if he was reciting a speech that had been memorized and filed away for a very long time.

James came down and said he had some errands to run. Guy told him he didn't need to hurry. When James left, Guy continued right away.

"I worried that it couldn't be right if it had to be a deep dark secret. Aaron didn't need to tell me—even though he did—I just knew. I felt terrible and wanted to tell somebody, like my father, but then I would think of Glen. So I just blocked out what had happened, the same way I blocked out the feelings I had when I saw a boy I was attracted to. I would try not to look, not to think.

"I had been very physical with my family, hugging and touching. But normal boys weren't supposed to be that way, so I stopped kissing my father good-night. I stopped hanging around with the girls at lunch, talking about hair and clothes. It was sad.

"I would hear things at school. I loved grape juice, until one day some kid said that grape juice was for faggots. Today, I toss those things off, but as a child I remembered it the next time I had some sort of urge or feeling. They were always right behind me, you know, like when you're running from monsters in a dream, but they catch up, so you keep running and running. You wake up so tired.

"Then I got my first girlfriend. My initial attraction to Melanie was that she was the most popular girl in the eighth grade—everybody wanted her—and I was only in the seventh grade. She didn't show much interest, but I just kept plugging away, knowing things would turn around eventually. A couple of the tough eighth-graders wanted to beat the crap out of me. I'm surprised I didn't die. When she picked me, I wanted to flaunt it, you know, parade around with her on my arm. That wouldn't have been a good idea.

"Do you think a seventh-grader can fall in love? I did. We learned about love together, slowly—there wasn't any rush. It was awesome. I couldn't believe how wonderful it felt to love somebody. Our sexual relationship evolved just the way it should, starting with little pecks. Then a couple of months later, we thought, well, maybe we can kiss each other and keep our mouths open. But don't stick your tongue in. Touch the skin above the bra, then under the bra. We talked about each step before it happened. We talked about actually doing it over four, five, six months. When we finally made love, I believed we had reached a very mature emotional level.

"We didn't tell anybody, even though people who did it were supposed to be cool, sophisticated. It was so special we kept it just between us.

"Even though I didn't know it then, it was intimacy I was experiencing with Mel. I don't think I had that again until James. And that's what I was trying to find again all those years.

"I thought my love for Melanie was going to overcome those other feelings, but it didn't, of course, so we broke up.

"High school was the hardest time of my life. I felt that the most popular, best-known person on campus would not be Japanese, so I devised a makeover: permed hair, blue contacts, a carefully calculated wardrobe, and under no circumstances would I eat rice in public. Inside I tossed and turned; the feelings were getting a lot stronger. To my friends, I was demanding, emotionally. I went from friend to friend, expecting them to give back what I was offering—constant presence and faithfulness. I was always frustrated.

"Then at the beginning of my sophomore year, I found a note on my locker. 'Gay Guy,' it read. Quickly, I got a new girlfriend and had sex with her to try to convince myself I was straight. It wasn't enough, and I couldn't even make myself feel what I'd felt with Melanie. I ended up hurting a very nice girl.

"I was fifteen years old. I figured, maybe guys don't feel anything when they're having sex. Maybe gay guys don't feel anything because they're men. But I had felt something good, close, and loving with Mel, except she was a girl. I knew what I wanted: to feel those things with a man.

"It got so I had to find out if that was possible. There was a joke going around school about a bar called Desperado's. Go there and see the fags.

"It all just kind of came together in the spring of 1983, toward the end of my sophomore year. Anne had a friend named George who made fake IDs. I asked him how he did it, and then I made one for myself. I arranged for George to drop me off at some house near the bar, acting like I was going to go inside. Then I walked to Desperado's.

"I was alone, nervous, shaking. Some man asked me to dance. I couldn't say no, because that wouldn't be nice, but I was so uncomfortable that after the dance was over I said thank you and left.

"I called George and asked him to pick me up. While I was walking back to the house, my heart was pounding. I wasn't supposed to be there—I was only fifteen, for one thing—but what hit me was that all those people were gay. I didn't know what to do with a whole bunch of people you know are gay. It was like, I belonged, because all of them had experienced the same feelings I had. But they were so much older. They weren't thinking about new clothes or homework.

"I went back again. It was more crowded, more people were dancing. I had something to drink: Nobody questioned my ID. It was getting easier.

"Pretty soon, I had two lives. School during the day, pep squad practice, biology tests. At night, as often as I could without my family and friends becoming suspicious, I went to gay bars. I drank more and more and felt more and more comfortable.

"People were having sex around Desperado's. I could feel it, but I didn't know for sure. Then one night I'd had a lot of beer, and I was in the bathroom. I saw this foot moving over to my side from the next stall. I thought, that's kind of weird. So I tapped my foot, to see if there was something he was trying to say, or was he just moving his foot? Then he motioned with his hand. Come here. I knelt down, and he pulled me toward him until I was flush against the wall of the stall, my lower body underneath. He performed oral sex on me. I didn't reciprocate.

"It was like the event just faded to black. I pushed everything down even more."

Guy stopped because the telephone rang.

"Do you want me to get it?" I asked.

"Yeah, then turn the ringer off, will you?" I ran upstairs and took a message for Jane. I returned to my place on the floor, but not before I gave Guy a little squeeze.

"I'm all right," he said. I nodded.

He pulled hard at the yarn loops, and then he held it up, and the weave of the afghan was loose and misshapen. Sighing, he let it fall to his lap.

"After that, there's a lot of fog in my memory. Other times with other men, but nothing like a relationship. Lots of drinking, fondling, rubbing, whatever. The hardest part was actually doing those kinds of things. It was easier to accept someone's doing it to me. If you're not doing it back, maybe you're not gay.

"Drinking was very important. I needed to cloud my judgment and become somebody I didn't really know.

"I didn't meet Mitch at a bar. He was a weight lifter, and we worked out at the same athletic club. The club was nice, but one time a man who I knew was married and had kids tried to touch me in the shower. I got out of there so fast. I thought, how can you do that? You're married, you're a father. You can't be gay, you can't want me. But it was a brief, fleeting moment, and he pretended he didn't know me after that.

"Mitch wasn't a hunk. He had muscle and was toned, but he needed to burn off fat to be good. He took me by surprise. Here was a guy who was totally butch, with this macho attitude. I never suspected he would be interested in me.

"I figured, this isn't Desperado's, he's thirty years old, maybe he wants a relationship. The first time was at my parent's house, in my room. I was lying there, and he started rubbing my back. He asked if that was okay with me. I said, yeah, that's fine. He said, are you sure?

"I don't know if he was asking permission. I only know he asked twice. That's how the initial contact was made. But I've always felt I made this choice.

"After that, he would call and I'd come over. He was nice, and the sexual things that were happening teased me, you know, gave me good feelings. Later, I thought about how I never kissed Mitch, and I always took my own clothes off. There's a difference, you know, when you kiss and help each other take your clothes off. It's the difference between romance and a sex session.

"One night he called and said come over, and I knew it was for sex. A lot of foreplay—the worst would be the oral stuff. There would be no penetration—I hadn't done that yet. I was waiting, I guess. I remember it was night. It was always night.

"When I got there, we went up to his room on the second floor of the house he lived in with his mom. We were together on the bed, and he was fondling me. It was musty, a stale-clothes smell. The sheets were clean, but not fresh like they'd just been washed.

"Suddenly, Mitch stopped. He went over and opened the closet, and there was a man in there. He brought him out and introduced him to me. Gary. He was in the Air Force. He was about twenty-five.

"I think I was hesitant, and Mitch said, it's okay, everything will be all right. I was looking at him, not really sure of what he expected to happen. The Air Force guy said not to worry, that he would get me ready. You have to relax, he said. He started to stimulate me sexually, around my rectum. Then I understood. I didn't resist in any shape or form, but I was afraid it was going to hurt.

"I don't remember much after that. Mitch watched, masturbating, I think.

"I went home feeling that I had given everything away. I had really wanted to do this with someone I care about. It was an underlying feeling—no consciousness at all.

"Two days must have gone by. It's kind of a blur. Then Mitch called and asked me to come over. I said I didn't think I wanted to. He asked me again, insisting. I said no. He offered me fifty dollars. I started to cry."

"Oh, Guy," I said, unable to hold back. I needed to say something. I couldn't chance him not understanding that I recognized it for what it was.

"You were raped."

"Yeah, that's what my father said."

I nodded, grateful not to be the first one, nor the only one, to have been allowed to view the remains of his past, exhumed after all these years. It was very difficult not to go to him right then, to gather him up and comfort him as I would my own child, hurting and fearful, needing to be told that everything would be all right.

Everything will be all right: For Guy, that had been the greatest lie of all.

"After that, I had sex with a lot of people. I did it all, thinking that allowing them to penetrate me was how I was going to grab them emotionally. One time, I don't remember who it was or the circumstances, but after he was done with me he said I had so much love to give, that I would be a really good boyfriend, or husband, for whoever took me up on it.

"So I would think, okay, if this one's not going to work, I'll try it with somebody else. More was better. It was wrong, morally wrong in my opinion, to have that many partners. What I was doing I was not at all proud of, and I thought I would never admit to any of it. But don't you see? My needs completely overwhelmed any judgment on my part.

"I started telling a few close friends I was gay. Anne was angry at first. Then the next day she came back and said it didn't matter. But for months, she acted like it mattered.

"Then I was HIV-positive. It hit me hard, yes, but I cast it aside, like a shirt that I tried on and rejected, because it just wasn't me. You asked me, was I worried about whom I infected? No. My priority was filling up the void, so I was never concerned about anybody else. It's not that I was out to deliberately infect people; it just wasn't on my mind. What was on my mind was getting my needs met.

"I thought Derek was going to be my first real relationship. I was very excited about it. Complete sex, all the time. I was blinded by the possibility that I had found what I was searching for, until Derek became possessive and insecure. I was a senior in high school, mind you. He was twenty-five and, as it turned out, emotionally and financially unstable.

"And then there was Keith—this gorgeous model—a god. Richie Rocket, my barber, introduced me to him at a party, and I fell instantly in love. I tried so hard with him. But he turned out to be as manipulative as Derek.

"Later, I found out he was positive. In fact, so is Derek. It used to be when my friends asked me how I got sick, I said it was a one-night stand with a bus driver. I was afraid for it to be someone I knew, someone I loved.

"Now, it would be a comfort." The hint of a smile visited Guy's mouth. He paused, obviously distracted by the thought, and the smile crept away quickly.

"Yeah," he resumed, "the day my mom walked in on us was the worst day of my life. Maybe even worse than the day I found out I was dying.

"Three months later, Greg died. I'm still angry at my mother for telling him about me and Derek. I wanted to tell him myself. And now they say he denounced me as his brother. That hurts so much. I try to focus on his letter, where he encouraged me and said I could still succeed. And our time in San Diego with him, when he still called me younger brother and it felt like nothing had changed. But now I'll always wonder.

"God, I missed him. I went to the DMV and said I was Greg Nakatani and I had lost my license. They gave me another one. My friends thought that was great. 'You look twenty-three,' they said. It wasn't so terrible, what I did, because every time someone thought I was Greg, the pain lessened, just a little.

"When Glen wrote to me after Greg died, he said he wished he could be home with me. I didn't wish that. He said he wished he'd spent more time with Greg. Too bad, I thought. He said things were really rough, whenever reality hit him. That part I understood.

"It always comes back to my oldest brother. When I was a sophomore in high school, I found out from a cousin that Glen was gay. I was furious that she had to tell me and that it hadn't been my parents. I also knew it must be something bad for them not to tell me.

"The only time I ever grieved for Glen was when I had to clean out his closet after he died. I turned on the light and started to look through his belongings, and then I broke down. I didn't want anyone to know I was crying, so I pulled the doors closed and hid there in the closet. I was surprised—he had some nice things, suits and ties and shoes, things I would have chosen. He had a little pile of CDs, and I took a few for myself. There was an old box of condoms. I laughed at that.

"Then, in the back of the closet behind his briefcase, I found a piece of Hawaiian artwork, a sculpture of three children, made of koa wood. One of the figures had a little chip, so I guess that's why it was in the closet. This is beautiful, I thought. Glen must have bought it because it reminded him of who we are.

"Suddenly, I was so angry at him. I wanted to scream and bang on the walls and destroy everything in the closet. I recognized everything. I recognized a life. I had to get out of there fast. I shoved everything to the back and slammed the closet door shut. I could still deny it."

The chocolate brown eyes, filling quickly, gazed at me. "I could still hide any evidence of our similarity." Guy blinked twice and his cheeks dampened.

"I remember the day after my mother caught Derek and me, my father came in to talk to me. He apologized for my mother. 'You're not just like Glen,' he said. God, I wanted to believe him. I wanted to explain about the feelings I was looking for, for him to reassure me that men can feel these things.

"But then he said, 'Maybe you aren't gay.' I don't really blame him. He knew I didn't want to be gay. Who would want that?

"He didn't know. I'm gay. Just like Glen. And I was dying. Just like Glen."

· · · ·

The afghan had slipped off our legs and lay discarded on the floor. Perhaps it was even hotter outside or the air-conditioner had given up; we just didn't need it anymore.

I felt many things. A great sadness, for the circles of ignorance and isolation that surrounded a family and slowly tightened their hold, a noose that choked away their lives. Anger, and shame, for the violence that had been done to Guy.

"It wasn't all your fault," I said, a little helplessly.

Tears poured down the face of the troubled little boy. "It's so hard for me to believe that. I let it happen, you know, so it had to be my fault."

"But they had no right to do what they did. They were the grown-ups, and you were a fifteen-year-old child. They took advantage of your youth and your vulnerability. They violated you in a hideous way. Even if you said you wanted it and begged for it, it would be their responsibility to take care of you."

Feeling utterly powerless, I watched Guy suffer. Hunched over, his body wracked with violent sobbing; he was grasping desperately at his chest. In that moment, I could almost hear his heart breaking, almost see a hole opening up, and the tube that fed him his medicine and kept his heart beating threatening to fall out.

"Guy," I said urgently, "there were so many things you couldn't control. It's okay to let go. It's okay."

His head jerked up, and his eyes seared into mine until I could feel the fire behind them.

"It's not okay, Molly! It's not okay at all. People are dying. I'm dying. I'm not okay with the decisions I've made, and I know some of this is not my fault, but until we all start being accountable for what's going on out there, it's not going to be okay."

"Yes," I stammered. "It's not okay. But you have to take a moment to separate yourself out . . ."

"I've been separated all my life!"

He made a sound, a low moan that didn't seem to be coming from him, really, like an injured animal was hiding nearby. It came to me that his spirit might be dying. But then, with great effort, he spoke.

"Oh, God. I just want to lie in my mom's arms and stay there forever. And stop, just stop. Sometimes I think, at least I'll have something to look forward to when I die."

"Don't die yet!" Through my panic, I experienced the odd sensation of my mouth opening and sounds continuing, although I had no
idea what to say next.

"I mean, uh, take another look, Guy. You're an amazing human
being. You've lived with more integrity and unselfishness in the past
few months than many people do in an entire lifetime. You know I'm
not making this up—you've made a difference. You've saved lives."

He seemed to be calming down. It wasn't that difficult to tell him
these things. They were obvious.

"You're very important." I pressed on. "And you've felt really good
about yourself. That's great. You should be proud of what you've done.
And you keep feeling that way, because, of course, you're right. You
deserve all the ovations you get. The past is . . . the past. Your accomplishments have surpassed all of that. You've moved beyond—"

I couldn't believe it. Guy was laughing.

"Take a breath, Mol."

"I'm just trying to tell you how I feel."

"You're doing a good job. My eyes are swollen."

"They're going to wonder what I've done to you."

We sat quietly for a while. I reached up and took his hand, entwin-
ing our fingers and squeezing tight, as if I might be able to melt us
together and he would believe me. He allowed the connection for a
while and then he smiled, pulling away gently—he didn't want to hurt
my feelings.

"I think of them," Guy said softly, "Aaron, Mitch, and Gary, and all
the others. They have to take responsibility for what they did. We all do.
But what is guilt and what is innocence? Maybe they discovered much
later than me that intimacy is what's missing, and that we're forced to
search for it in this tiny, scary space where we hope nobody sees us. We
all grew up in the same hateful world. Think about it, Molly. Maybe
they were even more troubled than I was."

Guy reached for the afghan and rearranged it over our legs. The
room had grown cold again, but we were okay.

IN FIRST PERSON

Sitting amid a pile of memories—photo albums, letters, reels of film taken with his old sixteen-millimeter camera—Alexander was enjoying himself. He felt better revisiting the past, now that the truth of what had happened to his family was taking focus. It was a recent comfort, a hesitant sense of calm still speckled with guilt and recrimination, tiny, broken rays of hope where he had thought the darkness to be inpenetrable and permanent.

I don't know when I first considered the idea that the fates of my three sons were somehow bound together. I know it terrified me. I was afraid I might be the connecting link.

I started thinking about it all the time. Had I made a mistake? Did I misperceive? I needed to know.

It became so clear. As much as I loved them, and I did love them so much more than I was ever able to communicate, I had fallen far short as a parent. Life dealt us lousy blows, but I had to own up to the part I played in it all.

My perceptions failed me, and for a person like me to have missed so much, to have unknowingly contributed to my sons' confusion and pain and isola- tion . . . don't you see? I participated in the problem, rather than the solution.

I understand now. Someone has to take responsibility for wreaking havoc on innocent lives. Our fear, our hatred, our collective ignorance— for God's sake, I was one of the voices of denigration. What's wrong with you? All the other boys are taking showers. Be a man. Stand up for what is rightfully yours. Don't act like a girl. Where's your substance? And worst of all I told them that failing meant dishonoring an entire family. Can you imagine what it was like for our sons to hear these things?

This is who I am, a person who needs to know what I did wrong so that the next time I'll manage the relationship better. The sad thing is that I have no children, no relationships left to manage.

Upstairs, the front door slammed. Alexander looked up to see his wife flying down the stairs toward him. Something must be up, he mused; her shoes were still on and evil spirits were being recklessly tracked into the house.

"People are so stupid," she announced, hands on hips.

"You're certainly right about that," he said, dumping over another box of photographs and spreading them out in front of him.

"No, Al, that's not what I mean."

He looked up.

"There was a story going around the faculty room about some mother who called up the school, hysterical, because we have a little girl in kindergarten who's tested HIV-positive and we didn't notify the parents."

"The school doesn't have to tell anybody."

"Apparently, our principal explained that to her. Laura also told this mother how bright the little girl is and that she knows exactly how to handle herself. If she falls down and scrapes her knee, she's supposed to call the teacher. She's not supposed to share her lunch, as if that would matter anyway. But just to be totally safe, this child and her parents have covered all the bases."

Jane flopped down in a chair. "You really should meet this little girl, Alexander. She's so cute, and to talk to her, you'd think she was much older."

"So what now?"

"We don't know yet. The mother was going to start a petition or go to the school board or something. She yelled at my principal on the phone, until Laura finally said she was going to have to hang up if she didn't calm down.

"Doesn't this woman know," Jane continued, "that HIV people are everywhere, on the street, standing next to her in the check-out line at the supermarket, serving her food at a restaurant? God, she'd probably die if she thought about that."

Their eyes met—yes, we didn't always know these things. No, we won't apologize anymore. We've earned a little righteousness.

"What are you doing, anyway?" Jane asked, surveying the floor.

"I'm visiting our kids," Alexander said brightly. Out of the corner of his eye, he saw his wife hesitate, gathering her courage. He handed her a photo—Glen, Greg, and Guy, as Count Dracula, Spiderman, and, in front of them, arms spread wide, a pint-sized tiger.

"Remember this?"

Laughing, she joined her husband on the floor. "I remember that Guy wanted to be Spiderman, like Greg. But Greg didn't want his younger brother to be the same thing he was, so Greg convinced Guy that what he really wanted to be was a tiger, but since we couldn't find a costume big enough, he was stuck with being Spiderman."

Al chuckled. "And I had thought Guy learned to be cagey from me. All the time it was Greg."

Jane sorted through the pile, searching for more-recent photographs. She finally found what she was looking for in a shoe box full of letters.

"Look, Al, these are from our trip to San Diego." She went through them slowly, handing them to her husband one by one. On the bottom of the pile, she found the photo that had been perched against the abalone shell on Greg's desk—Guy and Greg on the beach, arms around one another, heads thrown back in laughter, and her tears were instantaneous.

"I had so many hopes," she began. It was a recurring bitterness, one that Alexander recognized. "I never imagined things would turn out this way."

"How have they turned out, Jane?"

She turned to him, not understanding.

"Jane," he said gently. "I think we need to talk about what's happening."

She reached for the box of tissue next to the couch, blew her nose, and waited.

"Guy's finally being honest with himself. I think he's beginning to accept who he is."

She responded quickly, "He's mad at me."

"What do you mean?"

"He said that when I found him there with Derek, if I'd said it's okay to be gay, he wouldn't be sick."

"Oh, Jane." Alexander shook his head. "He was already sick."

"You don't know that for sure."

"Yes, I do. And so does he."

Jane sniffled and reached for another tissue.

"Anyway." Alexander began to arrange the photographs in stacks. "I don't think you committed the first sin. We'll give that one to me."

"What did you do?"

"Somewhere along the line, my kids got from me that they had to be perfect. My expectations placed tremendous pressure on Guy, and central to those expectations was his sexuality. He had a lot of reasons to believe that who he was would not be okay with me. It was as easy as that.

"And then he had this front runner Greg, macho and strong, and Glen, the antihero, acknowledged by the other two as being the most intellectually gifted. Glen left, and they made the pact. From that moment on, both he and Greg were locked in. It turned out to be a tragic promise, because it meant that in the future they could no longer come to us with anything they perceived would upset us. From that moment on, we were inaccessible.

"Things were much worse for Guy, because he was gay. On the outside, he hadn't disappointed us yet, but he knew he was a potential source. He had to push everything down even farther and keep that twenty-four-hour vigil at the closet door.

"When we discovered him, he was terrified that we'd reject him too. And we almost did."

Jane disagreed, "No, that was me. You were the one who went down the street and told him he could come home."

"But do you know what I did the next morning? I suggested that being gay was a mental illness."

"You did? I don't remember that."

Al took off his glasses and rubbed his eyes. "Then Greg died," he continued, "and Guy was right there, watching us break apart. By dying, Greg left Guy alone, the only one in charge of our destiny. How could he handle that, Jane? He had his secrets. He knew he was not doing what he was supposed to."

"It's good then," said Jane, "that he's telling the secrets now."

Alexander nodded.

"My God, Al, no one should have to go to his grave feeling that badly about themselves and what they did."

"You're right. I think of Glen. I never had a chance to acquit him, to raise him up. He never asked for anything from me, much less my unconditional acceptance. On that last night, I was able to say to him that I was sorry I wasn't a better father. He didn't give me anything back but a smile. He was dying, so he had other things on his mind. But a smile was everything.

"And now, with Guy . . ." Jane watched the soft lines around her husband's mouth quiver. "Please," he whispered, "I want something more than a smile." His head dropped, and a pair of tears spilled to the floor.

After a moment, he again spoke with a strong, clear voice.

"He's pierced the silence that has devastated this family, and, my God, I'm encouraging him. Don't you see? By speaking honestly of his past, he allows us back in. Finally, the pact has been broken. He's told us what's been bothering him, even if it hurts us.

"That's what's different. We can say we're sorry. We can do it right; we can tell him, 'Guy, it's okay to be gay. Guy, it wasn't all your fault.'"

Jane spoke up, continuing the litany. "Guy, we're so proud of you. We love you. You've always been everything a son could be."

Alexander choked back a sob, and they reached for each other. All around them, the air stilled, as if their embrace deserved a moment of silence; the spirits that dwelled in the house having come to honor them. And, sure enough, when they finally parted, there had been a change, and though they never spoke of it, they understood it had occurred.

. . . .

Jane and Alexander gathered the mementos of their family and replaced them lovingly in their boxes. Jane lingered over one last photograph: Glen, in a short-sleeve white shirt, standing on a road, the island of Maui behind him.

"Why is it," she said, fingering the image of her oldest son, "that I so easily assigned homosexuality to Glen?"

Alexander looked at her, marveling at the question.

"If you mean," he said slowly, "that his crimes against the family and the community relegated him to some dark side, then I guess I did that, too."

"I wasn't surprised he was gay," she went on, "not the way I was shocked at Guy. I imagined back alleys and drug dealers. You remember, I talked about expecting to get a call that he was dead."

Jane put the photo in the box and then picked it back up and placed it in her pocket. "I can't believe the way I acted."

They started up the stairs and turned into the kitchen. Anne had taken Guy to the doctor; they would be home soon. James would also be there for dinner, a meal that they would prepare together.

"We say we love our children," said Jane, opening the refrigerator and peering inside. "But we don't love them enough."

. . . .

It had been a week since Guy shared his story with me, the real story, not the one he'd imagined I'd be interested in, but the one he'd been afraid of, the one that ultimately liberated him.

Revelation Day, as I now referred to it, had left me shaken. A long talk with Alexander and Jane relieved my anxiety somewhat. I was not to blame for Guy's two-day bout with depression. It was time, they reassured me, for Guy to give himself away.

Nevertheless, as far as Guy and I were concerned, I felt it was his move. Finally, I received the summons, as I had so many times before.

Now, he stood at the top of the stairs, regarding me with amusement.

"You look guilty. Well, you shouldn't be. You shouldn't feel bad that I'm a mess. I've hardly been eating. I'm probably going to die soon. But don't worry about it. Come up here."

When I walked into his bedroom, he motioned for me to join him on his bed. A good sign, I thought, remembering the sacredness of his comforter. He lowered himself onto the down.

"Lean back," he commanded. "Close your eyes."

This wasn't what I expected, but I did as I was told.

"Envision, if you would, a warehouse that has been broken into apartments, and we're in the one on the second floor with the high ceilings and lots of windows. It feels open, and there's beautiful, polished wood floors and no furniture. Like a dance studio. Are you there?"

"Um hum," I murmured, busy imagining.

"On one side, the windows go all the way up the wall, and when the sun hits just right, the rays of light sparkle across the floor. Imagine a person by the window, the sun's coming through, and he's sitting with his arms around his knees pulled up close to his body. Go in closer. He's rocking a little bit, and you think it might be a child. But it's not, really. There's nothing wrong with him; he's just comforting himself."

"Are you the child, Guy?" I asked.

He was quiet for a moment.

"Yes."

"Do you want me to do something, go to him? Can I help?"

"Just look at him for a while. You'll see that he's going through a lot of insecurity and fear and confusion right now. That's what he feels like inside."

Suddenly, Guy sat up. I opened my eyes and raised up onto my elbows, watching him. "What I envision," I offered, "is lonely, this place, and, despite the sun coming in the windows, it's cold. The first thing I want to do is embrace the child, because I know he's troubled."

His eyes filled and his voice began to break. "I know how he feels."

I wondered which troubled child to address first. "Is it like you're watching a movie? Or are you blending together, you and the child?"

"It's never been hard to stay separate before. If I ever started to remember, I could handle it. I could just list the events, and I could address them and think about them, because it was like it wasn't me. It happened in the past."

"And now?"

"Now it's different. I look at the little boy and I want to cry, because the little boy is me. I can't disconnect anymore; the feelings just overwhelm me and pretty soon there isn't any safe distance between who I am now and who I've always been. I'm not in third person anymore, you know what I mean?"

"Yes, I do."

We sat next to each other, our shoulders touching, staring straight ahead. Finally, Guy said, "It scares me to talk to you."

"You don't need to say anything else."

"I know. There really isn't anything else to say. But it's just the feeling, of not knowing what's going to come out next or what I'll remember next and what I'm going to have to face next. I don't ever want to feel that way again."

"That would really scare me too."

"So I told my mom the other day, it's over. I'm tired of thinking and analyzing. I'm going to finish up with my work here and move to Hawaii. I always get better there."

"I think that's a good choice, Guy. You don't need to waste time thinking about it anymore."

"Right. I'm glad it came out before I died. I would hate to have died unenlightened. And I regret my behavior. It made me sick. But I didn't have many choices."

Guy stood up and I followed. I watched while he worked on the bedspread, smoothing it until all the wrinkles had disappeared, until it looked like we'd never been there.

Guy reached for a tissue from the box on top of his dresser. He glanced up at himself in his mirror, and at me, standing behind him. "I feel better now," he said, giving me a grin. His eyes moved back to his own image, and he leaned forward and tilted his face toward the mirror, running his hand over his chin.

"You know, I'm surprised I'm not breaking out over all this. Normally, when I'm this anxious, I break out."

• • • •

Guy never really "talked" to me after that day. And from then on, I no longer "interviewed" any of them. They continued to accompany Guy on his journey, and I went along, too, no longer the recorder of events, the journalist who sits with the candidate on the campaign train at the end of the day, getting the inside story that will humanize him for the rest of the world. That part was over. We were still on the train, Guy and his family and an assortment of friends and supporters, but somewhere in the middle of the night in the private quarters, the old goals, to win a race with death and educate the entire world, had been abandoned. It was a great relief.

I no longer had an excuse to be around, and I felt the need to ask permission to be included, even as more-frightening times loomed ahead. But they seemed unaware of my insecurity, and whenever I showed up, I was heartily welcomed.

"Where have you been?" Jane demanded when she found me on her doorstep after a five-day absence, "and since when do you knock?" Her questions, and the mock indignation with which they were delivered, were exactly what I needed to hear.

I was still an honored guest, but the nature of my visits changed, as I spent less time on the floor of the den and more around the slightly tilted kitchen table. Parenthood linked me deeply with Alexander and Jane, and constant, incalculable grief passed between us without resistance, soothed by the balm of our conversations.

With great tenacity, Guy held on to his life. For five weeks, beginning the day school started in September 1993, he shared his message again, honoring the commitments he had made as far back as January of that year. Sitting in a wheelchair, he spoke to larger and larger groups of students, unable to cope with anything more than a single morning session every few days. Between engagements, he suffered, complaining constantly of pain and exhaustion, his moods shifting unpredictably and harshly.

One morning in early October, Guy declared to the household that it was time for him to go back to Maui. "I still see the light, but it's getting dimmer," he told a quiet table over breakfast. "I know this is the first time you've heard me talk this way, but I've had it. No more. I've got to recoup. I can't do that here. I only get worse."

Alexander stood up and walked around the table to where his son was sitting. "Everyone will understand," he said, his hands settling gently on Guy's shoulders, his words floating over his son's head toward a tearful Jane and a silent James. "You've given and given, and now it's time to take something for yourself."

Guy smiled and leaned his head sideways until his cheek met his father's hand. "Thanks, Dad," he murmured.

Alexander called off the rest of Guy's fall speaking engagements, except for Saratoga High School, where he was scheduled to return for a third follow-up session during December.

"I promise I'll make that one," Guy told Pam Dunnett over the phone. "You helped me get started. I won't let you down."

Anne wasn't sure that Guy would ever come back. "You're not just visiting Hawaii this time, Guy. You're moving there."

Guy explained it in terms of airplanes. "I used to start my round-trip flights in San Jose. People in Hawaii would bring me over there to speak. Now I'll start in Hawaii, and schools will bring me back here to talk with them. I think it'll be cheaper that way, too."

Anne gave him a look of bewilderment. "I can't give you massages from two thousand miles away," she said crossly. Their eyes held for a moment, until Guy looked away, and Anne felt the unusual presence of vulnerability in their conversation.

"I have to change starting points. I can't start here anymore. Do you understand?"

Anne reached for his hand, but he grasped his wheelchair firmly and rolled away from her.

"You can visit me, Annie. By the time you come, I'll be doing much better. Hey," he said, giving his chair a wobbly half-twirl, "maybe I'll be able to toss this thing."

Anne went to James. "He thinks he's going to recover. He's living in a dream world."

James wondered if Anne was right. Guy spent almost all his time in his wheelchair now, too weak to walk more than a few steps without stopping to catch his breath.

"He's going to die," she wailed, "and I won't even be there."

James tried to comfort her, but he had other things on his mind. The problem is not that Anne might not be there, he thought. The problem is that James might not be there.

Guy expected that whenever he moved, James would move with him. They had been discussing the possibility for months, and initially James had gone along, because going along was easier than arguing with Guy. Better to invite a tsunami into the bedroom, he thought wryly.

That trip to Hawaii was our last wonderful time. When we laughed and teased each other, I remembered how it used to be. There was even a little kiss here and there, so long as he leaned first, but if I was the one to reach for him, I'd be in trouble. I told myself it was all right. I hadn't liked sex very much before Guy; I could hate it again.

That fall, I threw myself into two jobs. I went back to work part-time with the handicapped, and Nordstrom was still full-time, full-blast. We were gearing up for the Christmas buying season, and I was already counting the money I was going to make. I also worked out at the gym, because I was getting flabby. I was hardly ever home.

I could tell Guy was upset with me about being gone so much. In the back of my mind, I knew he was getting sicker. Everything was changing. I was finally independent, just when he was needing more and more. He knew it and I knew it, but we weren't talking.

Guy called Nordstrom and asked the store manager, an old friend of his, to hold James' job during an extended leave of absence.

"Guess what, James?" Guy greeted him at the door the evening he had announced his decision.

"Let me get inside, Guy," James' voice displayed a nasty tone. He knew what was coming, and he could feel his blood begin to boil before Guy got the words out.

"Norma says you can have a leave for as long as you want, and you'll have a job when you come back. Of course, she knows you're going to be with me . . ."

James brushed by him and went upstairs, taking the steps two at a time. He knew he wasn't being fair, because Guy would get out of his wheelchair and with great difficulty follow him up the stairs. Wrestling with his feelings, he commanded himself to stay put and stood in the middle of their bedroom, listening for the sound of Guy half-crawling up the steps.

Guy leaned against the doorway, panting. "That wasn't very nice, James," he snarled.

"I know. I'm sorry. But you shouldn't have done that."

"Done what?"

"Called Norma. That was for me to do."

Guy dropped down onto the bed, rubbing his knees. "I've been waiting for you to call Norma. I didn't want to wait any longer. We've got to make plans."

"If I take a leave, I might have a job when I come back, but I sure as hell won't be an assistant manager."

Being promoted to assistant manager was the most exciting thing that had ever happened to James. It was a goal that Guy had urged him to set, and now, just when everything was falling into place, James couldn't believe he was being asked to give it all up.

"I'm finally there, Guy. This is what you wanted for me."

"It won't be that hard to start over again," Guy argued. "I did it, after the leather jacket thing at Woodside. I was a manager again in two months."

"I'm not you. I've had to work harder to get where I am. The holiday selling season is coming; you know it's not a good time for an assistant manager to take off. And the thought of starting over, well, I don't know if I could do that."

Guy narrowed his eyes and went in for the kill.

"Would you do it for me, James? Do you think you could take some time off for me to die?"

What I remember most about moving into the Nakatani family was having dinner every night and everybody talking about death. I'd never talked about it once, in my whole life, and now all of this terrified me. I tuned out regularly.

On several occasions, they even talked about euthanasia. Guy was going to decide that the time had come to end it, and his father was going to help him. They discussed all the different ways they could do it. The discussion went on, night after night, until Jane announced she was going to get a machine gun and take care of them both.

All along, I never faced it. When he started getting sicker, I started pulling away, and Guy started pulling me back. When he announced we were moving, I kept saying that I didn't want to lose my position. That was true. But what was more true was moving meant Guy was dying, and as hard as I tried I couldn't imagine, not in a million years, going through it.

James sat on the edge of their bed, concentrating on untying his shoes. Guy struggled to his feet, bracing himself on the chair next to his desk. He looked down at James.

"Well?"

One shoe and then the other hit the floor with a thud. James hung his head, aware, as he had been many times before, of the power of Guy's presence. He's Superman, James would imagine, able to view my deepest feelings with x-ray eyes or overcome me easily with the pure strength of his will. Sitting there on the bed, he tried not to betray himself with a feeling or even the slightest movement, buying time, holding on to what was left of himself.

Slowly, James raised his head to meet Guy's gaze. The best offense, he reminded himself, was a good defense.

"I love you."

Guy's face softened momentarily. James watched while Guy thought this over for a few seconds, until the lines across his forehead constricted again and the fire in his eyes returned.

"What does that mean?" Guy demanded.

"It means that I love you."

"I love you, but what?"

James took a breath and stood up. He was an inch taller than Guy and he needed the advantage.

"I love you and I want to be with you, but I don't want to lose my position. Isn't there some way we can work this out?"

"There are places in Hawaii that carry Nordstrom shoes."

"I don't want to sell shoes."

The tsunami hit.

"You say you love me," Guy raged, "but you don't love me as much as your job. You say you want to be with me, but not enough to sell shoes for a couple of months."

James flinched, and Guy started to cry.

"That's right, James. The way I feel right now, I don't have very much time left. I had thought we would spend my last days together."

James took a tentative step toward him, and Guy met him, allowing himself to be gently enfolded in his lover's arms. His sobbing intensified, and James ran his fingers through his hair, murmuring to him as he would a child.

"It's okay, Guy. Don't cry. I'll come with you."

James felt Guy's body relax in his arms. His tears reduced to a sniffle, he pulled back and smiled at James. "I knew you would move with me."

"Not until after Christmas, Guy. I can't miss Christmas."

The grin disappeared, but Guy nodded, the irony coming to him quickly: I've created a monster.

· · · ·

Whenever anyone asked me, "How's the Nakatani family?" I had to refrain from responding, "Shrinking." Five to four to three, the numbers always came to mind. Inside, I contended they were still a family, that James and Anne helped to swell their numbers again, that even my presence, and the constant support of endless others, filled the house on Copeland Place with the stubborn sounds of life.

That Guy was dying was not a shock, not at all. Yet I found myself struggling with the truth, hauling it around with me like a heavy sack, as if anything less obvious might not remind me constantly, and I would be stunned and hurt after all.

Guy and I were uncomfortable. What had begun as a collaboration had mutated into a confession, and although we never spoke of it, I felt that we had left a friendship inside the darkened box where I had listened to his whispered recollections. It had been no different, I remembered from my Catholic childhood: I told my secrets to someone who was supposed to be a friend, whose face I knew, but who was lost to me once we began the ritual: "Bless me Father, for I have sinned . . ." For a while afterward, I would avoid the priest's eyes, even when he looked at me with affection. It was as wrong to me now as it had been then.

I came by to see him the night before his departure for Maui. It was raining, and in the entryway I propped up my umbrella and shed my coat and shoes. Anne appeared, embracing me quietly and pointing downstairs. It had been a bad day, she informed me.

Guy was lying on his side on the rug in front of the television. He didn't look up when I padded across the floor in my stocking feet, and I thought he might be asleep. His eyes were closed, his hair flopped across his forehead, his Polo sweatshirt, once carefully selected and proudly worn for fashion, now folded him in warmth and comfort. I curled up behind him and began to rub his back, very gently. Through the thickness, my fingers hunted for a softer piece of skin, one not next to bone.

"Hello," he said, and when I leaned over to see his face, he smiled.

"Hello." I waited.

"That feels nice."

I settled back down behind him, stroking his neck and the back of his head. The lingering scent of massage oil hung around us like incense, and I knew that Anne had been here.

"Rest up in Hawaii, Guy. Be good to yourself."

"Hmm."

Slowly, my fingers pulled away, until only a few strands of his black hair connected us. I lay listening to him breathe.

"I'll be talking to you," I whispered, rising carefully.

"Okay."

I sat on the top step and put my shoes back on. Laughter drifted in from the kitchen, where Jane, Alexander, James, and Anne might have been waiting for me, but I wanted to slip away. I wanted to examine what had just happened between us, to glorify the moment perhaps, to make it into a memory that would prove our friendship, despite everything.

From the floor of the den, I heard something.

"Molly?" Guy was calling me.

I went back down. He was still lying on his side, his eyes reaching up for me. He placed his hand on the floor in front of him, and I lowered myself down until we were facing each other, one arm crooked, our heads resting sideways on our hands. I felt the way I did when I held each of my babies, when time had no power and the world was held away by innocence.

His eyes fluttered a little as he took a breath. "I love you," he said, with much more sincerity than energy. "And I appreciate you."

He grinned, and I grinned back. Inside, I was tingling, my feelings for him spreading quickly through my body like a strong, numbing drug.

"I love you too," I said simply, holding back, as if I might bruise him with the surprising strength of my affection. "You're one of the best things that ever happened to me."

His smile broadened. "You're one of the best things that ever happened to me, too."

I touched his face and committed it to memory. "See you soon," I said. "God bless you."

"Ten times," he sighed.

He didn't move when I leaned over and kissed him. I ran up the stairs, past my umbrella and through the front door, losing my race with a torrent of tears just as I reached my car. In the rain, I cried for

Guy and his brothers, and for his mother and father and all of us, saints and sinners that we are, victims and executioners of our own inhumanity. And the heavens opened up and cried with me.

DYING WELL

Alexander and Guy moved to the house on Kea Road during the second week of October. Alexander wondered how it would be, just father and son and the disease—the third person in the house, with whom he would also have to struggle for control. He looked forward to January, when Jane would join them. Whether or not Guy would return to speak to Saratoga High School or whether the rest of us would ever see him again were questions left unanswered.

Alexander and Jane spoke every night on the phone.

"You won't believe what he made me do."

"What now," Jane laughed, anticipating a good story.

Alexander had been in the kitchen, trying to fix a broken burner on the stove, when he heard Guy calling to him from his bedroom. Alexander found him sitting in his wheelchair, frowning, his closet spread wide open in front of him.

All the way over on the plane, Guy worried about how wrinkled his clothes were going to be, so I hung them up the moment we arrived.

The next day, he called me into his room. Well, Dad, he said, we need to colorize and texturize. I didn't understand right away. I thought he wanted me to paint the closet.

But no. First he said the doors were too heavy. Down came the doors. Then he directed me where to hang the shirts, in order of color and texture within the color, and I realized we were re-creating his closet. First shirts, left to right, then trousers. All the greens together, the cooler stuff on the left, wools on the right, jackets last. I pretty much knew where everything went already, because of all the times I'd had to fetch things for him at home.

Order was very important to him. Probably because he felt so disordered himself. I just went along. At that point, I felt it was my job to please him. Within reason.

Jane found hope in the closet story. It meant that Guy was settling in, continuing his life, planning a future. She couldn't wait to join them.

"You two better have the doors back up by the time I get there."

Her husband groaned. "Have you seen those doors? They weigh a ton, and the screws are so old and rusty, I had only to turn the screwdriver a little bit and they broke apart. The doors fell off, Jane. And besides, do you want to be the one to fight Guy?"

"No," Jane admitted. "It's just, oh, God, that house . . ."

Alexander laughed and got to the point. "Don't worry, dear. The bathroom will be perfect when you arrive."

Other problems were not so easily fixed.

I don't know how it happened. Just the two of us in the house—I was there to be his slave, obviously. It got so I was doing everything for him, until one day I was overwhelmed. He became very angry, because I was acting overwhelmed, so he said if I was going to behave that way, he didn't want me doing anything for him anymore.

So I didn't. For two days, he tried to wheel himself around, and I could see him cringing in pain and becoming so frustrated. I felt very bad, but I held off, because he needed to work this out for himself.

I was outside when I heard him yelling for me. I found him in the kitchen, his wheelchair stuck between the refrigerator and the table. Of course, I helped him, and he said thank you, almost to himself really. I knew enough not to rub it in.

I had been running back and forth, doing it all. The one time I couldn't handle it anymore, he called me on it. He literally set out to punish me, and it almost worked. As a parent, it was a terrible moment for me.

One night, with Alexander out of earshot, Guy called his mother.

"I bought a new watch, Mom." As he might have convinced a customer at Nordstrom a few years before, he described it for her in glowing terms. "Do you think Dad might want it, you know, after?"

"I don't know, Guy. Why don't you ask him?"

"I was thinking you could ask him."

"What's going on, Guy?"

"I was thinking if Dad wants the watch, he can pay half now."

The next day, it was barely dawn in Hawaii when Alexander answered the phone.

"He wants to know if you want his new watch," Jane reported.

"Doesn't he want it?"

On that day, I had been aware of the purchase—the price of the watch and the credit card that bought it. I ignored it all.

It had been a good day. We were out and about, chatting about all kinds of things while I wheeled him around. It was just so nice, the two of us, no tension. He was looking at the watch in a jewelry store, and I could tell he might buy it. So I went outside. I gave myself that, you know, a moment of looking away.

I was worn down. Maybe I would have been able to talk to him about some of his thinking, like any father would, if he had not been ill. I was looking for a way to discuss integrity, but somehow, his dying precluded that.

When I wasn't with Guy, grief was my only companion, and I wasn't going to get much guidance from those feelings.

· · · ·

Back in San Jose, rumors were circulating that Guy would be living on Maui from now on. But just as the news was settling, he changed the plan. Guy would fly home the day before Thanksgiving and surprise

James. They would all be together for Christmas and then move to Hawaii for good.

There was no shortage of confusion over this new development. Guy's urgent flight to Maui had leaned heavily on each of his loved ones; it had been presented, anointed, as his last opportunity for quality of life. Now he seemed equally as obsessed with leaving the island and returning to James and to six weeks of chilling cold.

"He talks about James all the time," Alexander told Jane. "He came up with this idea of surprising him and, assuming something catastrophic doesn't hit him between now and Thanksgiving, he won't change his mind."

Jane agreed. His will would be the last thing to go.

Alexander didn't know what to say. Guy wasn't sliding downhill as quickly as he had been back before they went to Maui, but he wasn't getting any better—a detail their youngest son chose to ignore.

"Things are really turning around for me here," he wrote to Anne. And on the other side of the ocean, his old friend allowed herself a solitary moment of hope.

Alexander never challenged Guy's denial, yet he worried about other moments, when Guy moved so far out of touch with reality that his father wondered if the deadly CMV virus had begun to invade his brain. "He really believes he's getting better," he told Jane.

Was it hope or madness? I wanted so much to believe, as he did, that despite his rapid descent we had found one more plateau, firm ground where we could let down our guard just a little longer, assured that it wasn't yet his time.

But there were other signs, moments when I shuddered to think what might be happening to my son. Dad, he asked one day in the drugstore, sitting in his wheelchair, trying to write a check for a collection of body lotions and oils that he just had to have, How do you spell twelve?

Or when he talked like a child or whimpered and moaned in a new, disturbing way, unable to control the noises that came out of him. I felt like I was losing him then, as if all the wonderful things Guy had become were

*in terrible jeopardy, being sucked out of our hiding place even while I ran
to shut the windows and barricade the doors.*

The day before Thanksgiving, unbeknownst to James, Guy flew
home to the house on Copeland Place. That evening, he positioned a
few dozen friends and family members in the living room and told
them to act normal while he hid around the corner.

"What are you all doing here?" said James, understandably per-
plexed by the mob scene just inside the front door. Forgetting Guy's
instruction, a room full of eyes directed James toward the kitchen.

"What are you doing here?" he was heard to say again, and the conspirators made new conversation, conscious of the ambush that had
befallen James, and hopeful that Guy would not be disappointed. When
the pair emerged a moment later, properly beaming, they breathed a
collective sigh of relief.

*I was surprised and nervous for a few minutes, like everything had
changed, and Guy and I didn't really know each other and had never been
lovers. The audience in the living room didn't help.*

*When I saw how excited he was to surprise me, I got very excited, too.
Suddenly, everything was clear. He'd decided to come back to me, to support my career, and I would make him better, along with his family and
our friends. I had known all along that we could do as much for him as
warm weather and clear air.*

*I was so happy. We didn't talk about it for a couple of weeks, until one
morning he announced he'd made reservations to go back, forever, on
January 5. He said not to worry about the money for my ticket. He'd taken
care of it.*

December 1993. A month riddled with difficulties. Any other dying
person would have remained properly housebound, but Guy wanted to
go to the mall every day, except for Wednesdays, when his weekly eye
shot left him blurry and exhausted.

Preparing for a day of shopping was a lengthy ordeal for Guy's caregivers. He could no longer shower alone, and, after several unpleasant adventures with sponge bathing Alexander, Jane, James, or Anne simply climbed into the shower with him, following his instructions for washing his back and legs or shampooing his hair.

Dressing him began with his diaper, a cruel reminder of his state that set Guy's mood for what would follow. Outfits had to be carefully coordinated, and Guy changed his clothes several times a day and changed his mind several times each dressing. He would sit on his bed and bark orders, challenge the ideas of the weary dressers, and belittle anyone who accessorized badly.

The end product was Guy, dressed to the teeth, complete with hat, fur-lined boots, and leather gloves. Warming packets were placed inside the boots and the gloves, because AIDS had ravaged his circulatory system, creating a painful frostbite-like condition in his extremities.

At the shopping mall, trips to the bathroom were frequent and disastrous. If whoever was wheeling him happened to run into an obstacle, Guy pounced on them indignantly. He tired quickly. His helpers deemed the excursion a success if they actually spent a longer time at the mall than they had preparing him to shop or if no one had been publicly scolded.

"Just because he's dying, he doesn't have the right to treat us this way," Alexander told Jane when they huddled in their bedroom one afternoon.

"He needs to be in control, Al," she retorted quickly, reflecting her own frustration. "He's dealing with one piece of bad news after another."

"I know that. Don't you think I know that? Try living with him alone for a month. He's definitely still in control."

Sometimes I felt so alone. Was I the only one who was concerned about the quality of his dying? He had come so far with his living, and now it was all falling apart.

To make matters worse, Jane defended him. They were collaborators, just as they had always been, while I hopped around like a fool, trying to get someone to tell the truth.

Alexander sat down on the bed, deciding whether or not to simply let the tears come.

Jane walked over to her dresser and opened a drawer. She stared inside for a moment.

"Oh, Al," she conceded quietly, "you're right."

He regarded her gratefully. "You know what I'm really worried about? He's spending money he doesn't have, running up his charge cards, knowing he won't be around to pay."

Her back still to him, she pushed the drawer shut. "At first," she agreed, "I thought he would stop, once he reached a certain point. He's always known when to stop."

Leaning forward, Alexander propped his elbows on his knees and dropped his head into his hands.

Jane spoke to him softly. "Maybe his brain has been more affected than we think."

Her husband glanced up. "There's no doubt in my mind. The extreme moods, the baby talk, the forgetfulness—it's as though, not all the time, just sometimes, he's retreating to his childhood, forgetting what he learned about how adults act in the world."

Nodding, she walked toward him.

"You know," Alexander continued, "the doctor says those damn eye shots aren't doing any good."

"So that means," said Jane slowly, joining him on their bed, "he might as well stop them."

"And he might even feel better, just for a few weeks, with less medication."

"But he'll go blind."

"Yes. If he lives that long." They were silent then, hesitating, as they did sometimes to admit anything more out loud, in case giving voice to their fears could shape the future.

Al said finally, "I had always imagined it was good, putting that medicine right in his eye, so close to his brain. Now, without the gancyclovir, the CMV might really go wild."

"Oh, God. The dementia was always what he was most afraid of."

Sitting side by side, neither of them cried. For Alexander, the threat of tears had passed; he needed to be reasonable. Once the problems facing them were clear in his mind, it would be up to him to propose a plan that would respond to the new crisis. He would have to be sensitive to the feelings of the others; he would be the calm voice in the storm.

Jane, for the moment, felt nothing. The bottom of her emotional well was dry. She knew it was rare and temporary; she understood the pattern of her feelings. In no time, a clear vision of their reality would reenter her, and she would fill again, quickly and harshly, her tears loosening, spilling relentlessly and uncontrollably, from the raw, stinging interior of her soul.

THIS IS MY SON

Where once Christmas had been a grand event in the Nakatani house, that year, 1993, saw no fanfare, no mound of presents cascading out from under the tree, just here and there, some things of meaning. Jane received more than one frog: a frog charm on a gold chain, a frog key chain, a frog soap dish for the bathroom.

"I take frogs to Vegas with me," one friend explained.

"I should have started collecting them sooner," Jane remarked.

Guy gave me a bead necklace that he had made, an antique gold sun surrounded by brown and yellow eye-beads, named for the blue eyes in their centers. I had searched in vain for a gift for Guy.

"I thought I was getting a book about me," he teased, "you know, *A Guy Named Guy*. I was really looking forward to it."

"I'll hurry," I promised, and we exchanged a weighted gaze, until Guy nodded and looked away.

• • • •

The morning of January 4, 1994, Guy fulfilled his promise to Saratoga High School. Alexander and Guy waited to be introduced near the side door under a basketball hoop, the father with his backpack of his son's supplies, and Guy in his wheelchair, dressed in jeans and

265

several heavy sweaters. He was concentrating on putting his gloves back on, which he had pulled off to rearrange his red plaid hat.

"You look like Arnold Palmer," his father told him.

"Who's he?" said Guy, keeping a straight face.

The entire student body and faculty were present, as well as Guy's support group, which included his parents, Pam and Bob Dunnett, Anne, and me. When it was time, the lights dimmed, except for a spotlight in the middle of the floor. Alexander slowly wheeled his son into the bright light, his hand on Guy's shoulder. It would be the last introduction, the last public declaration of his feelings.

"This is my son, Guy Nakatani, who has brought honor to our family's name."

The room exploded. Guy reached up and touched his father's hand before Alexander backed away. Guy smiled and looked around him while the audience stood and cheered.

When I was in Maui in November with my Dad, I told myself if I ever have a chance to speak to kids again, I'll tell them that I love them and respect them, and I want them to know they're okay. I'd tell them to open up to their parents.

If things had been different, I would have done just that. I know in a heartbeat I would have. There wasn't anything I couldn't talk to my parents about other than my sexuality. I didn't want that connection with Glen.

You're okay, you're loved—the thought of being able to say these things to kids was so overwhelming, I just broke down and cried.

It took a long minute before the room was quiet.

"I'll tell you," he began, "you guys know how to do it right. I picked this school for my last talk because I love you guys the most."

Another minute of pandemonium shook the room.

"Okay," he continued, when the cheering stopped. "I'd better get organized here." Guy stopped to look down on his lap at his notes.

"He's never had to have notes before," Jane whispered.

Guy looked up. "If anyone here hasn't seen me before, you can interrupt me if you don't get it. For those of you in the back, I can't see so you've got to yell or something. I thought we'd just talk. You can ask me questions. Anything you want, just like always.

"But first, why am I here? I'm here because I want to continue showing you that things don't get better with this disease. They get worse. And it's going to keep getting worse. I need to warn you that I'm very emotional now. So if I can't make it all the way through this . . ." Guy stopped and gulped, and all of us on the bench held our breaths. ". . . My dad's going to cover for me 'til I get it back together."

Guy wheeled himself forward slightly. "What's changed? A lot of things have changed for me since I saw you last. You see this wheelchair? I live in it. I have to be wheeled around in my own home." His voice was getting stronger; he would find a way to perform, one more time.

"My body? It works to keep me warm. I have this circulatory problem and nerve damage, so only the main part of me stays warm. My hands and my feet are always cold and very, very sore. That's why you see me flexing my hands inside my gloves. I'm trying to stay warm. I can't walk, I can't stand on my own, really, and I can't open my hands all the way."

There was a long pause, while Guy looked down at the sheet of paper on his lap, and then absently at the crowd.

"Uh-oh," Anne said softly. "He's losing it."

Finally, he grinned. "I'm trying to remember what I'm supposed to be doing."

"You're okay, Guy," said a girl in the front row.

He nodded. "You're right. As I was saying, I can't really do anything. Do you remember what I told you the last time I was here? I said there would come a time when I wouldn't be able to wipe my own butt. Well, I'm at that point." Guy stopped to sniffle. "I can no longer wipe my own butt. I have to wear diapers, all the time, because I take in so much medicine, sometimes I can't control what comes out of me."

"I burp, I fart, I poop, I puke," he recited, "in front of everybody. I don't care who you are, if I gotta do it, I'm gonna.

267

"Believe it or not, that's my life. For entertainment?" His arm swept the room feebly. "You're my entertainment. Can't go to movies—can't hold up my head long enough.

"There's one thing that still gives me pleasure in life." He glanced at his mother. "Well, actually, two. I still shop! I love shopping and spending money. And I hang around with the people I love. I've got my mom and my dad."

Guy turned our way again and his voice began to tremble. "I talk to them constantly. You should try talking to yours, by the way. And my two friends. That's it. They make me happy. Any questions?"

"How do you feel today, Guy?" came a shout from the back.

"Pretty shitty. Oh, am I allowed to say that?"

The laughter was warm and pleasant; the audience was relaxing. Guy squinted out into the darkness that held the sea of people around him.

"Yeah?" he said, pointing and listening to the question.

"What's wrong with my legs?" Guy stopped to chuckle. "Nothing, other than they're skinny little chicken legs and my feet can't carry them around anymore. It's the nature of the disease. My friend hates that—I say it all the time. That's how we PWAs explain everything: It's the nature of the disease."

A murmur rose here and there.

"What's a PWA? Tell him, somebody."

"Person with AIDS," replied a group of voices.

Guy waived his arm to his left. "Yeah, go for it."

A girl stood up. "Are you afraid, Guy?"

"No," he said quickly. "I hope when I die, I'm ready. I'm trying to accept the idea that some things won't be finished. I guess that's the whole odyssey of dying."

The gymnasium was still—not uncomfortable, but pensive. The freedom with which the question had been asked and answered had transported nine hundred people to a different place, one where truth comes much more easily.

"Glen and Greg," said Guy, rocking back and forth in his chair, "they're my brothers, they'll be there to meet me."

Pam and I both reached for Jane, who was sitting between us.

"But no, I'm not afraid. I hope you guys are more afraid than me."

Guy leaned forward while a question was posed from the back. "How do I feel about what? He looked over at us, but we, too, were straining to hear. "Can somebody tell me what she's saying?"

Someone closer to Guy repeated the question.

"Wait," he said incredulously, "how do I feel about being Asian?" Everyone joined Guy in laughter. "Is that what she asked?"

Several voices were trying to help now, until finally Guy got it.

"Euth-a-nas-ia! How do I feel about euthanasia!"

We were all in hysterics. "Is this for real?" Jane poked me.

"It's *Saturday Night Live*," said Anne from my other side.

Guy's milky brown eyes widened. "If that kind of control is what you need, then go for it, I guess, or have someone who loves you do it for you. I thought about that once, but I've let go of it." Guy shook his head firmly. "Anyway, it's not quite my time yet. At least, I hope not."

How can gay kids go through what they go through internally and not want to die? And most of us go through it with smiles on our faces, making people believe we have no problems at all.

You scramble to find a place for yourself and a person you can pretend to be. You try to look at the way other kids act, and you do what they do, only you do it bigger and better, to make sure no one knows what else is going on.

I wasn't making choices—God, I was hardly conscious. I did what I had to do to cope. I played along, filled in the blanks like everybody else. When you're gay, you can live totally undercover, or you can live in opposition to society. Nice choices. Most of us try to float in the middle, just like the song says, looking for love in all the wrong places. Don't kid yourself. There's lots of kids out there just like me, and no one knows who they are.

"Next question?"

Guy waited, his gloved hands rubbing his thighs. Throughout the morning's conversation, he was never really still, pulling at his gloves or rocking slightly in his chair. Periodically, his voice would dim and the words would slur, and we could see him take a long, deep breath, as if he was willing himself to stay with us.

A tissue box passed up and down our row. Jane's emotions echoed Guy's: When his voice broke, so did her tears. Alexander stood next to the bleachers, around the corner from us, expressionless. He hadn't removed the backpack; whatever Guy's needs might be, he would be ready.

"Are you worried about catching a cold?" asked a boy in the front row.

"Why, have you got one?"

The student laughed and shrugged. Several of his friends started a movement to expel him from the gym. "Out, out," they began to chant, while Guy turned to us and grinned.

"You know," he said directly to the chagrined young man, "I can catch a cold going to dinner or shopping in the mall, and God knows I spend enough time there. I'm not worried. It's too late to worry.

"By the way," he continued, turning his eyes upward into the crowd, "I don't know if I explained to you, when you see me rocking like this, it's because there's something soothing about it for me. I'm not losing it or anything."

Anne leaned across me. "Yeah, right."

Jane giggled. "He should tell them about last week, when he took his pants off in front of the plumber."

Guy was provoking the crowd. "If you don't have any more questions, then I guess it's over. You have to go back to class."

To the left of him, a group of girls were selecting a spokesperson. Guy turned toward the commotion.

"C'mon, be brave."

A very high voice asked, "What did you get for Christmas?"

"Okay," Guy replied, rolling his eyes, "good question. What did I get for Christmas? We weren't supposed to exchange gifts this year, so I was pretty lucky, because we exchanged gifts anyway. The best Christmas gift I got, or I'm gonna get, is a dog. I want a shar-pei—one of those wrinkly ones."

Laughter filled the room once again. "So I asked people not to give me gifts. I asked them to contribute to my dog fund."

I nudged Jane. "What's this? I haven't heard about a dog."

"That's because I'm in denial."

To the right of us, Alexander was chuckling and shaking his head. Guy turned back to the center of the gym. A muffled voice asked the next question.

"What kind of music do I like?" Guy repeated. "I like music that makes me feel like dancing. The problem is that I can't dance anymore."

Guy went on, wistfully. "You know, the other night I had this dream. I was dancing, but it wasn't that I was dancing just in a dream, it was as if my body was actually dancing and feeling like I used to feel. I woke up and the feeling stayed with me for a few minutes and that was nice, because it took a little while before I remembered and it went away."

The room came to a complete standstill. Guy seemed to perceive our distress, because he said, reassuringly, "No, really. It was nice."

Members of the faculty were sitting together in the bleachers to Guy's right. "Have you tried meditation, Guy?" one of them asked solemnly.

"I don't hum, if that's what you mean."

The tension broke, and hands popped up all over the room.

"Has anyone ever given me a bad time?" Guy paused for a moment, and on our bleacher seats we pondered the question with him.

"No, I've been really lucky. Once in a while, I suppose, but I don't really remember the incidents because they were small and stupid, and I'm not going to waste my time with any of that. For the most part, people have really taken to me."

Whose fault was it? For years, I thought it was mine. I was account-able for my actions. It never occurred to me that anyone else was involved.

Everyone's involved. Me, you, every living human being. Do we really know what we're doing to each other? We call each other names, we push and shove each other out of the way, because we're so hateful and afraid.

Okay, I've taken responsibility. What about the rest of you? Why do you hate us so? Do you think we can make your son or daughter gay? Are you afraid we'll rub off on them? On you?

You don't get it. It's not contagious. It's who I am. Maybe it's who you are.

I need a new attitude—accept me, or I'll hit you with my purse.

Guy's time with the community at Saratoga High School was almost over. Alexander watched him carefully, monitoring the sound of his voice, his gestures, the content of his answers.

"I don't understand the question," he was saying, politely, to a boy way in the back. We all listened again. "What does the word *AIDS* mean to me? Hmm."

From the audience, several voices turned on the questioner, demanding clarification.

"No, I see where he's going with this. The word *AIDS* does mean something, beyond the disease. Come on, let's be honest. When you hear that word, you can't tell me you just think about t-cells and viruses and dying.

"AIDS is about how we treat each other and about how we treat ourselves. Is that what you meant?"

En masse, the audience turned and searched for the faceless voice in the darkness.

"When you hear the word *AIDS*, think about how we didn't care about this disease for a long time, because we didn't care about the people who were getting it. It's better now, but it's still not that great. So when you hear the word *AIDS*, remember you're the one it wants, you're the next one to get it, unless you take care of yourself.

"You know what I hope? I hope someday AIDS will be the disease that brought people together, even after it separated them. And I hope you'll say, oh yeah, AIDS, that disease nobody dies from anymore."

Applause rose around him, and Alexander moved out of the shadows to his son's side, pride brightly evident on his face.

Guy lifted a gloved hand. "One more question, Dad. That boy's been waiting."

Midway in the gym, a young man stood up. "What message do you want to leave with us, Guy?"

"What message do I want to leave with you all? I hope my being here today hits you so darn hard that if you ever think about doing something risky that could get you HIV, I'll pop right into your head. Abstinence is the only way you will not get this through sex. Take that to heart. There's a risk in anything else you do."

He grasped the arms of his chair as though he intended to stand up, startling much of the crowd. I felt them draw back in their seats.

Guy was simply gathering his strength. "Please remember me," he pleaded. "You don't want to have to go through this. And you don't want your mom and dad to have to watch you die.

"This is my last chance to tell you these things," he whispered, pushing away tears with the backs of his gloves. "I love you. Stop the abuse, please. Take care of yourselves. Take care of each other."

Alexander put a steadying hand on his son's shoulder, and there was a moment of sniffling around the room before someone proposed one more question. Guy glanced up, suddenly calm.

"You really want me to?"

"Yeah" came a round of voices.

Suddenly, it was the Guy of another, grander time. "Okay, I'll leave you a big picture of me. Poster size. You can put it in one of those windows, you know, with the trophies, or wherever."

The ovation rose once more, mixed with laughter and shouts of encouragement. Alexander waited until it had died down. "Let me just say this if I may. His mother, Jane, and I, we couldn't be prouder of him . . ."

He stopped, obviously struggling, until we felt the room swell, and the united will of nine hundred people, young and old, gay and straight, picked him up and held him high above us, above the devastation, above the past, so that their work could be brought to conclusion.

"Guy didn't want to be remembered as just one more victim of AIDS. He didn't want us to be remembered as that family who lost all their children. Guy has gone so far beyond all that. He's created a legacy for us, and a way to go on.

"All of you, and everyone who listened to him—you've been part of our family's resurrection. Thank you. Thank you very much."

. . . .

Guy was in a deep sleep when James climbed into bed next to him that night, moving slowly, careful not to disturb him or even touch him in the slightest way. Several hours later, James jolted awake, his heart pounding wildly as Guy's screams filled the pitch-black room.

"What's the matter?" he reached for Guy, who was thrashing about, entangled in the sheets and in his nightmare.

"Oh God, oh God," Guy whimpered, struggling to sit up. Is he dying? he wondered. Is this what dying is like?

"I'm not ready," Guy cried, falling back on his pillows. "I don't want to die."

"I know, I know," said James, caressing his forehead and kissing his hair. "I'm not ready, either." They rocked together gently, in time with Guy's sobs. What James heard next was the voice of the frightened child.

"Tomorrow I leave here forever. I knew this day was coming, but the closer it got, the more it's been happening."

"What's happening, Guy?" James murmured tenderly.

"The thought that death is chasing me and I can't get away."

James pulled him closer, as close as he thought Guy would allow. One by one around the bedroom, objects became discernible as their eyes grew accustomed to the faint light.

"James, please tell me again what it would have been like, if I hadn't gotten sick."

"We would have a house and a garden. And a dog of our own. We'd have friends over for dinner. We'd each do half the laundry."

Guy wiped his eyes with the sheet. They were quiet for a few minutes, and James understood that the immediate danger had passed. Indeed, Guy would not die now. He would be required to stay longer, growing weaker, unprotected as the cold night approached.

"James?"

"Hmm?"

"Do you ever say, 'What a fool I've been?'"

"Of course not. Why do you ask? Wouldn't you have stayed, if it had been me?"

"I don't know. The way I was then, I can't say for sure. I don't know if I'm capable of that much compassion, the way you were."

"I didn't stay because I felt sorry for you."

Guy turned his head on his pillow and regarded James with solemn brown eyes.

"I stayed because I loved you," said James firmly. Their faces were close, breaths mingling as they spoke. "I wanted to be with you forever." He studied Guy curiously. "You knew that, didn't you?"

"I always thought I fell harder for you than you for me. I thought I made you love me."

"You can't control everything, Guy. I was so in love with you I couldn't think straight."

In the dim light they saw each other smile, and a brief, bittersweet kiss sealed the moment. James waited until he was sure Guy was asleep, listening for his breathing to become even and calm, before he allowed himself to drift away.

Outsmarting the Angel

The next morning, January 5, 1994, James watched from the front porch as they drove away. Guy rocked in the front seat next to his father, clutching a stuffed dog. There were no wrenching good-byes to the house of his childhood, no heavyhearted glance back at its smiling windows. Guy simply ended his life there, chattering about Polo, the name he had chosen for his new pet, which was being flown in from Honolulu. Two days later, James followed.

Anne flew to Maui on Monday, January 24, and early the next morning she phoned me. "I think you should come," she said tearfully. "Now."

I wanted to be there. There was nothing left of the observer within me now; I had been fully taken in and given my special part. I couldn't imagine Jane and Alexander losing their last child unaccompanied by people who loved them, of which I was one. And secretly, I was hoping Guy wouldn't die without me.

Planning my trip had been difficult. "One should never try to outsmart the Angel of Death," I'd heard it said. "He will only work harder to fool you." So Anne's call was what I had been waiting for, some clue as to how the grim future might be arranging itself.

The urgency in her voice alarmed me. Only a few days before, he had been able to be up and around in his wheelchair, maybe even go on an outing; now, according to Anne's dreary description, he was languishing in the hospital bed they had set up in the living room.

The night before, the symptoms of his disease had exploded. His cough became deep and rough, his breathing labored, blood stained his sputum. The pain in his extremities intensified, keeping him wide awake, agitated, and frightened. After several hours of watching his son suffer, Alexander called the home care unit that had sent a nurse earlier in the week, asking for morphine—a request that for Alexander and Jane signaled the approaching end.

I asked to speak to Alexander, and he agreed the time might be right. "But it's your call, Molly. He could live for two hours or two months."

"That doesn't matter," I replied quickly, although it did. I got off the phone, talked over the details of the week I would be gone with my husband and children, and ran onto the noon flight.

That evening, at the airport in Kahului, I recalled walking the same long, breezy corridor almost six months before. "Welcome to Paradise," the wooden sign still read, and I gave it a second glance, noticing it was freshly painted—large red letters set against a brilliant blue sea and green, green gardens. Unreal, the thought came to me. We've fallen hard from paradise and been banished to a far less perfect place.

I worked my way through the tourists to the street. Sitting crosslegged on a concrete wall, Alexander was waiting. "Ah, there she is." He stood and greeted me, and I dropped my bag and embraced him.

"How's he doing?" I asked. Alexander opened the car door before I could do it for myself.

"Holding his own." He gave me a look. "It's hard to tell what's going to happen."

"I'm here because it was my time to come, Al. But it's not my time frame we're working with."

Alexander nodded. "You know, that's exactly it. This is Guy's show." He chuckled at this and pulled away from the curb. We drove for several minutes in silence.

"Well, that's not exactly true," he reflected. "Maybe he's ready to give away some control. Early this morning, the damnedest thing happened.

Something I've dreamed of, and just when I was beginning to think he would never reach that point," his voice caught faintly, "he did it. He finally let go."

We were already driving through Kahului, crossing the street where Jane's father's market had been, passing by the cemetery in Wailuku; we would soon be on the road up the mountain. Alexander recounted the previous night for me—Guy's severe distress, the anxious moments, their sense of helplessness.

"Did Anne tell you I arranged for morphine? I was shaking when I made that call, because once Glen got to that stage, he was dead within forty-eight hours. Finally, about 4:00 A.M., the pain seemed to let up just a little, but Guy was still awake, groaning and complaining that he was too hot and seconds later too cold. He asked for water, then for juice, then for food, but refused to eat anything we brought. He yelled at all of us—even Jane. He said that he still wanted to live, and Jane ended up in tears. After that, he started crying and telling us we were wonderful for staying with him.

"But within an hour, he started to cough violently; he couldn't stop. I became alarmed he might even have a heart attack, because of the coughing. When it finally stopped, he collapsed, just flopped his head back on the pillow. And then he asked for me."

Alexander leaned toward me. "You know, he's been asking for me more lately. He motions me to come, with his hand, you know, like this." He showed me how Guy had been summoning him with a weak little wave.

"So then Guy pulled me down next to his face. I don't think he wanted his mother to hear. Dad, he asked me, do you think it's coming closer?

"I said I thought we were getting pretty close. I knew to tell him the truth. Then he asked me if I thought he was ready, and of course I told him that he had done more in his short life than most people could do at all."

I nodded mindlessly, unwilling and unable to imagine how a parent faces these particular truths.

"There were just a few seconds of wondering, and then he took off the oxygen mask and said, 'Okay, I've had enough, I'm ready to go.'" Al paused, a broad, almost jubilant smile sweeping across his face. "Just like

278

that, he was ready, accepting. So many others just flail about, all the way to the grave. And ever since then, he's been calm, pretty perky actually. No coughing, not much pain. In fact, he's been saying good-bye to everyone."

"What do you mean, saying good-bye to everyone?"

"I mean he made us get out the address book and read off every name. And Guy would say, yes or no, and we would call all the yeses for him, and then he would tell them he was phoning to say good-bye. He even called Saratoga High School; they put him on the loudspeaker. I don't know if they could understand him, because every time he came to the good-bye part, he started to cry. He called Cat in Japan. She wasn't there, and so far he's left two messages."

I was speechless. I don't know why anything Guy did surprised me still, but the thought of nine hundred high-school students sitting in algebra and world history, listening to Guy's last words, was really quite extraordinary.

We were very close to the house on Kea Road. As Alexander negotiated the last curve, I reflected on my own strange conversation with Guy on the phone that morning. When I called to tell the family when my plane would arrive, Guy had asked to speak with me.

"Is that you, Mol? I'm calling to say good-bye . . ." His voice vanished, replaced by a sob.

Suddenly desperate, I felt myself grabbing for him, as though the phone was a tether that would keep him from drifting into deep space. "Guy, you don't have to say good-bye to me yet, because I'm coming to see you. Tonight. I'll be there. Hang on." Someone took the phone from him, and at that point I became obsessed with making my plane.

We inched down the steep driveway. I had fond memories of this house, but now Guy was dying inside. Alexander turned off the engine. I was about to climb out of the car when he reached over and touched me lightly on the arm.

"I guess you heard about James."

"I'm not sure," I replied slowly. "He's still here, isn't he?"

Alexander laughed. "Just barely. He came right after we did, you know, but he lasted only two days."

I settled back into my seat.

"From the minute he walked into the house, we could tell he didn't want to be here. He took no interest in Guy's medical care—he said Jane and I were in charge of that. He made Guy feel guilty because he wasn't able to go to the beach anymore. He argued with all of us about stupid little things and was mean to Guy, after Guy had been so excited for him to come. Jane and I were beside ourselves, but then Guy threw him out."

Alexander grinned at the look on my face.

"The straw that broke the camel's back was when Guy discovered that James never asked for a leave of absence. Instead, he took three weeks of vacation time."

"Oh, God," I said. "So he never intended to stay."

"Right. When Guy confronted him, there was a huge fight until poor Guy was exhausted, and he just kept saying, 'Get out, James. I don't ever want to see you again.'

"So James flew home and, apparently, got his act together somewhere over the Pacific. He took his leave of absence, said his good-byes—he even shipped his car here."

"You've got to be kidding."

"Eight hundred dollars. And he'll probably have to turn around and ship it right back."

Alexander slumped down in the seat and folded his arms. "You know, when I retired in 1992, it was a mutual agreement. The demands of the talks were overwhelming Guy; there were things he couldn't do alone anymore. I had to wait in the wings, sensing the right moment. Finally, I said, 'So, what do you think? Could you use a little help?' And he didn't disqualify me. But he also knew I was doing exactly what I wanted to do.

"Since then he's done remarkably well, delaying the moment when he would ask James to make this kind of move for him. The problem is that Jane and I are the models for his expectations; we continually change our lives, just to be with him. We both let go of our careers for him, and the choices we make every day—every minute, really—are based first on Guy's needs and desires. We have done all of this unquestionably. But James isn't a parent, and despite Guy's efforts to beatify their relationship, he isn't a spouse either. For James to mirror our behavior probably isn't a reasonable expectation."

"So how's he been since he came back?"

Alexander pursed his lips and studied the steering wheel. "A changed man," he said finally. "He ministers to Guy's every need." Alexander shrugged and lifted himself out of the car. "Guy wants him here for his final days," he said as we walked up the path to the house. "And whatever Guy wants, we want."

Jane greeted me at the sliding glass door. We hugged and cried a little. I tossed my sandals onto the pile and stepped into the living room, which was dominated by Guy's large bed that faced the same gorgeous view that had so captivated me months before. I hadn't remembered the walls were painted green. Next to the bed, a brick fireplace I had also forgotten from my previous visit, also painted green, divided the living room from the dining area. Guy's stereo and several trays of CDs were perched on the mantle. Grandpa's altar had disappeared.

She led me to Guy. His eyes were closed. He looked much thinner than the last time I'd seen him, a long three weeks before. The oxygen tube that was supposed to be under his nostrils and around his ears was hanging loosely around his neck.

Jane went around to the other side of the bed. "Molly's here, Guy," she said softly. I put my hand on his and he opened his eyes.

"Hi, Mol." He could still flash a prize-winning smile. "I'm glad you're here." His voice was like a bell, guileless, unwavering. "Today I called everyone to say good-bye." Two big tears escaped down his face, and Jane and I joined him quickly. "I'm dying, Molly."

"I don't know, Guy," his mother interrupted, sponging her cheeks with her hand. She rearranged his sheet and handed him the water glass he was reaching for. "I don't think you're going to die tonight. Not yet." She smiled at him lovingly.

"Where's James?" Guy asked.

"He and Anne went for a walk." Jane moved away from his bed, and I followed her. "He asks for James constantly," she whispered. "I don't know how Guy does it. I don't think I could be that forgiving."

Jane had my bag and was leading me down the hall. "You remember, there's only one bathroom." Be sure to get in the shower before James. He takes forever." She glanced through the door as we sped by. "Isn't it awful? I can't wait to tear it out." We ended up in the farthest bedroom, "the green room," she called it. "Grandpa didn't want to waste paint."

I sat down on the bed. The mattress was thin and hard. Jane was grinning, watching me test what I assumed were my sleeping arrangements. "We've all been sleeping in the living room," she informed me. "Except Al. When he's not with Guy, he escapes into our bedroom. By the way, you get the couch."

I was about to graciously protest when the sound of a bell came from the living room.

"We gave Guy a bell two nights ago. We should never have done that."

We were back at his side momentarily. "What do you want, Guy?" his mother inquired sweetly, moving the bell to the fireplace.

"Guava juice." I stood next to the bed while Jane disappeared into the kitchen. Guy sat quietly, opening and closing his hands, content to wait for his juice. I was silent, too, suddenly uncomfortable, not knowing what to say or do.

Just then Anne and James burst through the door, and Anne reached me first. "I'm so glad you're here! We need you," she cried, hugging me tightly.

"Probably not," I said, embarrassed, "but nevertheless, you've got me."

"Where have you been, James?" came a surprisingly firm voice from the hospital bed. "You were gone so long."

James sat down on the bed and took Guy's hand. "I'm sorry, Guy. We went for a walk. Did you miss me?" The rest of us stepped away.

"Well," I remarked as we walked into the kitchen, "Guy looks pretty good to me."

"Yeah," said Anne. "He really lights up whenever James is around."

"Huh." The sound that came out of Jane was not conclusive. She turned to Alexander, and they exchanged a look. "Actually," she said, keeping her eyes locked on her husband, "James has been great since he came back."

Just then James came into the kitchen to serve me my dinner, a large helping of tuna casserole he had kept warm in the oven. Alexander stayed in the living room with Guy, while Jane, Anne, and James sat with me at the kitchen table.

Jane was clearly exhausted. She asked what day it was. "Wednesday," we all answered.

"I can't believe that just two days ago, he was still making us take him shopping."

Anne spoke quietly. "No more, Guy. He's not going anywhere."

Jane poured me a beer. "Let's hope not. I don't know. Did Alexander tell, you Molly? Guy had enough energy today to make thirty phone calls."

"I heard." We collectively rolled our eyes. "Still shopping," I laughed. "What was he shopping for?"

"This is the latest," Jane replied, leaning forward so I could examine the huge gold charm that dangled from her neck. It was a circle, within it a mother whale with her baby on her back.

"It's beautiful," I said, turning it over in my hand.

"It's Guy and me. The jeweler let him trade in his wolf for this, and last night when Guy decided it was time to die, he gave it to me and made me promise never to take it off."

"His wolf?"

"He bought it because he thought it looked like Polo," Anne explained.

"Polo. Oh, the dog!" I exclaimed, suddenly looking around. "Where is he?"

"Gone," said Jane. "He was in and out of here faster than James."

"Be nice," said James, tossing a crumpled napkin Jane's way.

"He tried to eat the couch and attacked anybody who came in. Even Guy didn't like him. I couldn't handle Guy and a dog, so he just kind of disappeared."

Jane fingered the golden whales. More symbols, I thought, more meaningful things. Up until two days ago, Guy had still been a step ahead of the end, because whenever death threatened to catch up, he would cast another charm, raise another shield, create another symbol of his continuing reality. Just to buy a new shirt became an antidote for the poison within him: If I wear this magic cloak, it will keep me safe.

"You've had an exciting few weeks," I remarked to Jane.

"Oh, that's nothing. Guy and I had an argument, and he didn't speak to me for two days."

"Oh?" I said, looking over at James.

He shrugged. "I don't know. I wasn't here when all of this happened—Polo and the big fight."

"I hurt his feelings," she said somewhat regretfully, not because she had been wrong, I suspected, but because wounding him, even in love, was unthinkable for her.

Alexander had come into the kitchen. "He's asleep," he said. "Nodded off in the middle of a sentence." We all laughed, and then Jane continued.

"He wanted to go shopping all the time. It got so he was spending at least seven hundred dollars a day, maybe even a thousand."

I was incredulous. "On what?"

"Well, first he'd want to go to The Grand Wailea and brunch it up. Then he would make us wheel him in and out of the shops in the hotel, and of course nothing there is cheap. He bought clothes, a new stereo, all the CDs he wanted, and hundreds of beads—to make necklaces like the one he made you, Molly. He can't do any of that anymore, so then he tells poor Al what to do and how he wants them arranged.

"The biggest thing was the jewelry. His father lent him a heavy gold chain for the wolf, but he wasn't satisfied, so he bought another one. He ordered a ring for James that matches his and a diamond for his own. Later, when Alexander called the jeweler and explained Guy's situation, he said he suspected something like this—Guy in a wheelchair, looking so sick, throwing money around. The jeweler offered to help us by talking him out of the diamond. And then when we got rid of the dog, he let Guy exchange the charm, even though he'd worn it for two days."

She sighed, shaking her head. "I don't know what we would have done if he hadn't been so nice."

I understood now what had happened; Guy's death-bed gluttony had gotten to her.

"I told him, Guy, you've made a wonderful impression on so many people, young people, who've listened to you. Do you want them to see you doing these things, spending money irresponsibly and charging things on credit cards you know you'll never pay off? I just couldn't imagine that he would want to die this way."

"Without his integrity," added Alexander, his eyes downcast. "This would not be a good death, after such a good life and a heroic last two years." He turned to stare out the window at the sea, the white-cap spackled water, churning in the afternoon tradewinds.

"Guy was so angry at me."

Of course. Jane was his most faithful advocate and surest love; to have disappointed her must have posed a profound threat to his ego. And beyond that, he would recognize, despite his shame and his defensiveness, that she was telling him the truth.

"After two days, he came to me and said I was right and that the spending would stop."

"That was brave of him," I said.

"I think he meant it, too," Alexander interjected, glancing at Jane. A smirk passed between them.

"Was there any question?" I wanted to know.

"The next day he had me get him dressed to go out again. He could barely sit up. Naturally, I wanted to know where we were going."

Alexander started to laugh. "He said, very coyly of course, that he needed to go to Liberty House, you know, the classiest department store here on the islands. I asked, 'What are you going to do there?' 'I just have to get a few things,' he said. If you could have seen him, all dressed up in his Polo sweatshirt, his hat and his gloves, ready to go out in the Hawaii sun."

"We never even made it to the door," said Jane. A half-smile stayed with her for a moment. "You know, that was the thing. We would spend all this time getting him dressed, picking out the right shoes, anything he said; it was such a chore. And he just wanted to look cute! As soon as we got to Kahului Shopping Center or the drugstore, he would want to come right back."

"Time is nothing when you're dying," said Alexander. "The fact that it takes an hour to get ready and you're out for only ten minutes is irrelevant. The fact is, he did it."

Jane gazed at her husband. "And now his shopping days are over."

In the living room, Guy was clearing his throat. "Hello?" he called to us. "Hel-lo-o. I'm dying alone in here. I'm dying alone!"

Chairs scraped the floor, and four people rushed through the dining room, around the fireplace to Guy's side, where he looked us up and down, frowning.

"Who moved my bell?"

. . . .

We spent the evening gathered around Guy. As we talked, I kept an eye on the clear night sky and the slow illumination of a marquis of lights across the valley that stretched between us and the Haleakala Mountains. I watched a plane descend, first above and then below us, and land at the airport that bordered the ocean. The shoreline was clearly visible, as was the silhouette of the high country, and from his perch in the hospital bed Guy could behold the wondrous view whenever he wanted to.

At about ten o'clock, Anne brought out mattresses and sets of sheets and pillows. She created three beds on the floor, while Jane and I arranged mine on the couch. Alexander talked quietly with his son.

Just as we were finishing, a feeble voice rose from the bed. "I need you, Mom."

She went to stand next to Al. Anne went over, too, and then Guy called for James.

"Molly," said the voice. I didn't move. I wasn't convinced that Guy remembered I had arrived.

"Mol?" he repeated, and Alexander motioned to me. "I think he wants you to come and sit with him."

I experienced a wave of pleasure that Guy had asked for me. None of us could have guessed what was coming next.

As the five of us settled around his bed, Alexander and Jane on his right side, James at his foot, and Anne and I on the left, Guy whispered something to his father.

"He wants us to touch him," Al instructed. Jane and I began to stroke his arms gently, while Anne and James gave his legs a light massage. Alexander caressed his son's forehead and brushed back his hair. Guy closed his eyes and began to breathe deeply.

We listened to him inhale and exhale. After a while, he added a sound to each breath. Twenty minutes stretched into forty, and Guy's mantra of gasps and moans continued while we kept watch silently, until we began to raise our eyes to one another, questioning.

After an hour, we all understood, but none of us knew how to get out of it. Alexander rescued us. Leaning down, he put his mouth up to Guy's ear. He continued to stroke his son's hair with such tenderness, that I too could feel his touch.

"Did you want to die now, son? Is that it?"

Guy kept his eyes closed and nodded.

Alexander's expression dimmed for a second. Then he took a deep breath, as if to summon his love to the surface and find the words that would communicate to his son that the moment was, indeed, sacred.

"Not tonight, Guy. It's not your time quite yet."

"I know" came a whisper from the bed. "I tried, but I didn't feel any different."

Alexander glanced up, and we all smiled despite ourselves. "You rest now," he told his son. "Maybe tomorrow."

On cue, Jane, Anne, James, and I moved away from the bed. Alexander continued to run his fingers through Guy's hair for a few more minutes, and soon Guy's breathing quieted and he slept.

Alexander joined Jane and me on the couch, which was long enough for the three of us to curl our legs underneath us and snuggle in. "Can you believe it?" he whispered, smiling not with disrespect, but with the limitless affection of a father fascinated with such innocence. "He thought he could make himself die. Everything was perfect. Molly had arrived, and we were all around him. This morning he made the decision, today he said his good-byes, tonight he goes—just like that."

Al had a way of offering a soft chuckle, even in the most dire moments. "And I thought he'd let go at last." Alexander stood up and shrugged his shoulders. "No way."

The soft, grateful sounds of our laughter followed him down the hall until he disappeared into the darkness.

• • • •

Twenty-four hours went by and Guy lived on. We relaxed a little, and over the next few days a routine was developed—to bathe him, bring him the plastic container for his pee, and sit with him when he was in the mood to chat. James and Anne made a list of "Ways to Make Guy More Comfortable"; they informed me privately that the real title of the list was "When Dying Isn't Fun Anymore."

> Give him a sponge bath
> Give him a massage
> Put lotion all over his body
>> (must be Keri lotion)
> Put cold compresses on his head
> Reposition him to relieve bed sores
> Swab his nose with Vaseline on Q-tips
> Empty his bladder into the pee bucket
> Feed him Apple Jacks
> Tranquilize him
> Read off all of his CDs
>> (even though you know it's going to be
>> Barbra or Mariah)

James wanted to add, "Touch his penis lightly," but was overruled.

The tasks were handled by his four principal caregivers; I saw that my job was behind the scenes, supporting them. But on Friday night, after I'd been there two full days, my job description changed, and my status unexpectedly rose.

James, Anne, and Jane were sleeping on the floor, and I was awake on the couch. Listening to Guy breathe was a reluctant pastime of whoever happened to be up during the night; we counted the seconds between the time he let out his breath and the time he inhaled anew, imagining, from our places around the room, what we would do if he failed to breathe in again. It was a situation that was not conducive to sleep.

Guy stirred and I got up and went to him.

"Hi," he said. Light from the full moon filtered through the windows and onto Guy's face.

"Hi there," I replied.

"I need to pee."

Okay, I thought, I can do that.

"The plastic thing's in the bathroom. Could you go get it? Bring the toilet paper too."

I brought the container and the toilet paper. Guy pulled his T-shirt up and pushed at his knit boxer shorts. "It's easier if you hold it for me."

I tried not to change the expression on my face as inside I was shrieking, hold what Guy, hold what?

"Don't worry, I'm a pretty good shot," he said pleasantly. I understood then that he wanted me to hold the container. Thank you, God.

I put it in position. "Okay, fire away."

When he was finished, he put out his hand for the toilet paper. "I don't like to drip," he explained, but I was already on my way down the hall to the bathroom with his pee, which I emptied into the toilet. I rinsed the container and put it back on the floor, feeling good, trusted, like a real insider.

Guy was waiting for me when I returned, so I pulled up a chair and sat down next to him. Side by side, we faced the windows and the night beyond.

"Are you comfortable?" Guy asked. I leaned back and propped my feet up next to where his formed a little mound under his sheet and blanket. We sat that way for a long time. Periodically, he slept, but I didn't leave him; I reflected that there was no place else I'd rather be than next to my dying friend, listening to him sleep, very peacefully now, and, in front of me, without my having to do so much as shift in my seat, a sight that rivaled heaven. As the horizon of light emerged from behind the mountains and slowly replaced the starry night with soft, near white color, the plants and flowers outside our windows turned translucent, as if lumens of light had seeped inside their leaves and petals, and their very molecules were radiating from within.

"Do you see my magic plants?" Guy asked drowsily.

"I see them, Guy. I'm trying to figure out what makes them glisten like that."

Guy yawned. "I don't try to figure out anything anymore. I just accept." He gave me a devilish grin. "How 'bout a drink?"

My feet hit the floor. "What would you like? Water? Juice?"

"No, a *drink* drink. Whadda we got?" He tilted his head toward the dining room. I went around the corner of the fireplace and found the liquor cabinet.

"Well?"

I read off the labels. Guy settled on vodka and guava juice.

"No way, Guy" came a voice from the floor. Jane had awakened, probably from the clanking of the bottles. Sheepishly, I returned to my post next to the bed.

"Wait 'til she drops off," he whispered, patting my hand.

"I can't, Guy. She'll kill me. I'll go before you do."

He laughed out loud at this, and Jane's head popped up once again, shooting us a dagger look of suspicion. Guy closed his eyes, still smiling, and I waited until I was sure he was asleep before I climbed back into my bed on the couch.

· · · ·

Later, those hours I spent with Guy were designated his "last good night." The pain had relentlessly returned by Saturday afternoon, and Alexander, guided by Charlotte, the home nurse who had been visiting us almost daily, made the difficult decision to give his son liquid morphine. But after only one dose, Guy reacted violently, waking, trembling and terrified, from fitful sleep, over and over again until night ran into day and he had been up for twenty-four hours straight.

"Ativan and Duragesic," said Charlotte on Sunday. "We'll try the patches—a higher dose this time. Forget the morphine for now."

The Ativan sedated him, and the Duragesic patches worked almost instantly to lessen his pain. When Guy fell into a deep sleep, the rest of us collapsed on the couches.

"We're into pain management now," Alexander told Jane. "Anything it takes."

Just one good death. Practically every day, I would tell Alexander— that's all I ask for. Greg had died violently, with us so far away and unaware. And Glen—I was right next to him, and still I couldn't keep him from dying badly.

And now Guy. I would do anything to break this terrible pattern, to take away his pain, to make sure he was never alone. In these last days, I would do anything to let him know he was the most special child in the universe.

CALL ME TOSH

For most of the next few days, Guy slept. He never asked for food or drink, and Alexander decided that waking him up for any reason would be cruel; the agony of the past forty-eight hours would not soon leave the father's memory. As more time went by, and Guy's body seemed to be disappearing before our eyes, Anne began to panic.

"We're starving him to death!" she ranted to Charlotte, who had accompanied us on a long walk down Kea Road. We stopped at the place where both sides of the ocean were within our view.

"You're helping him die, Anne," said Charlotte gently. "Sometimes we have to abandon our old notions of what it means to sustain life. Inside a hospital, death is the enemy, and so life is prolonged, often at the cost of a good death. Outside the hospital," she put her arm around Anne, "where people like me find wonderful caretakers like you, we can more fully respect the wishes of the patient and even befriend the dying process."

"I don't think Guy wishes to die."

"His father tells me he does. But if I were you, his best friend, I wouldn't want him to go. What will happen though, is that Guy will sense that you're holding him here. He'll worry about what's going to happen to you, and then he'll hold on, too, which will only cause him more pain."

Six years of dread and pervading sorrow seemed to take hold of Anne in that moment. In Charlotte's arms, her body shook uncontrollably. Then it was my turn, and when I felt her despair crushed against me, I better understood the depth of her pain and the love she held for her friend.

After a long time, she looked at me through red, swollen eyes. "I'm studying to be a physical therapist." Although subdued, desperation leaked out between her words. "I'm learning how to help people cope with their pain so that they can live again. It's hard for me to understand any other goal."

"Oh, Anne," said Charlotte, her face softening, her compassion evident. "This isn't about fixing him so he can get better. It's about accepting, in the end, that some things are unfixable."

· · · ·

Eventually, Guy came back, if only temporarily. For another day or two, he had many wakeful moments, during which time Anne struggled to say good-bye, James continued to tease and make him smile, and Alexander and Jane guarded constantly against the insistent enemies, anxiety and pain.

More than a week had passed by since I arrived on the island. I hadn't discussed my departure with anyone, but during a transient, unwelcomed moment of reflection, I toyed with the facts: I couldn't stay past Thursday, and Guy was going to outlive my visit. The thought having been briefly considered, I tossed it away and ran back to my spot in the circle.

On Wednesday evening, I took Anne to the movies, after Jane had pulled me aside earlier in the day. "Anne needs a break," she observed. Only occasionally now, the Guy that Anne had known revisited. But she still fretted about the decision to sedate him when, inevitably, his suffering returned.

"He must be down to only eighty pounds," she declared during lunch, and her accusation was not lost on any of us. It was then that Jane pressed me into service.

We returned from the movie just before ten. Standing outside the screen door, kicking off our shoes, we could see Jane, Alexander, and James surrounding Guy's bed, staring at him intently, like a group of interns on rounds.

Jane motioned to join them and we did, although our walk across the room slowed considerably as we looked into their somber faces and began to suspect the worst.

"Oh, my God," said Anne, reaching Guy's bedside before me. Feeling the stinging rush of fear, I stepped in next to her.

He was sitting up, as he had been for the past few days, even when he was sleeping. His head was thrown back, tilted to the side, his eyes were closed, his mouth gaping. A freighted moment passed, and then, just as Anne made the slightest movement toward him, he pulled his head up into her face.

"Boo."

He delivered his line to perfection—not loudly, but with grand conviction. Anne almost toppled over on me, but grabbed the bed somehow and then began to swear and laugh, and the conspirators joined in, reveling in the success of their prank.

Except for me. I backed away, shocked at what had just happened, surprising myself with an array of feelings, of which I realized anger was the one that would prevail. While everyone congratulated Guy on the high degree of distress that had registered on our faces, I escaped into the kitchen to attend to my rage.

I could hear them, their laughter waning reluctantly, laying out the beds, saying good-night to Guy, who was exhausted after his performance. I waited for quiet before I got ready for bed and crawled under my sheet.

But Jane was waiting for me. She gave my legs a gentle push, and I allowed her onto the couch.

"What's the matter?"

"I feel like my emotions have been shamelessly violated," I answered, and as quickly as it had entered me, the anger was gone. She considered me intently. "I was wondering when you were going to start letting your feelings out. You're grieving, too, Molly. Why don't you just let go?"

And immediately I did, as if all I needed was permission to turn on my tears. While I was weeping, Jane kept one arm around me, and with the other handed me tissues.

"I have to go home," I said finally, still sniffling.

"I know. And it's time. Go home and be with the living."

• • • •

When I awoke to the sound of giggling, several hours had gone by.

"I've been telling you, Guy," Jane was saying, "we need a sign." I turned on the couch, trying to make them out in the darkness. Had that been laughter I'd heard or my imagination? I listened, curious, never considering the idea that I was eavesdropping.

"I tried to arrange something with Glen. I kept asking him if he saw Greg or Grandma."

"I remember," Guy murmured, speaking slowly, slurring his words only slightly. "Didn't Glen finally flip you off?"

"Oh, Guy." The laughter again. "He just gave me this look, like, c'mon Mom."

"Tell you what. When I see Greg and Glen, I'll put my hand up and wave."

"Remember, the first thing I want you to tell them is how mad I am at them for dying." She paused. "No, don't say I'm mad. Say that I miss them."

"Don't worry, I'm going to tell Greg that he was a stupid shit to get himself killed. And then I hope we'll just keep going like we always were."

"And Glen?"

"That I'm sorry I didn't talk to him before he died and I understand what he was going through."

"You look just like him now, you know. I told Al the other day, Guy has disappeared and only Glen is left."

My eyes had adjusted to the light, and I could see them now, except for Guy's face. I wondered what he would say. If Jane had uttered those words only a short time ago, she would have been taking her life in her hands.

I heard a deep sigh. Finally, Guy spoke, so quietly that I had to lift my head up off the pillow and direct both ears their way. "I know. He's my brother. We're Japanese. Gay. Infected. Mixed-up. How aren't we alike?"

"You found a life for yourself, Guy, a wonderful life. Glen never did that."

"He never had a chance."

I put my head back down and listened to the silence between them. After a minute, the sound of an enormous yawn filled the room.

"My goodness, Guy," said Jane.

"That's how you yawn, Mom. A full-mouth yawn." He did it again, and I had to bury my face in my pillow to keep them from realizing I was spying on them.

Jane was giggling again. "Go to sleep, Guy."

"I have to pee."

"Just a minute." Jane went to get the pee bucket. I continued to watch Guy's silhouette on the bed, smiling to myself.

I heard Jane's footsteps coming back down the hall, and so, apparently, did Guy, because just as she entered the room, he waved limply at the curtains and said, "Hi, Greg. Hi, Glen."

I couldn't help myself. "You little shit," I said as Jane went by, stepping between the mattresses on the floor.

She gave me a little nod. "You better believe it."

We started to giggle, loudly, helplessly, until we had awakened the rest of the house. Guy's joke was replayed, and the room filled with our reckless, defiant laughter.

• • • •

The next morning, while I packed, Anne tended to Guy. At one point, as I rushed past them to retrieve some clothes I'd left in the dryer, she appeared to be writing on his arm. Later, as I closed my suitcase, I could hear the drone of Guy's voice coming from his bed, almost like he was chanting.

"Let's go, Mol." Alexander stood at the door of the green room, his hands on his hips. "You're going to miss that plane." I had put off the moment as long as I could. I followed him out into the living room. "I'll be in the car," he said, grabbing my bag from my hands.

I took a few steps toward Guy's bed and stopped, fascinated by what he was doing.

"*Ai shi te i ma-su.*" Out of the sheets came one bony arm, until it was bent in front of his face.

"*Ai shi te i ma-su,*" he repeated. I suddenly realized he was reading his arm.

"*Ai shi te i ma-su,*" he raised his eyes to me as I moved to his side. The smile I got was dazzling and I would not forget it.

"And what does that mean?" I asked, taking his free hand and leaning down close to him.

"I love you."

I pulled back a little, attacked by feeling. I hadn't wanted to cry my way through this good-bye.

"See, Annie wrote it on my arm so I could remember. I told her to write it on my heart, but after she was done we figured out it had to be upside down for me to read it. So she did it again, but it came off with all the oil and lotion."

Guy sighed and his eyelids drooped a little, as if the explanation had depleted him.

"Could you say it just one more time?" I asked him gently.

"*Ai shi te i ma-su.*"

"Me too." I kissed the cool, tender flesh on the back of his hand and then bent down to his face, closing my eyes, memorizing the feel of his forehead under my lips.

"I've got to go," I whispered against his skin.

"Thank you for coming to see me."

I could only nod and move away quickly.

"Oh, and Molly?"

I turned and took one more look at the back of his head. "Yes?"

"Call me Tosh."

I joined Alexander in the car and left Guy Toshiro Nakatani, who had finally come home, to die without me.

· · · ·

Friday, February 4, 1994. Only the circle remained.

The monitoring of Guy's medication remained Alexander's biggest problem. He struggled to find the right combination of tranquilizer and painkiller that would keep Guy comfortable yet still allow him to communicate his needs. But complications were overtaking them. Open, oozing bedsores had to be treated, and moving his tender body even slightly made him cry out in misery. He sometimes asked for food or water, but refused to eat or drink when anything was brought to him.

During wakeful periods, he was agitated and frightened. The agonized sounds he made alerted them to his constant pain, until Jane told her husband she couldn't stand anymore. After consulting with Charlotte, Alexander began to administer morphine directly into Guy's heart through his catheter, beginning with the lowest dosage, hoping his body would not again reject the potent painkiller.

This time, the morphine worked. Guy slept for almost seventy-two hours, rising to consciousness for only brief moments here and there, hardly communicating, with one terrible exception.

It was late Sunday night. Guy woke suddenly and called out for Alexander.

"Daddy? Daddy?"

Around him, everyone was alert, and Jane got up quickly. "Al," she called, but he was already there, striding across the room as if he'd heard the sound of his name before Guy uttered the words.

As he often did now, Alexander bent down to caress Guy's forehead and whisper to him.

"I'm here, son."

"Where am I?"

"You're in Maui, Guy, in Grandpa's house."

"Is there a steep driveway?"

"Yes."

A long silence, and then Guy spoke again.

"Why am I at Grandpa's house?"

Oh, God, I thought, and a familiar fury rose within me. What a terrible twist of fate, to have struggled so hard and so valiantly to accept his life, even to the point of letting go of it, and then to forget that he's dying and have to be told all over again. The moment devastated me, and I cursed the mind and its harsh infidelity, its steel-blue coldness, playing such a callous trick on an innocent child. Nevertheless, my son needed the truth, and it was my responsibility to give it to him.

"You're dying, Guy. We're taking care of you until it's time."

There was an almost imperceptible pause.

"Oh."

Alexander waited, never lifting his hand from his son's face. The luminous brown eyes made their way to his and rested there for a moment. "Are you ready, Dad?"

Alexander was startled, but he recovered quickly, as understanding raced through him. "Yes, son, I'm ready. We're all ready. You can go now and we'll be fine."

"Okay," Guy sighed, and the lids fluttered closed.

Alexander's head dropped, and with one arm he reached for Jane. "You have to tell him to go," he murmured, pulling her close. "He wants to know we'll be all right."

Alexander moved over and Jane took Guy's face in her hands. "Guy," she intoned, repeating his name until he was staring at her. "It's time. I want you to go.

"I'll miss you," she said with surreal strength. Like a white-hot flame to the end of a needle love had purified her pain, and now glowed with her resolve.

"But I'll be okay, Guy. You don't have to worry."

Jane sat beside him, holding his hand, never flinching, until Guy went back to sleep.

I was proud of Jane, for understanding so quickly what she needed to do, and for doing it so courageously.

This would be the last time Guy was able to let us know what he wanted. For six years, I had dedicated myself to his needs. It was Guy who made the decisions about everything—the dosage and administration of medicines, the regimen he would follow to maintain a certain level of health—he did it all. This included asking for help. Sometimes it had been difficult for me, waiting for this to happen, but, unlike Glen, who never communicated a need, when Guy finally made his demands, he was often very noisy about it.

It was clear that for the last week he had been asking me to help him turn off the machine, and not to unnecessarily prolong his transition from this life to the next. So naturally, certain tensions arose among the care-givers when I determined, for instance, that we needn't offer him some-thing before he asked for it. If he made a little noise in his sleep, it was okay not to respond instantly. Of course we responded to anxiety and pain; in that case, I was often frantic to help him.

Each person had to subordinate their needs to support Guy's. As con-flicted as people were, they adjusted eventually. It had fallen to me to champion this, his last cause. After all, I was his father.

Thursday, February 10. Anne sat next to her friend, who lay on his tender back with its gaping bedsores, his eyes half-open in sunken sock-ets, the skin of his face hanging from his cheekbones. He stirred and gave up a little whimper. Searching for ways to comfort him, she began her routine by checking the diaper; but he hadn't urinated. She knew he hated to be wet. But in order to pee, she thought bitterly, he needed fluids.

She picked up the plastic cup from the table by the bed. "Want some ice, Guy?" she said softly, lifting a spoon to his chapped lips. His mouth opened a little, and she carefully inserted two small ice chips. His mouth closed.

Anne sat back, satisfied. Guy seemed to be holding the chips on his tongue, and she waited for him to swallow. But instead he started to choke, suddenly, violently.

"Oh shit." Artfully, Anne put her arms around Guy's back and head and lifted him up. "It's okay, Guy, it's okay. Just try to swallow." His mouth fell open and what was left of the ice chips dripped down his chin onto his shirt.

Anne lowered him down and calmly inspected the damage. "Now I have to change your shirt." She knew him. He wouldn't want to stay in a wet shirt.

She chose one of Guy's favorites, a brown T-shirt printed with a familiar Hawaiian petroglyph. Carefully, she began to ease one arm through the sleeve of the wet shirt. He grimaced and she stopped. His face relaxed and she tried again.

With surprising force, he delivered a deep moan. Anne pulled back, and watched Guy's eyes flutter open; wide, brown, liquid pools regarded her solemnly.

"What is it, Guy? What do you need?"

His mouth moved soundlessly.

"Yes?" Anne leaned close. "Tell me again, Guy."

Slowly, he drew in a breath and opened his mouth.

"Bye."

Al and Jane had been telling me that I needed to say good-bye. James said that even the slightest touch might hold him back. He'll feel your fear, they had warned me, and he'll stay here on earth needlessly because he's worried about you.

Nobody worried about how I felt. An incredible grief lived in my heart, like a ton of bricks resting on my chest. It was a tear-everything-apart-knock-things-over-throw-shit-scream-my-lungs-out-cry-until-my-ducts-are-dry feeling. It was a deep, forever, brother/sister agony.

Secretly, I believed I knew Guy best. And believe me, he wanted to live! So you tell me, what was I supposed to do? He trusted me.

As if she could keep time from moving forward, Anne didn't move or even take a breath. What was Guy trying to say? Was this it?

His lips parted again, and his chin thrust forward slightly, as if he was focusing every still-functioning part of his body toward forcing a sound up through his throat.

" 'kay?"

"Oh, Guy." Despite the warning she had been given and the promise she had made to herself, Anne wept.

I realized at that moment that they were right. Guy wasn't trying to say good-bye to me. He wanted me to say good-bye to him. And he wanted to know I would be okay. So I made myself stop crying and I told him to go, that I would be fine, that I didn't want to hold him here.

It might have been my imagination, but as I said those things, Guy smiled—just a tiny little flicker. He always knew when I wasn't telling the truth. I could almost hear him saying the words—nice try, Annie. I hoped it was enough.

Several hours later, Guy came back again to the surface of consciousness, groaning, whimpering, his arms coming up off the sheets as if to point out his pain, but falling back helplessly, the effort far beyond him. All through the night and into the next day, his suffering intensified.

When Charlotte arrived, she found a house in anguish. Alexander pulled her into the kitchen.

"My God," he cried, his desperation unchecked. "Doesn't he deserve peace and a comfortable passing? What has he done? What is it that any of us have done to keep him here now, hurting . . ." He shook his head, summoning calm. "We're all hurting, you know, my wife . . ." His tears began again.

Charlotte stood with Alexander, one hand resting lightly on his arm, her face serene and accepting, and he felt comforted. After a moment, he was ready to discuss the next step in Guy's care, and Charlotte agreed with him: The morphine dosage should be increased— within prescribed limits—to ensure that Guy would be free of pain.

Jane waited next to her husband, her fingers entwined with her son's, while Alexander filled Guy's catheter with morphine. In only a few moments, she felt the stiffness leave his hands, and she massaged warmth and color back into them. For the moment, he was peaceful.

"Whatever it takes," Alexander murmured.

Jane concurred. "Please go, Guy," was her constant prayer while she sat with him in a determined vigil.

Just one good death.

It was decided that only Alexander and James would administer the morphine. "The stronger the dose, the more chance it could cause respiratory failure," Charlotte had warned them.

Alexander told his wife, "There's no need for all of us to bear the burden." So it was he, or James when Alexander had finally given in to sorely needed sleep, who injected the morphine into Guy's heart.

I agreed with Al that we should be the ones. But the first time I had to do it, my hands were shaking so much I could hardly get the needle into the catheter.

One look at Guy and you knew he needed as much morphine as he could stand. And I didn't want him to suffer anymore; none of us did. Even Anne had come around. The dear girl—every time she sat by him now, she was telling him to go and that she would be fine. I wanted to tell her: Anne, he gets the point.

We tried everything to send him off. Charlotte said to create a peaceful atmosphere, so we closed the drapes and kept the lights dim at night. It was too bad, because we couldn't light candles with the oxygen. We even looked through his CDs and found some good dying music.

I couldn't believe how quickly we'd lost him—only a week before, I was walking by his bed and he reached out and tried to grab my balls. Naturally, I acted shocked. Guy! I said, what are you doing? He just smiled. It was so wonderful. He'd forgotten we didn't do that anymore.

10 P.M. Saturday, February 12. Exhausted even beyond their limits, Alexander and Jane slept.

In the living room, Anne lay sprawled on the floor with a pillow over her head. "I just need an hour of sleep," she had told James. "I can't make my eyes focus anymore."

James stood next to Guy's bed and glanced at the clock. It had been two hours since Guy's last dose of morphine. He fitted the syringe into the catheter and pushed the medicine into Guy's body, flushed the catheter out with saline solution, and filled a third syringe with Heparin to keep his blood from clotting. He placed the empty syringe on the table next to the others.

Suddenly Guy lurched, gulping for air. James froze, watching, waiting.

I thought, what should I do if he dies? Should I yell for everybody to get up? That didn't seem like a good idea. How could he die in peace with me yelling and everyone frantically running in here?

As it turned out, it wasn't quite time. He even opened his eyes, and he seemed to be looking at me. I'm here, Guy, I told him. I was desperate and I didn't know what else to do, so I gave him a little kiss.

Now you might doubt this, and I'm not sure I believe it myself, but he said something to me just then. His mouth opened and he formed the words, no sound, just movement. I love you. I read it on his lips.

As gently as I could, I put my arms around him. I love you too, I whispered, I always will.

2 A.M. Sunday, February 13. Alexander gave Guy another dose of morphine. Quickly, his breathing slowed. Alexander took his pulse, stroking his son's wrist as he counted: forty beats per minute. He went into the bedroom, where his wife lay sleeping.

"I think it's time," he said. She got up instantly, awakening Anne and James as she moved through the living room.

They took their places around Guy: Alexander at the head, Anne and Jane at his sides, James leaning forward over Guy's lower body, closing in the circle. Alexander put his lips to his son's ear, his fingers tracing the lines of Guy's face and lifting strands of his hair. After a few moments of utter quiet, he spoke, with a softness the others could feel, each word brushing against them weightlessly.

"It's safe, Guy. It's safe." Guy blinked once, twice. As if warming their hands over a fire, they covered his chest, his heart, until they understood that his life had been extinguished.

There was a space in time, and then piercing the silence came a wail, the sound of a mother losing the last of her children.

• • • •

One of the two paramedics who responded to the call from 310 Kea Road pronounced Guy dead at 2:55 A.M. "No more pain, brother," he said as he gently covered Guy's face with a sheet.

The coroner arrived after the paramedics and the police had gone. In a tone of quiet respect, he questioned Alexander until he was satisfied. He asked everyone to leave the living room while he had Guy's body taken out, and so they stood in a knot in the middle of the bedroom that had been Guy's, trying to maintain their composure.

"What does he think we're going to do?" James asked.

"He doesn't want it to get messy," Anne speculated. "He's worried we'll throw ourselves on Guy and then the bed will topple over and his body will be on the floor."

"He's just trying to be kind," Jane said quietly. "He doesn't know what we're capable of."

While Jane made phone calls, James and Anne sat on the couch in the living room and watched Alexander busy himself with a variety of tasks. He removed the oxygen tank, and then the bed, to the porch outside, and put away the medical supplies that littered the table and the fireplace. By five o'clock that morning, the room had been transformed back into a living space. Outside, the sky was lighting up; dawn would be upon them momentarily.

Jane came around the corner, holding the portable phone. "Aren't you hungry?" she asked Anne and James as she was dialing. "I'm taking everyone out to breakfast," she declared, before they had a chance to answer. One hour later, joined by Charlotte and various friends and relatives, they took over two large booths at the International House of Pancakes in Kahului.

Out of the corner of her eye, Jane watched the waitress approach.

"How are you this morning?" the woman asked pleasantly. "Do you know what you want?" She turned to Jane. "Let's start with you."

I walk around and I'm different from everybody else. I know there's something good about how I'm different. Of course, the little things aren't important, but that's what everybody says when they're grieving, and then they get over it, and the little things start mattering again. That won't happen to me. I'll be forever immune to trivial pursuits, because all of my children are dead.

There will never be a day in my life when I don't think about my three children. But they are alive in me. I know that people look at the two of us and wonder; Alexander and I are alone, without our sons, without a future. But we are more than we appear to be. We will go on. We are still a family.

HONOR THY CHILDREN

Guy had two funerals. The first was held in Maui at the
Kahului Hongwanji Mission, where Guy's urn, the antique
mailbox he had found in the mountain town of Makawao, sat center
stage, surrounded by maile, the vine of Hawaiian royalty. To the right
of Guy's shrine was his portrait, a robust and healthy Guy, a confident,
almost cocky young man, an image I never really knew. The face I will
remember was thinner, softer, more vulnerable than striking, more
childlike.

It was an intimate gathering of family and friends and of Maui
AIDS activists who had been drawn to the Nakatani family story. Anne,
Cat, and James told their tales of Guy in wonderful eulogies, and afterward Alexander cradled his son's ashes in his arms on the way to the
spot where Guy's urn would be buried next to those of his brothers.
The next morning, for the first time, Jane watched over all of her children from her kitchen window.

Almost a month later, one thousand people, mostly teenagers,
packed into the gymnasium of Saratoga High School to celebrate Guy
and to grieve with his parents. I remember the date, March 5, because
it was my forty-fifth birthday, a detail I found to be somewhat amusing, considering Guy's gift for taking over whatever space he happened
to be inhabiting. Make no mistake, I gladly gave over the moment to his

memory. Besides, he had made us promise to go to a gay bar after his funeral, so all day I looked forward to a party.

This was the memorial service Guy had planned, beginning with his requiem, a breathtakingly beautiful piece of music written and performed by one of Guy's closest friends. He chose other special songs, and the high-school jazz ensemble that would sing them. He chose those who would give his eulogies, including a local congressman. Even the napkins (not those thin ones!) were Guy's design. Of course, the day took on a life of its own. Stories of Guy's heroism during the last two years of his life were retold by many; the young woman who had contemplated suicide until Guy spoke to her high school; the group of friends who had gone together to be tested and then celebrated their good fortune by starting an HIV and AIDS Awareness Club; the boy who wrote an essay on Guy entitled "Saving Myself" that won a national award and a college scholarship.

Guy believed he could change the world, and ultimately he succeeded, because he opened doors that had been closed and created opportunities for transformation to take place. As for me, if I were to have walked with Guy and his family and not come away changed, I would have missed the lessons of the journey.

From the onset, it was hard to ignore Guy's last-minute accomplishments. He demystified HIV and AIDS to 40,000 people before he died, revealing it as a lethal, immediate, and indiscriminate danger which has, to date, killed 4 million people worldwide, infected at least 20 million, and continues to invade the bodies of new victims at the rate of 7,000 each day. AIDS is the leading cause of death of Americans between the ages of twenty-five and forty-four; one in four infected with HIV in 1995 was twenty years old or younger. Promising new drugs will slow and even block the advancement of the virus, but are unavailable and unaffordable for most of the AIDS population worldwide. A vaccine, the only hope of stopping the pandemic, is entirely possible, but research and development are still of low priority and sinfully underfunded. The most chilling truth of AIDS persists: Whoever it infects, it eventually claims.

Guy knew for five years that death was waiting for him, that the life that had served fairly well would soon burn out. But rather than being consumed by anger and sadness, Guy Nakatani caught fire.

It was as if he were able to breathe life into his illness and bedazzle whatever threatened to limit him. Where he had been self-absorbed, he became compassionate; where he had been superficial, he became noble; and in the end he gave everything he had left so that someone else might live. And he did all these things with flare. Come, he said, I will show you my secrets.

Ah, the secrets. Guy didn't understand that his integrity, and his humanity, would eventually get the best of him. He imagined a story of a hero; he told me the story of a human being. And so with a pad of tracing paper in hand, we revisited his life. At first, he held the pencil, constructing carefully a few simple images in dark lines. But, ultimately, I had to be the artist; and as each thin page descended, one upon the other, adding shading and color and details, the picture was filled in, deepened, until we began to see all that was there.

Each of us should be able to relate. Each of us has a simple image of ourselves that begs for fullness. As a parent, I am responsible not only for allowing my self-portrait to be unveiled, but for encouraging my children to embrace theirs, without fear, knowing I will love them no matter what the canvas reveals.

With this in mind, Chuck and I decided to have a conversation with our children, say, over the dinner table, about "gay being okay." Certainly, the idea had floated through our house before, but we were after something different, something that recognized a wholehearted, open-ended acceptance of their sexuality, whatever that might be, without hitting them over the head with it. I remember sharing the plan with Suzanne, a gay friend, who laughed hard at our efforts. Bear with us, I asked her, and she stopped laughing and agreed that we were on the right track, despite our clumsiness. So Chuck and I continued to sort it out, before we actually tried it.

First, we considered who we were dealing with. At the time, our oldest daughter, Melissa, was a junior at the University of California at

Berkeley. She and Guy had become close friends; she was an occasional overnight caregiver before he moved to Maui; she communicated with him in a dream after he died. As mother and daughter, we had shared our personal struggles with sexuality. She wouldn't be around that dinner table, but we counted on her to be the third adult in this ongoing discussion.

Mark, our oldest son, was just beginning his freshman year in college. Through the many months of Guy and his family being so engaged with our own, we hadn't really discussed sexuality with Mark on a personal level, but we thought he might have something to say at the dinner.

Mark had been mesmerized the first time he heard Guy speak and was with the rest of us the night before he left for Maui the last time. "Come here, Mark," Guy said from his place on the couch, where he was holding court for myriad friends and supporters. He commanded Mark to sit down and drape his legs over him, as if Mark was sitting in his lap. James snapped the photo—Guy with a twinkle in his eye, Mark, smiling widely.

Nicholas and Gino, aged sixteen and fourteen at the time, and our younger daughter Kristen, twelve, had followed along on the journey with the Nakatanis as they would any other Fumia family adventure. Once in a while, one of them asked me how I would feel when Guy died.

"How will you feel?" I asked them back.

"Sad," they would reply. They were scared for him and for me. Just before I left for Maui in January 1994, Gino came to me, worried about my having to go through the ordeal of watching Guy die. And again, we were given the opportunity to talk at length about death, about losing a friend, and about saying good-bye.

They loved Guy and James, Al and Jane, and Anne. No questions asked. Whenever Chuck and I imagined our discussion, it was with Nicholas, Gino, and Kristen in mind. Our youngest child, Joel, was only five. "He's a little young for this," Suzanne advised me, "but let him sit in." I agreed, and it was nice to hear it from an expert.

In the end, the conversation was short and sweet. But that was the point. Over barbecued hamburgers, it went something like this:

Chuck: As you grow up, you'll become more and more aware of your sexuality. Everyone spends a lot of time figuring all that out.

Molly: If you don't know already, you'll eventually know whether you're gay or straight. (I didn't address the fact that some people find themselves poised in between. I figured we needed something to talk about later.) You'll be able to tell by your feelings, the people who attract you, and with whom you imagine sharing love and intimacy.

Chuck: So. We just want you to know that despite what you may have heard, gay and straight are both okay, normal, just fine, and we're here for you, whenever you want to talk. About anything.

Nicholas: We know all this. Can I have another hamburger?

The "discussion" ended. But saying those things, however obvious we wanted them to be, produced an odd sensation—at least in me. Uninvited, shamefully, came the feeling that we were encouraging them to be gay. No, no, I defended myself—we're encouraging them to be who they are! And in that moment, sabotaged by ancient fears, I felt like I was betraying everything I ardently believed.

The truth is that even in the most open of us, the hidden weaknesses, the tiny tears in the lining of our souls, allow those powerful forces in. We are so easily scared. How many times have I heard it said that gay is fine, but what a hard life he or she will have. Or that one of my best friends is gay, as if the "lifestyle" is not really acceptable, but since affection and relationship preceded the knowing, an exception will be made in this case. Or, worse, that a son or a daughter has been accepted, so long as their private life is kept separate, hidden from those it might unknowingly taint.

Love—with conditions. Despite our deepest knowledge to the contrary, homosexuality continues to be seen as an affliction, not as one of the ways a human being breathes in and out. Accordingly, such attitudes make it impossible, in the mind of a confused young person, to deemphasize sexuality and emphasize self-esteem, because the heart of his or her character is judged to be sick or even evil.

I've come to believe that the way we, as a society, are in relationship with the gay adults and children among us testifies to the way we are in relationship with all others, including ourselves. From the outside, homophobia is the last great human rights issue, because in order to deal with it, we must start from the inside. To say that the suggestion of homosexuality strikes fear in the hearts of many members of our society is not an overstatement. Alexander Nakatani gives a clear example of this issue:

"Many men are afraid of gays because they really can't imagine the act of sex as love. That's because homophobia is also about the denigration of women by men for whom sex is not about love but about power and domination. If in his heart, a heterosexual man is behaving as a predator, he is threatened by homosexual men, whom he imagines to be capable of dominating other men. Perhaps he could be dominated, too. This is the threat.

"Any man who understands sex as an act of love has a better chance of imagining two men loving each other and expressing their love sexually."

For even more of us, the claim is made that ignorance is at the core of our fears. But how long can one claim ignorance? As the nineties rush by, we are presented again and again with the facts. Sexuality is not chosen, but inherited, God-given if you will, a birthright. Love, commitment, honesty, respect—these are the measures of good, lasting relationships between any two people and, ironically, as my long ago Catholic upbringing taught, the ground rules for sexual love.

As some might suggest, we could dismiss this discussion as old news, if not for the children of Jane and Alexander Nakatani and an infinite number of others. Their story outlines the consequences of ignorance. Their legacy is that ignorance can no longer be our excuse. If we lose a son or daughter to self-hatred, we are making a choice. We are sending them out into a world we have not made safe for them.

• • • •

Today, Alexander has taken on Jane's old role. He has become the itinerant teacher, on the road with his story in hand, armed with his memories and his courage. Whatever his classroom, he jumps right in.

To a group of parents assembled in a library in San Francisco, he has this to say: "You're not asking the right questions. Don't ask me about statistics. You have to be able to speak truthfully, as both a participant and a parent, about sex. You're wasting your time if you wonder about what's happening out there. Wonder about your own child and share with him or her how you felt when you were discovering your own sexuality. Unless you nurture an environment of trust and communication, you may never know if he's troubled. Worse than that, you may aid in the destruction of her spirit, without even knowing it."

In San Jose, surrounded by high-school students whose lives were changed by his son, he speaks with utter respect and affection. "If Guy were here, he would say that he believes in you. Unfortunately, Guy's gone from us now. So if you would permit an old man a moment, I want you to know that I believe in you, too. Not only will you save yourselves from his fate, but you will save others in the process, because you are strong and wise."

And, finally, to a group of teachers in Los Angeles, Alexander Nakatani proclaims the following: "The failure to develop good self-esteem and then to engage in high-risk behavior is not solely the province of young, gay men. Straight kids also abuse themselves, chain themselves to alcohol and drugs, impair their judgment, take chances, get into bad relationships, and become suicidal. If nothing else, we should have figured this out by now.

"Ultimately, my family's story is not about AIDS or homosexuality, but about what happens to all of us when a child is denigrated, whether it be because of race, gender, sexual orientation, size, or shape—the reason doesn't matter, and the damage is the same. Anything that wounds the self-esteem of a child is the enemy we should all be fighting.

"We have to care about every child as we would care about our own."

• • • •

313

The memory of Guy rests gently on the minds and hearts of others who loved him. After two years of grieving, James still awaits a new love. But when he looks in the mirror now, he sees a man he likes and a new confidence that he carries with him every day to his new job—one he chose on his own.

Guy's sidekick Anne has grown into an exceptional young woman. "In the end," she remembers, "I felt like we said a thousand good-byes, like an echo, 'good-bye, Guy, good-bye, Anne.' Until one day, he didn't answer, and I was free to go." She recently began her career as a physical therapist, a vocation she was born for.

For a while after Guy died, friends of Alexander and Jane Nakatani noted their sanguine smiles and apparent resiliency. Talk of Glen, Greg, and Guy came easily and defying all logic it seemed possible their broken hearts might mend. But six months after her third son's death, Jane suffered a major heart attack, followed by triple bypass surgery. Physically recovered, she and Alexander spend most of their time on Maui now, in the house on Kea Road. They exercise daily, cook heart-friendly food, and entertain guests from the mainland. Miraculously, they still laugh. They are rarely apart.

In March 1996, my daughter Melissa and I visited them. A highlight of our time together was dinner at Mama's Fish House, where it was as if the great meal, the merriment, and our celebration of each other begun two and a half years before simply continued where we'd left off. At the end of a wonderful week, we accompanied them to the cemetery below their house. Melissa and I stood close by as mother and father tended to their children. The sun was setting. They were tucking them in for the night.

Alexander cut the grass around the flat bronze markers and polished each of their names while Jane filled three vases with fresh flowers and greens from her garden. They worked silently, side by side, the ritual memorized and well practiced.

Melissa and I shared an unspoken thought: This was all that was left, this small, tender act. And yet, I knew with certainty that it had an integrity and sacredness of its own.

The next morning, Jane took us to the airport. She looked into our eyes and just before the tears began pulled us into an embrace. Melissa and I understood what she wanted for us: to savor each other's presence now and in the future. Promise me, we could almost hear her saying, that you will make the way you honor one another a tradition, to be passed on forever.

I remember a discussion we once had about tradition. Eventually, we got around to the Judeo-Christian commandment: Honor thy father and mother. It may be a commandment, Jane had said, but it's also a Japanese assumption.

And then we all agreed: We'd gotten it wrong. Children come into the world owing us nothing. We owe them everything. It is children who should be honored.

It came to me then that Alexander and Jane Nakatani, although deprived of any further occasion to parent their children, had, in their courage and their grief, bequeathed to us this awareness. They will be remembered as two people who helped families experience what, sadly, eluded them—the richness of life together.

Theirs is a story of almost unfathomable transformation. In the telling, they allowed their woundedness to send them into the world, rather than withdraw from it. They offered the wisdom born of their suffering as gift. These are extraordinary acts, as was their mere survival in the face of such conclusive tragedy. And this may be the noblest of their deeds, because their willingness to survive beyond their precious children almost certainly ensures the survival of others. For this possibility, we can all be grateful.

Guy

Alexander and Jane Nakatani, December 17, 1960.

1995 in Kauai.

Greg, Glen, and Guy.

Greg

Glen

Guy with Mark Fumia, January 4, 1994. The night before the final move to Maui.

James and Anne, 1993.

Guy and Molly Fumia in Maui, August 1993.

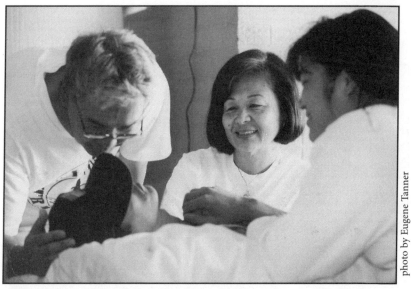

Guy and his caretakers, Al, Jane, and Anne, January, 1994.

photo by Eugene Tanner

photo by Eugene Tanner

Al and Jane two days before Guy's death, February 11, 1994.

Guy, 1992.

Molly Fumia is the author of two previous books that explore the transformative nature of grief: *A Piece of My Heart: Living Through the Grief of Miscarriage, Stillbirth, or Infant Death* and *Safe Passage: Words to Help the Grieving Hold Fast and Let Go.* The mother of seven children, one of whom died in infancy, she holds a master's degree in Theology from the Graduate Theological Union in Berkeley, California. She resides in Los Gatos, California, with her husband Chuck and their children.

She is wearing The Bracelet from the Until There's a Cure Foundation, sales of which support the international AIDS Vaccine Initiative. For more information, call 1-800-88UNTIL.